A Step-By-Step Guide for Coaching Classroom Teachers in Evidence-Based Interventions

A Step-By-Step Guide for Coaching Classroom Teachers in Evidence-Based Interventions

Dana D. Marchese

Kimberly D. Becker

Jennifer P. Keperling

Celene E. Domitrovich

Wendy M. Reinke

Dennis D. Embry

Nicholas S. Ialongo

OXFORD
UNIVERSITY PRESS

Oxford University Press is a department of the University of Oxford. It furthers
the University's objective of excellence in research, scholarship, and education
by publishing worldwide. Oxford is a registered trade mark of Oxford University
Press in the UK and certain other countries.

Published in the United States of America by Oxford University Press
198 Madison Avenue, New York, NY 10016, United States of America.

CIP data is on file at the Library of Congress
ISBN 978–0–19–060957–3

9 8 7 6 5 4 3 2 1
Printed by Webcom Inc., Canada

PATHS® Curriculum is a registered trademark of Channing Bete Company, Inc. PAX Good Behavior Game® is a registered trademark of PAXIS Institute. Rather than use a trademark symbol with every occurrence of these trademarked
names, names are used in an editorial fashion, with no intention of infringement of the respective owner's trademark.

This book is dedicated to Dr. Nicholas Ialongo. Thank you for the tremendous contributions you have made to the field of Prevention Science and determining the most effective ways to implement evidence-based interventions in schools. Your passion, commitment, and dedication to improving the lives of students, teachers, and families is truly inspiring. We are forever grateful to have had the opportunity to work with you.

Contents

Preface

Welcome, coach! You are about to embark on an important mission: to support teachers' proficiency in delivering evidence-based prevention programs in their classrooms. This book will help prepare you to perform your job successfully. After reading it, you will have acquired a working knowledge of the following:

- **Background and rationale for classroom-based prevention programs**. You will see how evidence-based programs promote positive student development with regard to social–emotional learning, behavioral functioning, and academic success.
- **Core coaching principles**. You will develop a framework for your coaching that involves effective relationship building and behavioral principles.
- **Universal coaching model**. You will discover how these coaching principles are applied in a flexible yet systematic way to enhance teacher skill development.
- **Indicated coaching model**. You will develop an appreciation for barriers that arise during delivery of evidence-based programs and insight for how to apply your coaching skills effectively to reduce the interference of these barriers and promote teacher skill proficiency.

This book highlights the consultation strategies used by the coaches on the PATHS to PAX Project with the Johns Hopkins Center for Prevention and Early Intervention working with classroom teachers in Baltimore city public schools. The PATHS to PAX Project is the integration of two of the most widely disseminated evidence-based, universal school-based preventive interventions, The PATHS Curriculum and the PAX Good Behavior Game (GBG). Because many of the strategies in the PATHS to PAX Program are common elements of other social-emotional and classroom management interventions.

Overall, this coaching model parallels the public health model of prevention by defining systematically the target (e.g., teacher implementation) and potential adverse outcomes (e.g., low teacher implementation), developing strategies to promote positive outcomes, and implementing and evaluating these strategies. The coaching strategies specified in the model also reflect a public health approach to prevention such that *universal* coaching strategies are used with all teachers. *Indicated* coaching strategies are used with only those teachers who demonstrate implementation challenges. This volume contains detailed descriptions of the various coaching activities as well as handouts to facilitate meetings with teachers. We envision these resources supporting you during your training as a coach of evidence-based programs and serving as references when you are out in the field. We hope your experience as a coach is rewarding, inspiring, and, ultimately, triumphant in promoting teacher proficiency and student success.

This manual begins with a description in Chapter 2 of the core coaching principles that serve as the foundation for our model. Chapter 3 describes the universal coaching model and details the specific coaching procedures used with all teachers. In Chapter 4, the indicated coaching procedures used with those teachers who have been identified by coaches as having the most difficulty with program implementation are specified. Chapter 5 presents the lessons learned through coaching teachers and presents case examples to highlight various strategies. In Chapter 6, the process for selecting, training, supervising, and evaluating coaches is discussed. Finally, a summary of the guide is provided in the Conclusion.

Forms in the Appendix are also available from the *Oxford Clinical Psychology* website, where you can print, save, and complete them electronically. You may access the forms at www.oxfordclinicalpsych.com/coachingteachers.

A Step-By-Step Guide for
Coaching Classroom Teachers
in Evidence-Based Interventions

Overview

This book reflects collaborative efforts to establish systematic procedures for supporting teachers in the implementation of classroom-based universal prevention programs targeting the promotion of social–emotional learning and the reduction of disruptive and aggressive behavior. This chapter describes the rationale for classroom-based prevention programs and sets forth the purpose of this book.

Objectives

- Provide the rationale and benefits for universal school-based prevention programs.
- Describe the PATHS Curriculum and the PAX Good Behavior Game prevention intervention.
- Relay the importance of coaching in obtaining quality implementation of prevention programs.

Universal Prevention Programs

Children who enter school with behavior problems have more difficulty adjusting to the demands of the kindergarten classroom. They often fail to engage in learning and miss classroom instruction when they are removed from the classroom, which causes them to fall behind academically. Children with early disruptive and aggressive behavior often have poor emotional understanding, self-regulation, and attention, which contribute to multiple social skills deficits. As a result, these children are at risk for peer rejection, which undermines their social adaptation and contributes even further to poor achievement (Ladd, Kochenderfer, & Coleman, 1996, 1997; O'Neil, Welsh, Parke, Wang, & Strand, 1997). Children who exhibit disruptive and aggressive behavior in elementary school are also more likely to experience conflict with teachers as well. Over time, disruptive and aggressive behaviors in early elementary school have been shown to predict subsequent mental disorders, substance abuse, and school disruptions (Kellam et al., 2008; Petras et al., 2008; Schaeffer, Petras, Ialongo,

Poduska, & Kellam, 2003; Schaeffer et al., 2006). In addition, positive student–teacher relationships are associated with high academic performance both in the short and long term (Hamre & Pianta, 2001; Peisner-Feinberg et al., 2001; Pianta & Stuhlman, 2004).

A considerable body of evidence has been obtained from carefully controlled research studies that indicates risk factors and processes, such as those noted earlier, are modifiable (Furr-Holden, Ialongo, Anthony, Petras, & Kellam, 2004; Ialongo, Poduska, Werthamer, & Kellam, 2001; Kellam et al., 2008; Petras et al., 2008; Storr, Ialongo, Kellam, & Anthony, 2002; Wilcox et al., 2008). Universal preventive interventions that promote social–emotional skills and modify the environmental conditions that support the development and/or maintenance of maladaptive behavior have been shown to improve student behavioral outcomes (Catalano, Berglund, Ryan, Lonczak, & Hawkins, 2002; Greenberg, Domitrovich, & Bumbarger, 2001; Hahn et al., 2007; Park-Higgerson, Perumean-Chaney, Bartolucci, Grimley, & Singh, 2008; Weissberg & Greenberg, 1998; Wilson & Lipsey, 2007). Moreover, the risk of later psychiatric symptoms and disorders can be reduced over time (Greenberg et al., 2001; Hoagwood et al., 2007; Ialongo et al., 2001; Kellam et al., 2008; Petras et al., 2008; Wilcox et al., 2008).

Benefits of a School-Based Prevention Program

The school setting is a primary context in which disruptive behaviors occur, and chronic disruptive behavior interferes with the educational goals of schools. Early onset of mental disorders predicts early termination of schooling, particularly failure to graduate high school (Breslau, Lane, Sampson, & Kessler, 2008). Public schools in the United States graduate only about 70% of their students (Swanson, 2004). There are significant barriers to mental health care utilization, particularly for inner city youth (McKay & Bannon, 2004; Neal & Brown, 1994; National Institute of Mental Health, 2001; US Public Health Service, 2001); thus, providing a prevention program in a school setting could not only reduce the occurrence of such mental and behavioral disorders, but also the associated impairments in educational and occupational attainment as well.

There is clear need for evidence-based prevention and intervention programs. Early and accurate identification of children with mental and behavioral disorders, along with the implementation of effective preventive and early intervention services would have a significant impact on the lives of many children and families. Despite this striking need for services and the dire consequences associated with mental and behavioral disorders, many children do not receive services for their behavior problems (US Public Health Service, 2000). Even when services are offered in schools or communities, they are often inappropriate or ineffective (US Public Health Service, 2000). For instance, one study showed that children with mental and behavioral problems who received community treatment for their symptoms had comparable levels of improvement as children with mental and behavioral problems who were not treated at all, indicating the need for implementation of interventions known to be effective (Weisz, Jenson-Doss, & Hawley, 2006). Thus, bridging the use of evidence-based intervention for youth and offering it in our schools where many youth can benefit are needed. In fact, there is a growing body of evidence highlighting the benefits of implementing evidence-based prevention and early-intervention programs among youth in schools (National Research Council & Institute of Medicine, 2009). A recent Substance Abuse and Mental Health Services Administration, Center for Mental Health (2007) report to Congress highlighted both the promise of school-based interventions to improve mental health and the need for more research and services. And, indeed, emerging evidence suggests school-based interventions can have beneficial effects in promoting positive adolescent mental health (Gillham et al., 2007; Neil & Christensen, 2009).

Furthermore, there is increasing evidence that social–emotional skills have the potential to promote engagement in learning and long-term academic success through their influence on the social and cognitive mechanisms that underlie the learning process (Durlak, Weissberg, Dymnicki, Taylor, & Schellinger, 2011). Because of their constant presence in the classroom, teachers are vital to promoting students' skill development and practice throughout the day (Grossman et al., 1997; Hawkins, Von Cleve, & Catalano, 1991; Weissberg, Barton, & Shriver, 1997). For this reason, most universal intervention models use teachers as implementers and deliver instruction at the classroom level.

The PATHS Curriculum

Students' development of social and emotional competence enhances their learning and academic achievement (Adelman & Taylor, 2000; Greenberg et al., 2003; Zins, Weissberg, Wang, & Walberg, 2004), and the PATHS Curriculum is one classroom-based program that targets social–emotional development. The PATHS Curriculum is based on the affective–behavioral–cognitive–dynamic model of development (Greenberg & Kusche, 1996; Greenberg, Kusche, & Speltz, 1990), which places primary importance on the developmental integration of affect (and emotion language), behavior, and cognitive understanding as they relate to social and emotional competence. It is a universal, teacher-taught, classroom-based prevention intervention that has been shown in large-scale randomized controlled trials to have an immediate and beneficial impact on aggressive, disruptive, and off-task behavior (Conduct Problems Prevention Research Group, 1999, 2010; Greenberg, Kusche, Cook, & Quamma, 1995; Kam, Greenberg, & Kusche, 2004; Kusche & Greenberg, 2012). Furthermore, the efficacy of PATHS in terms of reducing off-task and aggressive/disruptive behavior and increasing prosocial behavior, social competence, inhibitory control, and verbal fluency in the elementary school years has been demonstrated in a series of randomized controlled studies (Conduct Problems Prevention Research Group, 1999; Greenberg & Kusche, 2006; Greenberg, Kusche, & Riggs, 2004; Riggs, Greenberg, Kusche, & Pentz, 2006).

The PATHS Curriculum is designed to improve skills in four domains: (a) prosocial friendship skills, (b) emotional understanding and emotional expression skills, (c) self-control/emotion regulation (e.g., the capacity to inhibit impulsive behavior and organize goal-directed activity), and (d) problem-solving skills that, in turn, are expected to improve problem behavior and social–emotional skills. About 40% of the Lessons focus on skills related to understanding and communicating emotions; 30% focus on skills related to the increase of positive social behavior (e.g., social participation, prosocial behavior, communication skills). Additional Lessons address making/sustaining friendships, using good manners, taking turns and sharing in games, expressing one's viewpoint, listening to others, conducting social problem solving, and demonstrating self-control.

PAX Good Behavior Game

The PAX Good Behavior Game (GBG) (Barrish, Saunders, & Wolf, 1969) is a universal preventive intervention for use in elementary classrooms that allows teachers to use social learning principles within a team-based, game-like context to reduce aggressive/disruptive and off-task behavior and, consequently, to facilitate academic instruction. The PAX version of the GBG represents an adaptation of the original GBG (Embry, Staatemeier, Richardson, Lauger, & Mitich, 2003). Like the original GBG, the PAX GBG (also referred to in this book as "the Game") is essentially a group-based token economy in which the groups or "teams" are reinforced for their collective success in inhibiting inappropriate behavior. The team-based nature of the Game allows teachers to take advantage of positive peer pressure in managing student behavior at the individual and classroom levels. Students are rewarded for displaying self-control and emotion regulation, and not attending to the misbehavior of others. The rewards for winning the Game are usually nonmaterial and include activities such as listening to music, getting to sit on soft cushions, or blowing bubbles.

The GBG has been shown to reduce aggressive/disruptive behavior in early elementary school classrooms (Brown, 1993; Dolan et al., 1993; Ialongo et al., 1999). Follow-up studies suggest that some effects of the intervention are maintained in middle school (Kellam, Rebok, Ialongo, & Mayer, 1994) and early adulthood (Kellam et al., 2008; Petras et al., 2008). The GBG (Bradshaw et al., 2009; Ialongo et al., 1999; Kellam et al., 2008; Petras et al., 2008) has been shown to improve students' on-task and prosocial classroom behaviors (Dolan et al., 1993; Ialongo et al., 1999) and to have beneficial impacts in terms of increased high school graduation rates (Bradshaw et al., 2009) and reduced risk for substance abuse, antisocial behavior, and mental disorders (Kellam et al., 2008; Petras et al., 2008).

PATHS to PAX

PATHS to PAX is the combination of two of the most widely implemented and researched interventions: the PAX GBG and the PATHS Curriculum. Research has shown that for children to learn social–emotional skills they need instruction, opportunities for practice, and reinforcement. By combining the PATHS Curriculum and the PAX GBG, students are provided with all three essential elements necessary to develop these skills.

Furthermore, there are a number of reasons why one could expect additive if not synergistic effects as a result of combining the two interventions. First, the PATHS Curriculum seeks to accomplish reductions in aggressive/disruptive and off-task behavior via teacher-led instruction aimed at facilitating emotion regulation (particularly anger management), self-control, social problem solving, and conflict resolution skills (Greenberg et al., 1995; Kam et al., 2004), whereas the GBG is based on social learning principles and provides teachers with an efficient means of managing student aggressive/disruptive and off-task behavior via reinforcement of the inhibition of these behaviors within a game-like context. The GBG, by increasing attention to task and reducing disruptive behavior in the classroom, may facilitate the acquisition of the emotion regulation, social problem-solving, and conflict resolution skills taught in the PATHS Curriculum. Second, the social learning-based GBG may increase the likelihood that students' newly acquired skills would be prompted and reinforced appropriately by teachers and school staff. Consequently, the PATHS Curriculum skills would be better learned and used more frequently. Third, the increased teacher and child success, as a result of combining the PATHS Curriculum and the GBG, should minimize teacher and child discouragement and subsequent failure to participate or comply fully with the intervention regimens. Last, the combination of PATHS Curriculum and the PAX GBG resulted in a wider array of intervention effects than the PAX GBG alone.

PATHS is being used throughout the United States, Canada, and Europe. Information on training, materials, and costs is available on the PATHS training website (http://www.pathstraining.com/main/). Like PATHS, the PAX GBG is being used throughout the United States, Canada, and Europe. Information on training, materials, and costs is available on the PAXIS Institute website (www.Paxis.org).

Coaching and Implementation Quality

Published findings regarding the implementation of other programs suggest that implementation tends to be low after one-time workshop trainings (Miller, Yahne, Moyers, Pirritano, & Martinez, 2004; Sholomskas et al., 2005). Qualitative reviews (e.g., Fixsen, Naoom, Blasé, Friedman, & Wallace, 2005; Herschell, Kolko, Baumann, & Davis, 2010; Stirman, Crits-Christoph, & DeRubeis, 2004) and empirical research (e.g., Kelly et al., 2000; Lochman et al., 2009; Miller et al., 2004; Sholomskas et al., 2005) indicate that ongoing coaching (e.g., consultation, feedback) may enhance skill development and program implementation above and beyond what is demonstrated after initial training.

This book outlines the PATHS to PAX Coaching Model and offers strategies for monitoring, enhancing, and troubleshooting teacher implementation. The coaching strategies and techniques described in this book serve as an exemplar model for working with teachers to implement similar evidence-based practices in their classroom. Our model reflects what we know from the literature in terms of best practices on training and coaching. It is based on a conceptual model of school-based implementation that incorporates theory and empirical research regarding the factors associated with variation in implementation, including characteristics of the intervention, the support system, implementers, and the organizational context in which the intervention is being conducted (Domitrovich et al., 2008). In addition, it incorporates theory regarding the process of providing implementation support to promote change in teacher behavior (Han & Weiss, 2005).

Our training and coaching model is based on the research on the factors influencing fidelity of implementation of evidence-based practices in school settings. Han and Weiss (2005) offer a model of the factors influencing implementation of evidenced-based interventions in school settings, drawing on extant theory and empirical findings (see Figure 1.1).

Phase 1 ⟶ Phase 2

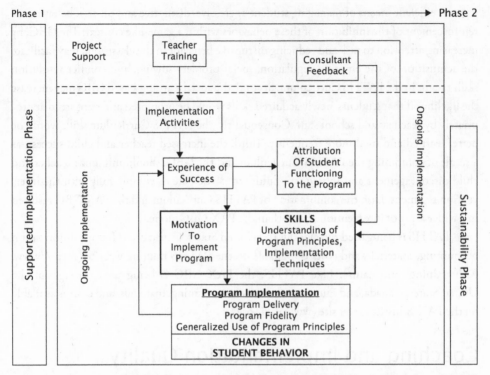

FIGURE 1.1 Han and Weiss's (2005) Model of the Sustainability of Teacher Implementation of School-Based Mental Health Programs. Reprinted with permission from Han, S. S., & Weiss, B. (2005). Sustainability of teacher implementation of school-based mental health programs. *Journal of Abnormal Child Psychology, 33*(6), 665–679.

Our training and coaching model is based in large part on their model and on the research on optimizing implementation of evidence-based practices in school settings. Han and Weiss distinguish between the supported implementation phase (or the period including the initial training and consultation/coaching/mentoring) and the sustainability phase, following the supported implemented phase, when consultation/coaching is no longer available. Implementation fidelity and sustainability are defined by Han and Weiss as (a) the quantity of the intervention delivered, (b) the quality of the implementation with respect to the standards set by the program developers, and (c) the use of the core principles of the intervention in dealing with behaviors not addressed in the training and consultation phase.

The emphasis by Han and Weiss (2005) on the training/consultation protocol in establishing and sustaining implementation fidelity is consistent with extant theory and empirical findings. The findings suggests there are characteristics related to the intervention and immediate training/support system that foster high-quality implementation, including (a) program content based on a well-articulated theory of cause (Gottfredson, 1997; Tobler & Stanton, 1997; Tobler et al., 2000; Wilson, Gottfredson, & Najaka, 2001); (b) program standardization, including manualized intervention materials (Blakely et al., 1987; Gottfredson & Gottfredson, 2002); (c) provision of training to implementers (Dusenbury, Branningan, Falco, & Hansen, 2003; Noell, Witt, Gilbertson, Ranier, & Freeland, 1997); (d) ongoing consultation of implementers (Aber, Brown, & Jones, 2003; Gorman-Smith, Beidel, Brown,

Lochman, & Haaga, 2003); (e) a process for monitoring implementation that is linked to professional development (Scott & Martinek, 2006); and (f) a training and consultation phase long enough to ensure a thorough working knowledge of the core program principles and their translation into practice (Rose & Church, 1998; Leach & Conto, 1999). Each of these six elements is reflected in our training and coaching model.

The body of literature on coaching (or training/consultation) is relatively small. Although models are being developed (e.g., Neufeld & Roper, 2003a, 2003b; Poglinco et al., 2003; Showers, 1985), there are few step-by-step guides to coaching. Thus, this book provides a detailed guide for coaches working with classroom teachers. It outlines the fundamentals of effective coaching, as well as a case formulation approach that can help a coach decide which coaching strategies to use and when. Moreover, many of the principles that underlie the PATHS to PAX Coaching Model generalize to the coaching of other school-based interventions.

Throughout this book we discuss in more detail some of the general coaching strategies that have been shown to be effective in the literature, such as building positive relationships, providing effective training, practicing new skills, modeling, informal modeling, coteaching, conducting observations, giving personalized feedback, discussing barriers to implementation, planning action items, helping teachers plan Lessons, videotaping the teacher, observing highly effective teachers, connecting the teacher with highly effective teachers, and using resources and materials. See Box 1.1 for examples of each of these general coaching strategies.

BOX 1.1. Coaching Strategies for Working Effectively with Classroom Teachers

Positive Relationship: Build a strong, positive relationship with the teacher that is collaborative, respectful, and nonjudgmental. Encourage and support the teacher. Keep your conversations and observation data confidential.

Effective Training: Provide the necessary training for the skill, curriculum, intervention, or program.

Practice/Role-play: Have the teacher practice the new skill.

Modeling: Schedule a time to model in the teacher's classroom (modeling may need to be scheduled frequently in the beginning until the teacher's skill level/implementation increases).

- Ask the teacher to complete the Good Behavior Game Modeling Checklist (Appendix A) if the coach models a Game.
- Discuss the completed form and the teacher's feedback/reaction to the modeling, students' engagement, and so on, after modeling.

Informal Modeling: Spend time in the teacher's classroom modeling the targeted skills informally (e.g., praising students, ignoring Spleems, reinforcing positive behavior). (*Note*: A Spleem is a made-up word that refers to anything that is not PAX or anything that gets in the way of PAX.)

Coteaching: Schedule a time to coteach a Lesson with the teacher in the classroom.

Observation: Observe the teacher during a Lesson. Schedule a time to review detailed feedback privately with the teacher.

Personalized Feedback: Provide feedback that is individualized and specific. Highlight the teacher's strengths. Model frequently the use of behavior-specific praise with teachers by giving them written and verbal praise regarding the things that are going really well in their classroom. Tootle Notes (an example of which is included in Appendix B) can be used as a fun way to provide written compliments to the teachers as well as model the Tootle Note process for teachers so they can use Tootles with their students.

Barriers Discussion: Discuss with the teacher the potential barriers to implementing the specific skill specifically (e.g. behavior-specific praise, planned ignoring). Then, develop collaboratively a list of ways in which the teacher can avoid or respond effectively to the identified barriers. As a coach, assess whether the barrier is a performance or skill deficit.

Action Planning: Set specific goals collaboratively with the teacher, including what the behavior will look like, when it will occur, and how long it will occur, and document that it occurred.

Planning: Schedule a time to help the teacher plan a Lesson. Complete the Coach–Teacher Collaborative Planning Sheet (Appendix C).

Video: Videotape the teacher teaching a lesson and then schedule a time to watch the tape together so the teacher can reflect on his or her teaching practices. Provide the teacher with feedback on implementation. Schedule a time to watch and discuss a videotape of a highly effective teacher.

Classroom Visit: Schedule a time for the teacher to observe a high-implementing teacher's classroom (preferably the same grade level in their school or visit another school). After the observation, discuss the teacher's reaction to the observation, what he or she thought the high-implementing teacher did well, the positive classroom environment, and so on. If possible, schedule time for the teacher to talk to the high-implementing teacher and ask questions.

Connection: Provide the teacher with the contact information (e.g., e-mail address, phone number) of a highly effective teacher in the school to answer questions, brainstorm ideas, provide support, and so on.

Resources/Materials: Schedule a time to review training slides, curriculum/Lessons, videotapes, and so on, regarding the targeted skills with the teacher.

Chapter 1 Reflection Questions

- Why is it important to intervene early with students entering school?

- What are some of the benefits of a school-based prevention program?

- Why is it important to teach students social–emotional skills?

- How can coaching be beneficial to teachers?

- How do you think this book would be helpful in your work with teachers? What are you hoping to learn from this book?

Core Coaching Principles

Overview

The coaching model described in this book was developed based on a review of the existing literature on topics such as coaching, training, supervision, and school-based consultation, as well as on many of the key principles that guide the PATHS to PAX Project. This chapter provides a brief review of the literature and describes in detail the core coaching principles of the coaching model we developed and use: engagement, collaboration, supported skill development, constructive feedback, and positive reinforcement.

Implementation reflects the degree to which a program is delivered as intended (Domitrovich et al., 2008). Two seminal articles by Domitrovich et al. (2008) and Han and Weiss (2005) provide models for enhancing implementation relevant to the PATHS to PAX Coaching Model. First, they assert that program implementation depends on characteristics of the programmatic intervention itself (i.e., PATHS to PAX GBG). These characteristics might include the ease with which teachers understand and learn program components; the degree to which the program fits the needs and goals of the teachers, students, and school; and the extent to which students find the program engaging and enjoyable. Second, program implementation depends on the support system established to assist teachers with delivering the intervention (Domitrovich et al., 2008; Greenberg et al., 2001). Facets of the support system include training, coaching (*you!*), and ways that school administrators support program delivery (e.g., providing designated time for teachers to deliver the program). Although the field has made significant advances in the development of effective interventions, the body of literature on the support systems that enhance implementation is in its infancy.

The coaching model is based on empirical findings and current research literature regarding factors influencing implementation of evidence-based interventions in school settings as well as mechanisms (e.g., teacher-training processes) that affect teachers' program implementation. These factors are related characteristics of (a) the school (e.g., administrative support), (b) the teacher (e.g., self-efficacy beliefs, professional burnout, perceptions of program acceptability), and (c) the program (e.g., teacher training and performance feedback) (Domitrovich et al., 2008). Throughout this manual, we refer back to these school, teacher, and program factors that influence teacher implementation of a new program.

Teachers' preimplementation beliefs regarding a program, including how it compares with current practice, its effectiveness, and whether it is compatible with the needs, values, and experiences of the school (Elias, Zins, Graczyk, & Weissberg, 2003; Pankratz, Hallfors, & Cho, 2002; Parcel et al., 1991; Ringwalt et al., 2003; Rogers, 2003), can impact their initial acceptance of and motivation to begin an intervention significantly. This, in turn, affects the amount of effort teachers devote to the process and, ultimately, the level of program fidelity and sustainability they achieve. Thus, your initial interactions with teachers are crucial to the development of positive impressions about the program. To capitalize on teachers' positive expectations of a new program and therefore increase their motivation to implement the program with fidelity, training procedures and your subsequent coaching should aim to increase teachers' understanding of the program's principles and should build on teachers' existing experiences and skills related to the intervention (Han & Weiss, 2005). For high-fidelity implementation and sustainability, teachers require your ongoing support. The best outcomes of training are achieved when classroom practice is combined with your feedback on ways to improve teachers' classroom implementation of the skills learned in training by using verbal comments, written notes, or graphs (Noell, Duhon, Gatti, & Connell, 2002).

Through supported implementation, you and your teachers will engage in an ongoing process of implementation support, teacher skill development, and student behavioral change/skill development (Ringwalt et al., 2007; Han & Weiss, 2005; Noell et al., 2002). Teacher growth and success with program implementation increases self-efficacy beliefs and attributions of student gains to the intervention, thereby providing reinforcement and increasing motivation for teacher implementation (Han & Weiss, 2005). Over time, continued motivation, reinforcement, and teacher and student skill development are the positive outcomes of this feedback loop (Han & Weiss, 2005).

As a coach, you play an integral role in supporting teacher implementation. Consultation is a key factor in the feedback loop process and has two main functions: to enhance teachers' implementation skills and to increase teachers' motivation to implement the program in their classroom (Han & Weiss, 2005). This is accomplished through didactics, coach modeling of program components, classroom observations of teacher implementation and student response (e.g., improved behavior/skill development) to the intervention, and performance feedback regarding teacher implementation (Noell et al., 2002). In their seminal meta-analysis, Joyce and Showers (1995) demonstrated that didactics, modeling, practice, and coaching feedback produce similar gains in teachers' understanding of theory and skills. Only performance feedback was associated with teacher application of skills in the classroom. Additional studies have also demonstrated the importance of performance feedback with regard to promoting high-quality program implementation (e.g., Mortenson & Witt, 1998; Noell et al., 2002).

We used the models of Domitrovich et al. (2008) and Han and Weiss (2005) as guides in the development of this coaching model. In the sections that follow, we present the core coaching principles of engagement, collaboration, supported skill development, and constructive feedback. In addition, positive reinforcement and a description of the association of each of these principles with teacher implementation are reviewed. Furthermore, each of these principles are discussed in Chapter 3, in which we describe our Universal Coaching Model in detail.

Objectives

- Develop understanding of the core coaching principles: engagement, collaboration, supported skill development, and constructive feedback.
- Recognize the importance of positive reinforcement in the coaching relationship.

Engagement

A productive and collaborative partnership between you and each teacher is predicated on building relationships with teachers, engaging them to be active participants in the coaching process, and obtaining and maintaining their trust. Just as students who are engaged with the teacher, school, and learning are eager to participate in academic Lessons, so, too, are engaged teachers enthusiastic about trying new techniques and about asking questions or voicing concerns when they are having difficulty. In one study of a comprehensive preschool intervention, this type of openness to consultation was associated positively with higher levels of implementation quality (Domitrovich, Gest, Gill, Jones, & DeRouise, 2009). Without engagement in learning, students' academic effort suffers (Christenson & Thurlow, 2004; Furlong et al., 2003). Similarly, teachers who are not engaged with their coach or who are not open to consultation are likely to use the program inconsistently. They may also be more likely to discontinue the program when challenges or concerns arise, rather than asking you, the coach, for assistance.

Engagement is an ongoing interactive process between the coach and teacher that is influenced by your personal and professional characteristics and behaviors, and the individual characteristics and experiences of the teacher. *A coach who is perceived as similar to the teacher, likeable, empathic, credible, and collaborative may have an easier time engaging teachers than one who is perceived as too different, insensitive, incompetent, and critical.* One way to engage teachers is to emphasize similarities between yourself and the teacher (e.g., share your own experiences working in educational settings). Likeability can be enhanced by using a warm tone of voice, choosing words that validate a teacher's frustrations (i.e., empathize), providing encouragement (e.g., "I know you've got a challenging class, but I know you can do it!"), and displaying friendly body language (e.g., unfolded arms, smiles, nodding head). Credibility is developed by exhibiting professional behavior (e.g., punctuality), knowledge of the program, and the ability to apply program components to meet the needs of the individual teacher or classroom. To demonstrate collaboration, strive to recognize and appreciate genuinely the knowledge and skills that each teacher brings to the classroom, and to develop a partnership with each teacher (e.g., "I'll help you figure out a solution" or "Together we can develop several solutions"). In addition to these strategies, the most successful coaches find ways to inject their own personality into the coaching relationship, such as through the use of humor or finding common ground unrelated to teaching (e.g., discussion about hobbies, children) to enhance the relationship-building process.

Just as you may develop an immediate positive connection with certain teachers, it is entirely possible that your preexisting beliefs, values, and personality could also interfere with engagement. This is completely natural and should be expected at times (Kemp, 2009). Introspection and supervision are important processes to help you develop self-awareness about interpersonal interactions and your effect on others (Kemp, 2009). These issues are discussed further in Chapter 6.

Collaboration

The coaching model is designed to develop and maintain a partnership between the coach and teachers to improve teacher–student interactions in the classroom and to create a classroom environment that fosters student academic learning and encourages the development of positive social–emotional skills and behaviors. The collaborative model implies a nonhierarchical relationship based on equal use of your knowledge as a coach and the teacher's unique strengths. Collaboration includes respect for each person's contribution and leads to a relationship based on trust and open communication. Encourage teachers to participate actively in setting goals and providing feedback to you so the intervention is sensitive to the needs of the teacher and the classroom (Sankaran, Dick, Passfield, & Swepson, 2001; Sutherland & Wehby, 2001).

It is recognized that student behavior is determined by many factors and that strategies that are effective in one classroom may need to be adjusted somewhat to be as effective in another. In a collaborative relationship, a coach works with teachers by involving them actively in the dynamic process of sharing experiences, discussing ideas, and problem solving. Using this approach, the coach should express genuine interest in learning about the cultural, school, and classroom contexts in which the teacher works. Soliciting regular feedback from teachers regarding program feasibility and implementation, as well as the teacher's perspective about your effectiveness at understanding and addressing their concerns fosters a sense of teamwork. Instead of presenting yourself as an "expert" who gives one-sided advice and lectures, portray yourself as a useful resource with tools the teacher may want to add to their teaching toolbox—someone who can work with the teacher to try some of these new "tools." Both the coach and the teacher are experts; teachers function as experts concerning their students and have the ultimate responsibility for judging what works best in their classroom and particular school, and the coach serves as an expert and master teacher concerning children's social–emotional needs, behavior and classroom management principles, and implementation of the program within the context of academic instruction. When both types of expertise are combined through the collaborative process, the intervention is shaped successfully to the unique characteristics and needs of each classroom. In this way, your role as coach becomes one of understanding teacher perspectives, clarifying issues, summarizing important ideas raised by teachers, and reflecting them in a sensitive way (Neufeld & Roper, 2003). When teachers request assistance, possible alternatives can be suggested. Through ongoing coaching and reciprocal feedback, teacher confidence and self-efficacy may be increased. A sense of ownership of the outcomes increases the likelihood of persistence in the face of difficulty. Increased motivation and commitment, and reduced resistance may also be seen. As coach, you then serve as a model for being objective, enthusiastic, and hopeful in their problem solving (as opposed to admiring the problem).

Collaborative coaching that involves a partnership between the coach and teacher is conducted differently from more traditional, directive instruction. Directive, noncollaborative coaching is nonparticipative; the coach teaches and the teacher listens. There are rigid right and wrong methods presented without regard for teacher and classroom goals, values, and life circumstances. The following example illustrates a noncollaborative approach to coaching as well as an example of the collaborative coaching process.

 COMMUNICATE!

Example Dialogue of Noncollaborative Coaching

Teacher: I don't understand why that student will not listen to me! I tell him over and over to keep his hands to himself and not to hit other students, but he turns around and does it right in front of me again.

Coach: You're not being consistent with your consequences. That's why he is not respecting you. I have a better method to use with this student. It works in other classrooms and I am sure it will work in yours.

Example of Coach Using Collaborative Coaching

Coach: It sounds like you've really been working hard with this student. It's frustrating when children are aggressive and don't listen. Are there any strategies you've tried with him that are sometimes effective at stopping his aggression? How have you handled other children who have trouble keeping their hands to themselves? Have you noticed that the strategies you use are effective in reducing that type of behavior? Would you like to hear about some of the strategies I have seen other teachers use in similar situations? One way that some teachers respond to a child who is aggressive is to use a timeout.

In the noncollaborative example, the coach puts blame on the teacher and tells the teacher what he should do. In this example, the teacher may feel the coach does not have enough information, does not understand the situation, or is disrespecting his classroom management skills. In contrast, the collaborative coach reinforces the teacher for trying hard, empathizes and acknowledges the difficulty of the task, invites the teacher to help solve the problem based on the teacher's experience with similar situations in the past, and asks for the teacher's permission to provide some advice about the situation based on strategies other teachers have found helpful, effective, and successful.

Thus, the collaborative process involves *stimulating* teachers to come up with relevant ideas and appropriate solutions based on individual needs and circumstances. This is accomplished by modeling good problem-solving skills the teacher will be able to implement in future situations. As a collaborative coach, you can then *reinforce* and *expand on* important points that teachers have brought up. You can provide examples of strategies that have been used successfully in other classrooms to stimulate problem solving and to facilitate learning. New strategies are introduced by tying into the needs, concerns, and ideas teachers have expressed. As a collaborative coach, you persuade by *explaining the rationale* for the components of the program in such a way that teachers can see the connection to their own stated goals. Finally, you *review, summarize*, and help teachers *generalize and adapt* what they learn to their particular classroom.

This approach can be tricky at first, especially if you are used to working from an expert (i.e., hierarchical) model. In addition to affecting the teacher–coach relationship negatively in an expert model, it can also be problematic in situations when the coach "tells" the teacher a very specific thing to do. If it does not work, the teacher may blame the coach or may think the coach is not credible. With practice, though, you will find the process of collaborative coaching enjoyable. A collaborative approach relieves you from needing to have a "magic pill" or solution to a problem. It can be a relief to know that, in the role of collaborative coach, you are *facilitating* solving problems rather than trying (unrealistically) to come up with a "quick fix" or allowing the session to be used to admire the problem rather than working on a solution.

Supported Skill Development and Constructive Feedback

Supported skill development and constructive feedback are integral components of the coaching model. Although didactic training occurs at the outset, weekly coaching sessions in the classroom are structured to enhance teacher skill development through the use of active techniques. Specifically, you will model program techniques for teachers, observe teachers practice techniques with their students, and provide constructive written and verbal feedback to maximize teacher skill development. Coaching is an adaptive process such that the nature and degree of coaching support are determined on an individual basis and are guided by the teacher's progress. For example, as teachers demonstrate skill acquisition, the coach likely scales back modeling and instead relies on observation and feedback. Eventually, the coach relies on the teachers' report of their progress after observing them demonstrate consistently sound implementation. In this way, coaching represents an ongoing professional learning opportunity in the classroom context, rather than a professional development opportunity disconnected from the school setting (Webster-Wright, 2009). These learning experiences provide the opportunity for teachers to master new skills, thereby increasing their self-efficacy for bringing about student learning and success (Tschannen-Moran, Hoy, & Hoy, 1998).

Ideally, to promote long-term sustainability of evidence-based programs and practices, teachers have to understand the rationale of the programs and practices thoroughly, and how to generalize and adapt program components and practices. Toward this end, and in keeping with the spirit of a collaborative approach, pose open-ended questions as frequently as possible to help teachers develop insight regarding program implementation. Moreover, make an effort to provide structure for teachers to reflect on classroom situations when you observe something critical happen that would be important for them to realize. For example, rather than saying, "Alexander sat down immediately when you told the class to come back into the room from the hallway. That was an opportunity to praise your student," a better strategy to foster insight is to say, "Did you happen to notice that Alexander went right to his seat and sat down after you told the class to come back into the room from the hallway? Can you think of anything you can do that might make it more likely he'll follow instructions next time too?" Through these types of discussions, teacher skill development can be supported in terms of assessing the effectiveness of program components, making changes when necessary to strengthen the use of program components, and generalizing program principles to everyday classroom situations.

Positive Reinforcement

Positive reinforcement is a core behavioral principle that refers to the increased likelihood of the occurrence of a particular behavior following the reward of that behavior. The coaching model relies on positive reinforcement to motivate and reward teachers for consistent program implementation. Positive reinforcement is not reserved just for exceptional program implementation; rather, it is an integral, ongoing part of coaching that plays a complementary role to supported skill development and constructive feedback by shaping teacher behavior throughout the process. Positive reinforcement also helps to generate excitement about the program so it is not viewed as a burden by teachers.

Positive reinforcement generally takes one of two forms: praise (written and/or verbal) or tangible items (e.g., prizes such as classroom supplies or teacher gift card). There are a number of strategies coaches can use to maximize the effectiveness of positive reinforcement. First, identify the specific behavior the teacher demonstrated. For example, saying "I like the way you used your harmonica to quiet your students" conveys to the teacher the value of using the harmonica as opposed to saying "Good job!" Second, when using praise or providing a reinforcer, convey sincerity and enthusiasm through tone, body language, and word choice—for example, "I was excited to see that you added new Tootle Notes to your Tootle Board! You earned this week's incentive for doing that!" (Tootle Notes are written compliments that teachers write to students or students write to their peers. A Tootle Board is a bulletin board in the classroom that displays the Tootle Notes to help promote a positive classroom climate.) Finally, aim to provide reinforcement contingent on teacher behavior— in other words, closely following observation or evidence of the teacher's use of program skills.

Praise is one of the best reinforcers, so always keep an eye out for ways to praise teacher skill and to point out gains made in skill development—for example, "You've come a long way! Remember how hard it used to be to deliver the Lessons while your students were misbehaving? Now you've become really good at ignoring minor misbehavior." Focus on the specific things the teacher has done to promote change in the classroom and students rather than on the changes made by students, unless they are a direct result of the teacher's behavior—for example, "I noticed that Joe is really responding to your praise! That's terrific! Keep it up!" A number of positive reinforcement strategies are discussed in detail in Chapter 3.

This chapter provided a foundational theory and literature on which the coaching model rests. In addition, a brief overview of the core principles of the coaching model were introduced: engagement, collaboration, supporting teacher skill development and constructive feedback, as well as the use of positive reinforcement with teachers. Overall, coaches play an integral role in the skill development of teachers and, ultimately, the effectiveness of interventions in their classroom.

Chapter 2 Reflection Questions

- What are the four core coaching principles discussed in this chapter?

- What is collaborative coaching? How is it different from noncollaborative coaching?

- As an effective coach, what types of things will you do to support teachers' skill development?

- What are some ways to use positive reinforcement with classroom teachers?

- Think about your current strategies for working with teachers. Are you currently using the four core principles in your coaching? What do you think you are doing well? What could you do differently?

Universal Coaching Model

The Universal Coaching Model represents a collaborative coaching approach that includes specific coaching activities and strategies used with *every teacher* involved with delivering the program. The collaborative approach, as well as the coaching activities and strategies described in this chapter, provide the foundation for implementation support. Many teachers implement the program successfully when coaches rely on the strategies included in the universal model (Chapter 4 focuses on coaching strategies for teachers who need a more *intensive approach* to support their implementation). The first half of this chapter provides specific information about a pacing guide for carrying out these strategies whereas the second half of the chapter provides detailed information describing the process of being a collaborative coach. Data collection and feedback are discussed, common early implementation challenges are presented that you will likely observe as teachers implement the PAX GBG for the first time. Last, common coach challenges are presented.

Objectives

- Learn the importance of timelines and pacing guides in successful implementation of a prevention program.
- Understand the process of becoming a collaborative coach and how to provide support and structure to the coaching sessions.
- Learn how to use data to provide feedback, set goals, and provide positive reinforcement.
- Navigate through the common early implementation challenges of first-time implementers of the PAX GBG.

A Multiphase Approach for Supporting Teacher Implementation

Coaching in the context of the Universal Coaching Model begins the week following teacher training. There are preparatory tasks in which coaches may be involved before coaching begins, such as meeting administrators, training teachers, and delivering materials. Coaching activities are grouped into three phases: (a) connect, (b) cultivate, and (c) consolidate (Chorpita, Becker, Phillips, & Daleiden, 2011). Table 3.1 provides a pacing guide for each coaching activity involved in the Universal Coaching Model, the purpose of each activity,

TABLE 3.1 Pacing Guide for Coaching Activities in the Universal Coaching Model

Coaching Phase	Timing (after training)	Coaching Activity	Purpose
Connect: Set the stage for teachers to achieve high implementation through relationship-building preparatory activities.	Week 1	Establish the coach–teacher team	Begin to establish rapport. Identify a time to visit the classroom.
		Visit the classroom for the first time.	Assist the teacher with preparing the classroom environment. Establish a plan collaboratively for implementation.
	Week 2	Engage students as active participants.	Deliver Lesson 1 (Creating a Classroom Vision) and Lesson 2 (PAX Cues). Set the stage for the PAX Good Behavior Game by using language and behaviors that promote PAX.
		Support the teacher's initial efforts.	Continue building rapport. Visit during scheduled Lesson time to reinforce regular use of program elements. Provide feedback about the Lesson and the environment.
	Week 3	Enhance students' on-task behaviors.	Deliver Lesson 3, Beat the Timer. Continue to check in with teachers throughout the week to assess and possibly assist with the implementation of other Lessons.
		Observe Kid of the Day.	Assess teacher implementation of Kid of the Day by observing the classroom environment, teacher behaviors, and student involvement.
Cultivate: Use active learning strategies to support teachers in achieving high implementation.	Week 4	Kick off the Good Behavior Game	Model Game implementation. Encourage the teacher to play the Game. Observe and provide feedback.
	Week 5	Set the stage for social–emotional content Lessons.	Review and plan first few content Lessons collaboratively.
	Weeks 6–8	Polish teacher skills.	Conduct weekly observations and feedback.
Consolidate: Solve problems that create barriers while supporting sustained implementation.	Weekly, ongoing throughout the school year.	Maintain implementation and address minor challenges.	Check in regarding the frequency and effectiveness of the Games and Lessons. Solve collaboratively problems that create barriers to implementation and address minor student behavior challenges.

and the timeline according to which activity is conducted, and descriptions of each coaching activity.

Phase 1: Connect

The Connect phase of the Universal Coaching Model is all about laying the foundation for successful implementation of any evidence-based program. Important themes include building rapport, creating a positive classroom environment, planning regularly and collaboratively for implementation, providing coach-supported teacher introduction of program components, and reinforcing teacher skill development.

Week 1
Establish the Coach–Teacher Team

After the teachers are fully trained, your role as a coach is to help each teacher and the entire school staff get the program up and running. However, before jumping into coaching, it is necessary to establish positive working relationships with teachers; therefore, the primary goal of the first meeting with teachers after the training is for the coach to begin developing rapport with teachers.

Imagine you are a teacher and someone new is entering your classroom to support you in a program you learned recently. What thoughts might you have about this situation? Is it reasonable that you might think the coach is evaluating you or is going to report to the principal about what is going on in the classroom? Is it reasonable that you might not want to follow the program because of competing demands (e.g., "one more thing on your plate")? Is it reasonable that you might not want to follow the program because you do not think it will be helpful or because you already have control of your class?

The answer to all of these questions would be a resounding yes! It is absolutely reasonable that teachers might be apprehensive about having a coach come into their classroom and that they might not want to deliver the program to their students. This is a completely normal response to the introduction of a new program into a school and it is one the coach should expect. Therefore, it is important for you as coach to lay the groundwork for a successful coach–teacher collaboration by beginning to establish rapport and by clarifying roles at the first meeting with teachers after their training.

How should you begin to establish rapport with teachers? If this is the first time you are meeting a particular teacher or group of teachers, introduce yourself by way of providing your name and some background about your relevant experiences as a teacher, school-based professional, or coach. Then, provide teachers with the opportunity to introduce themselves and to talk about their professional experiences. Be mindful of teachers' verbal and nonverbal reactions to you and the things you say. Smiling, making eye contact, and contributing to the conversation spontaneously are indicators of positive rapport, whereas looking away, frowning, engaging in other activities (e.g., grading papers, checking e-mail), and providing short answers may indicate teachers are not engaged with you.

It is helpful for you to clarify your role as the coach from the onset. One way to lead in to this discussion is to ask teachers what they think the role of the coach is using open-ended questions.

COMMUNICATE!

Coach: So now that we've introduced ourselves and talked a little about our backgrounds, I wanted to talk about our roles with the PAX GBG. What do you think my job is as a coach?

Teacher A: I think it's to help us do the program exactly the way it's supposed to be done.

Coach: OK, so your thought is that there is a strict way to do the program and that I am going to work with you so you do it in a certain way.

Teacher B: I think that too, and that you'll probably have meetings with the principal to tell her how we're doing.

Coach: **(With Humor)** Ah, okay, so I'm kind of like a spy too? If those two things are true—that there's a right way to do the program and that I am going to tell the principal how people are doing—what are your thoughts about that?

Teacher B: I don't really feel comfortable with that.

Teacher A: I don't even want you in my classroom if that is the case, but I guess I can't do anything about it.

Coach: Well, I appreciate you both being so candid. A lot of teachers have similar thoughts and it gives me the opportunity to clarify a few things. I want us to be a team. We each bring skills and expertise to the table. You are the expert on your school and classroom, and I have experience with the PAX GBG. My job is to support you in using the tools that are part of the PAX GBG, and I know that not every teacher finds every tool useful. Therefore, we'll start with the basics of the Lessons and the Game and we'll see how they best fit into your classroom. We'll do that together and I'll count on you to give me feedback about how things are going. It's true that I'll also observe how things are going in the classroom, but I will not be sharing details with your administrators. In fact, I go out of my way to avoid evaluating teachers in that way. That's not my role. If the administrator wants to visit your classroom to see the program, that's one thing, but I won't be reporting to the administrator about how teachers are doing, except to say something positive!

As in this sample script, open-ended questions provide teachers with the opportunity to share their initial thoughts. The coach in the sample uses some praise as well as simple reflection with humor and then also normalizes the thoughts of these teachers before providing clarification about the coach's role. In addition, the coach conveys a collaborative approach by using the word *team* and stressing the importance of teacher feedback. Furthermore, the coach also dispels any perceptions that he or she will be evaluating teachers to report back to the administrator.

In addition to initial rapport building, the introductory meeting provides an opportunity to ensure teachers have all necessary materials, to check in about classroom preparation, to answer questions, and to schedule a time to visit the classroom to help teachers prepare the classroom environment.

Visit the Classroom for the First Time

The goals for the initial visit to the classroom are twofold: (a) to assist the teacher with preparing the classroom environment and (b) to collaboratively create a plan for introducing the program to the students.

Prepare the Classroom Environment

A positive classroom environment provides a favorable context for the PAX GBG. Teachers receive many materials to create a positive classroom environment, including visual thumbs up/thumbs down cues to be displayed on students' desks, PAX and Spleem posters, and the PAX Quiet harmonica. Assisting the teacher in displaying materials (e.g., posters), creating a prize box and PAX Stix, and posting a Tootle Board (which, as mentioned earlier, is a bulletin board hung in the classroom that displays Tootle Notes, which are written compliments from teachers and students) provides an opportunity for the coach to continue building a positive working relationship by lending a hand and also by taking advantage of the unstructured time during which you and the teacher can talk about neutral topics as well as the intervention. Here's an example:

 COMMUNICATE!

Coach: I like what you've done with regard to hanging materials on the wall. It looks like you have a section of the wall devoted to math and a section devoted to vocabulary. What are your thoughts about where to hang the PAX and Spleem posters?

Teacher: I think it would be helpful to have them up front so they are within sight and reach during instruction.

Coach: That's a great idea! I think having them be easily accessible is really helpful. Have you thought about your Tootle Board yet?

Teacher: Not really. It's just a bulletin board, right?

Coach: It can be. I've seen teachers do it a variety of ways. Some have it on a bulletin board in the classroom and some post the Tootles on the door. Other teachers have a space set up where they post Tootles as well as the Feelings Faces that you'll talk about during the Lessons. You can really be as creative as you want, but it's ideal to post the Tootles in a spot where the students can see them regularly.

Teacher: To help provide structure during transition times, I thought that I might put a Tootle envelope on the door so that when students enter the classroom in the morning and after lunch they can pull a Tootle and begin writing.

> Coach: That's a terrific idea! What a great way to make Tootles part of your daily routine! I am definitely going to suggest that to other teachers who are looking for ideas.

In this exchange, the coach uses open-ended questions to elicit the teacher's ideas before offering his or her own, thereby acknowledging the teacher's expertise. Even those ideas that are offered are framed as what the coach has observed other teachers do, thereby reducing the perception of the coach as the expert. The coach offers multiple ideas from which the teacher might choose and praises the teacher for coming up with a novel idea. In these ways, the coach guides teachers but encourages them to play an active role in preparing the classroom for the PAX GBG.

By week 2 after the training, teachers are at a variety of stages in terms of preparing their classrooms for the program. In many classrooms, the coach assists the teacher with classroom preparations. However, when arriving in another classroom, you might find that a teacher has already hung the posters, displayed the desk cues, and created the Tootle Board. In this situation, offer verbal praise, a written Tootle Note, and possibly even a tangible reward, such as pencils, to reinforce the teacher's enthusiasm and participation. The coach may want to provide the teacher with a copy of the Tootle and Tootle Board Flyer (Appendix D), which lists tips for using Tootle Notes and a Tootle Board to create a positive classroom community. In addition, there is a Tootle Board Checklist (Appendix E) the coach can complete and leave with teachers to provide feedback on their Tootle Board.

The first visit to the classroom also provides the opportunity for the coach and teacher to develop a plan for implementation collaboratively. Ideally, each teacher delivers two Lessons each week and plays three Games per day. It is helpful to ask the teacher to identify times when they will deliver the Lessons and play the Game. Although teachers can adjust scheduled times as needed, this type of verbal commitment increases the likelihood that the Lessons and Games will be incorporated into the classroom routine, and provides means of scheduling when the coach can visit the classroom to observe program implementation. As a coach, it is also important to assist teachers with identifying any potential barriers to Lesson delivery and Game playing, and work to identify solutions to these barriers to help them stay on track.

 COMMUNICATE!

> Coach: I like your idea of delivering your Lessons Tuesdays and Thursdays after morning announcements. Sometimes things get in the way of teachers delivering the Lessons. Can you think of anything that might interfere with your Lesson delivery?

> Teacher: Well, it's possible there might be an assembly or fire drill at that time. Other than that, I think it's a good time to do the Lessons because it will help the students transition to academic instruction.
>
> Coach: So it sounds like, on occasion, there might be something unexpected that could interfere with the Lessons. What do you think would be a reasonable backup plan if this should happen?
>
> Teacher: Well, I could probably make up a missed Lesson on Friday afternoon. That time is usually flexible for us. Either that, or I could do both Lessons back to back one morning.
>
> Coach: You've come up with two possible solutions. Which solution is preferable to you?
>
> Teacher: I would prefer to make it up on Friday afternoon so that I have more time. However, if I can't, I could make it up the following week and do them back to back.
>
> Coach: I agree that making up a Lesson on Friday is probably preferable in terms of timing and ensuring students understand the main points of each Lesson. If, for some reason, making up on Friday doesn't work out, let's plan to talk and we can figure out how to make up the missed Lesson.

In this exchange, the coach deferred repeatedly to the teacher and elicited her opinion about when to deliver the Lessons. The teacher's opinions regarding potential barriers and potential solutions were elicited by the coach. Moreover, the coach offered reinforcement for the preferred solution and expressed intentions to help the teacher solve the problem of missed Lessons collaboratively.

A similar conversation can be held to identify times when teachers intend to play the Game. Although playing the Game can be spontaneous, it is helpful for the coach to recommend that teachers start out playing during low-demand classroom situations, such as independent seatwork, while the students and teacher are first learning to play the Game. After students are successful at winning the Game and teachers feel confident in playing it, the Game can be played during increasingly demanding classroom situations, such as transitions (e.g., returning to the classroom after lunch, changing classes), group activities, and academic instruction.

A pacing guide with a schedule for delivering the Lessons can be provided and explained to each teacher (Appendix F). The pacing guide was developed to reduce the likelihood that teachers feel overwhelmed by a program manual filled with tasks and Lessons. Breaking down the program into weekly activities helps teachers develop self-efficacy related to the program, and helps the teacher and coach monitor implementation. Note that in the pacing guide, the first seven Lessons are preparatory Lessons that set up the program in the classroom. The coach assists the teachers with implementing many of these Lessons. Point out to the teachers that the pacing guide reflects the school calendar and the expectation for Lesson delivery is adjusted on the weeks when there are any missed school days (e.g., Spring Break). When unexpected closings take place (e.g., for winter weather), teachers may fall behind with implementation. Ideally, the coach and teacher develop collaboratively an adjusted pacing guide and plan to be used in these situations (e.g., doubling up on Lessons, having the coach teach a Lesson).

Week 2
Engage Students as Active Participants

Creating a coach–teacher team and preparing the classroom are two integral steps to successful implementation; however, the students are the key to the success of this program. Students who are engaged learners are more likely to develop and use the skills taught in the program than students who are not engaged.

The coach's first involvement with students occurs when assisting the teacher with the activity of creating a PAX vision for the classroom/school (Lesson 1 in the pacing guide). Together, the coach and teacher can engage students in creating a PAX vision for the classroom by asking students what they will see, hear, feel, and do more of in a PAX classroom/school. Students often come up with things such as see more smiles, hear more nice words, and feel more comfortable and relaxed, and they do more work or spend more time helping one another. As the students call out these ideas, the coach and teacher generate a chart that is then placed in the classroom as a reminder of this vision and can be referenced throughout the school year.

Conversely, the coach and teacher will also want to ask students what they see, hear, feel, and do less of in a PAX school. Students often say they see less hitting, hear fewer angry words, and feel less stressed, and that teachers and students do less yelling. Again, all these responses should be noted on a chart that can be hung in the classroom. After these two charts are created, they can be labeled. For example, what will happen more is labeled "PAX" and this chart is the guideline or goals throughout the year; what will happen less is labeled "Spleem."

This activity helps students understand the expectations of a PAX environment. Next, it is time to *practice PAX*. The coach and teacher move from words to deeds by using a language that promotes PAX, constantly referring to PAX and PAX leaders, and modeling PAX for others to copy. Remember to use lots of praise when you see PAX behavior in the students as well as the teacher!

Support the Teacher's Initial Efforts

After delivering Lesson 1 (Creating a Classroom Vision) collaboratively, many teachers will be excited to move ahead with implementing the rest of the program. There are five additional preparatory Lessons that need to be completed in the first three weeks: PAX Cues (Lesson 2), Beat the Timer (Lesson 3), Kid of the Day (Lesson 4), Are You a PAX Leader? (Lesson 5), and The Golden Rule (Lesson 6). In addition to Lesson 1, you should aim to be involved in the delivery of Beat the Timer (Lesson 3). Although you might not be able to be involved with delivering the other preparatory Lessons, it is important for you to plan and review each Lesson with teachers to ensure they understand each program component they will be introducing to the class. Each Lesson plan includes an objective, materials, and how to carry out the Lesson that should be reviewed with teachers. In some cases, teachers are so enthusiastic about the program they want to do more than two Lessons per week. This is perfectly acceptable and be sure to praise teachers who are this eager!

Any time you are in the classroom, there are many things you can do to gauge the quality of teacher implementation for Lessons that you do not observe directly. First, look around the classroom environment. Are signs relevant to PAX cues displayed in a central location? Second, observe teacher behavior. Does the teacher refer to PAX cues? Third, assess the students. When the teacher uses PAX cues, do the students respond in a way that demonstrates they understand the cues? If the teacher does not use the cues spontaneously, you can use the cues (e.g., blow your harmonica) to observe student responses. You can also ask students questions about program components (e.g., "What does a zero-inch voice mean?") and provide lots of praise for students who know the answers (e.g., "I am so impressed, Ms. Forrest. You have a classroom of PAX leaders!").

One thing that is useful for you to orient yourself to is whether the teacher is maintaining a regularly scheduled Lesson time. As opposed to delivering a Lesson whenever there is a "convenient" time, a regularly scheduled Lesson time helps make the Lessons part of the classroom routine and reduces the likelihood that teachers will prioritize something else over teaching the Lessons. Popping in at the identified time is informative in this regard. If the teacher delivers the Lesson at the designated time, be sure to provide verbal and written reinforcement (e.g., Tootle Note) for Lesson delivery, and perhaps even an incentive to reinforce the teacher.

Sometimes a teacher no longer intends to deliver a Lesson at the designated time. In these instances, find out more about what is interfering with Lesson delivery so that barriers can be reduced before they really interfere with program implementation. Use a nonblaming and noncritical approach to elicit specific information about the barriers to Lesson delivery (e.g., "Most teachers are unable to deliver a scheduled Lesson at one time or another because something gets in the way. What's getting in the way of your Lesson today?"). Next, identify potential solutions collaboratively and assist the teacher with identifying the one that has the best chance for success. Then, be sure to return at the time when the Lesson is rescheduled so you can provide reinforcement for Lesson delivery or continue to work with the teacher to solve barriers if the teacher is unable to deliver the Lesson again.

Week 3
Enhance Students' On-Task Behavior

Beat the Timer is the second preparatory Lesson (Lesson 3 in the manual). The Beat the Timer game challenges students to complete a task in less time than what is set on the timer, thereby increasing efficiency and decreasing off-task student behaviors. This activity is particularly effective during transitions, such as moving from the carpet to desks, putting away materials, and lining up.

Before delivering the Lesson, the coach and teacher should meet briefly to discuss the Beat the Timer challenge and to plan its introduction to students. Allow teachers to determine whether they would like to conduct the entire Lesson themselves or whether they would like the coach to play a role in presenting the concept to the class.

Immediately before introducing Beat the Timer, remind teachers of the purpose of Beat the Timer and orient them to look for how students respond to the timer challenge. After playing Beat the Timer, find out the teacher's perceptions? of how things went, identify any anticipated obstacles to implementation, pinpoint times when the timer challenge might be useful, and provide praise for a job well done!

Observe Kid of the Day

Although it is not necessary to observe the Lesson during which teachers introduce the concept of Kid of the Day, it is very important that you observe a time when the Kid of the Day activities are underway. Find out when teachers select a new Kid of the Day (this is likely first thing in the morning) and be present in the classroom at that time. Provide the teacher with the Kid of the Day Flyer (Appendix G) for tips on implementing the Kid of the Day successfully in the classroom, and the Kid of the Day Guidelines (Appendix H) for six questions teachers should ask themselves regarding implementing Kid of the Day.

- Does the teacher select a student randomly to be the new Kid of the Day and have a method for keeping track of who has had a turn? Ideally, teachers use sticks with each student's name on them to select a new Kid of the Day at random, then removes the sticks from the container of students who have had a turn. Kid of the Day selection is not based on behavior and is never removed as punishment.
- Does the classroom have a Kid of the Day identifier (e.g., visor, hat, ribbon)? The special identifier helps the Kid of the Day feel important and also serves as a visual reminder to teachers to enlist the help of that particular student throughout the day.
- Look around the classroom environment. Is the name of the Kid of the Day displayed in a central location? Again, this is an indication that the teacher incorporates Kid of the Day into the classroom routine.
- Observe teacher behavior. Does the teacher complete the full-page Tootle and post it in the classroom? Is a copy sent home with the Kid of the Day? Tootling serves as noncontingent reinforcement to students and develops a positive classroom environment.
- Does the teacher select the Kid of the Day for special roles and tasks? Assess the students to gauge implementation when you are not present. For example, you can ask students to raise their hands if they have been selected as Kid of the Day to see how many times the teacher has implemented it. The coach can also ask students who have been Kid of the Day with which special tasks or classroom activities they got to help the teacher.

Following Kid of the Day activities, provide teachers with verbal praise as well as a written Tootle Note to model using Tootles. Also, provide feedback regarding teachers' strengths of implementation and areas on which they can work.

Phase 2: Cultivate

Now that you and the teachers have put a lot of time and effort into laying the groundwork for successful implementation of the program, you'll begin to incorporate coaching strategies such as modeling, observation, and feedback, which will help elevate teacher skills to a desired level of implementation.

Week 4
Kick off the Game

Although teachers leave the training with increased familiarity with the PATHS to PAX Program, teachers benefit from seeing the coach model before they begin playing the Game. There may be enthusiastic teachers who have already started playing the Game, but it is still important to model the Game in the classroom to make sure students understand the concepts and the teacher plays the Game correctly. There are three main aspects of the modeling visit: (a) setup and providing rationale, (b) modeling, and (c) debriefing.

Before modeling the Game, explain to the teacher what you are going to do as the coach and provide the teacher with a structure for observation. Provide the teacher with a copy of Ten Easy Steps for Playing a Successful Game (Appendix I) with students as well as a copy of the Good Behavior Game Modeling Checklist (Appendix A). Using the Good Behavior Game Modeling Checklist, teachers are able to make notes about each element of the Game the coach demonstrates when modeling.

Set the stage for the Game by delivering Lesson 6 (Introducing the PATHS to PAX GBG). During this brief Lesson, the coach introduces the rules of the Game (e.g., directions of the activity), identifies teams, and elicits types of Spleems (e.g., disruptive behaviors) from the students as well as the teacher that will be counted during the Game. Different teachers have different expectations for their students, so it is helpful to include the teacher when going over for which Spleems the coach will be looking during the Game. In addition, ask teachers about their personal preferences for zero-inch or three-inch voices based on the norms for their classroom.

Play the Game while the students do an independent activity. In kindergarten and sometimes the first grade, the coach can instruct students simply to draw a picture of themselves being a PAX Leader in school on a blank piece of paper or provide them with a copy of My Most Wonderful School (Appendix J) and have them draw a picture of the most wonderful school . In older grades, it may be helpful to instruct students to write a few sentences and/or draw a picture that shows them being a PAX Leader in school or provide them with a copy of The Greatest Classroom (Appendix K) and have them draw a picture or write a few sentences about the greatest classroom. (Providing choices seems less threatening to students who may have academic difficulties).

Keep the Game short (e.g., one to two minutes for early elementary grades, three to four minutes for upper elementary grades) to ensure student success, and use lots of praise for students/teams displaying positive behavior, particularly when you see students get back on track after displaying a Spleem. Find as many opportunities as possible to enlist the teacher's assistance while you model the Game. For example, have the teacher blow the harmonica to start and stop the Game, set the timer, help count Spleems, and/or pick a prize at random from Granny's Wacky Prize Box. Giving teachers an opportunity to get their feet wet will help pave the way for playing the Game independently.

After modeling, elicit teachers' perspective regarding the Game components as well as student response to the Game. This can be done well by using the Good Behavior Game Modeling Checklist (Appendix A) as a guide for the discussion. This debriefing provides the opportunity to assess the teacher's enthusiasm and ambivalence regarding the Game, to identify potential modifications that might need to be introduced to fit the Game into the classroom, to emphasize positive student response to the Game, and to foster the teacher's self-efficacy for implementation.

A key element of the modeling visit is to have teachers play a Game *immediately* after the coach models it. If teachers are willing, genuinely praise them for their efforts/enthusiasm, sit off to the side and observe, offer support if they need help, and complete the Good Behavior Game Modeling Checklist (Appendix A) to provide feedback to the teacher after the Game (feedback is discussed later in this chapter). Sometimes, teachers are reluctant to play the Game immediately, perhaps because of practical concerns (e.g., lack of time) or personal concerns (e.g., nervousness). If needed, make an appointment to come back at another time that week with the expectation that the coach will observe the teacher play the Game at that time. Most teachers only need one modeling visit, then observation and feedback to implement the Game independently and successfully, although some coaches find it necessary to conduct multiple modeling visits if a teacher needs additional support.

Until the teacher gets used to the Game, they should play it only during independent student activities (e.g., seatwork) and when activities have a specific educational purpose (e.g., a math worksheet practicing a skill the teacher taught recently and practiced as a group). When teachers are more comfortable with the Game, they can begin to play it while teaching, during small-group work assignments, on the carpet, and during transitions, such as in the hallway or moving between classes.

After the Game is introduced successfully into the classroom, it is time to focus on the social–emotional Lessons.

Week 5
Set the Stage for Social–Emotional Content Lessons

Although the Game involves multiple elements that are unfamiliar to teachers, delivery of the social–emotional Lessons parallels classroom instruction; therefore, modeling a Lesson is not necessary for the majority of teachers (although may be helpful for new teachers or those who request it). Instead, it is helpful for the coach to assist teachers with developing a method to prepare for the Lessons.

When possible, plan for approximately 20 minutes alone with the teacher to look over the first few Lessons in the manual. Locate and organize materials specified for each Lesson. Review and discuss with the teacher the Lesson objectives, notes about what to look for, and the content. Use the Coach–Teacher Collaborative Planning Sheet (Appendix C) to facilitate discussion, highlight main concepts, and plan preparation tasks. Also, highlight the "self-checks" noted on the bottom of the form. These teaching behaviors reflect principles of effective teaching and are ideals for which teachers should strive when teaching the Lessons. In addition, as the coach, you will look for these behaviors when you observe Lessons. You can also provide the teacher with a copy of the Guidelines for Conducting a High-Quality Lesson (Appendix L) that lists tips for teaching a high-quality Lesson.

Although the Lessons could be delivered as the teacher reads the manual word for word, encourage the teacher to identify points where they can insert their own personality and examples into the Lessons to engage students and make them more enjoyable and personal.

 COMMUNICATE!

Coach: One of the main things we have found with these Lessons is that if students are engaged and interested, they are more likely to remember the material and use the skills at other times of the day. Now that we've talked about the general purpose and content of the Lessons, what are your thoughts about how you might deliver the Lesson to hook your students?

Teacher: I have some good examples of times when I experienced the different feelings in the Lessons. I know the students always enjoy when I tell them stories of when I was a child.

Coach: That's a great idea! I can picture your students having fun listening to your stories and imagining you feeling happy or frustrated. That must really help them connect to you.

In this example, the coach provides a rationale (but no suggestion), seeks the teacher's perspective, and reinforces the teacher's idea, thereby demonstrating collaborative principles. Having the teacher think about these things ahead of time will help them deliver the Lesson seamlessly. The coach can also emphasize the importance of Lesson generalization to student skill development by helping the teacher identify situations during which she could refer back to or reinforce Lesson content.

 COMMUNICATE!

Coach: I think this Lesson [On Accident/On Purpose] really hits home because it seems people are often likely to assume someone's negative behaviors were intentional. Are there situations when you think it would be helpful to refer back to this material to help your students deal with uncomfortable feelings or potential conflict?

Teacher: Absolutely! On a daily basis someone gets upset at someone else for supposedly doing something intentional and it turns out that it was more likely an accident—especially during transitions! Students are moving in all different directions and someone gets bumped and then a fight brews.

Coach: Ah, that's a great example. What are your thoughts about how you might generalize the material from the Lesson to that kind of situation?

Teacher: I could blow the harmonica to regain some order and have the students take their seats. Then I could ask the students to name the problem—you know, that the student was bumped. Then, we could name the kinds of things that would tell us whether it happened by accident or on purpose. So, by accident might be that the person who did the bumping was looking the other way or that he apologized. On purpose might be that the student had a mean look on his face. Then we could see which of these most likely reflects how things played out.

Coach: That is a fabulous idea! That's really spelling out a great method for the students to use these skills. And to facilitate that, it might be helpful at the end of the Lesson to let students know this is what you are going to do, and perhaps even practice it at a time when things are calm so that it provides a rehearsal for what you'll all do when this kind of situation arises.

In this example, the coach begins with a collaborative approach by soliciting the teacher's ideas about when the Lesson material might be useful during daily classroom life. The coach reinforces the teacher's participation in the discussion by providing praise and then asks her ideas about how to generalize the materials. Following the teacher's response, the coach again provides verbal reinforcement and then expands on the idea with a suggestion of her own to help set up the teacher's plan for success.

To wrap up these planning sessions, the coach could ask teachers if they feel comfortable delivering the Lessons or if they would prefer to observe the coach or have the coach present for assistance. Encourage teachers to have the Coach–Teacher Collaborative Planning Sheet (Appendix C) handy following the Lesson to prompt the teacher to do a self-assessment using the principles of effective teaching (e.g., stating the objective clearly, staying on topic, pacing).

Weeks 6 through 8
Polish Teacher Skills

During the preparation phase of coaching, the teacher was observed and the coach provided feedback on a weekly basis around a set of circumscribed topics (e.g., specific preparatory Lesson, classroom environment). After modeling of the Game is completed, the coach should still be present in the classroom to observe a Game and Lesson on a weekly basis for the remainder of Phase 2 (approximately three weeks). However, the evidence used to assess how well PATHS to PAX GBG is working in each classroom has now expanded, as described in the following paragraphs regarding the Good Behavior Game Implementation Rubric (Appendix M) and Good Behavior Game Rubric Rating Form (Appendix N).

During the Lesson portion of the rubric observation, the coach rates the teacher on four key domains of the Lesson: (a) Teaching of PATHS to PAX GBG Concepts, (b) Level of Disruption during the Lesson, (c) Pacing of the Lesson, and (d) Teacher Affect and Energy during the Lesson. Each domain of the rubric is scored by a zero- to four-point response.

For example, to gain the highest score (4 points) on the Teaching the PATHS to PAX GBG Concepts domain, teachers must state the purpose, relate the Lesson to other learning, related the content of the Lesson to the Lesson topic, and be well prepared, understand the concepts, and assess their students. For the Level of Disruption during the Lesson, Pacing of the Lesson, and Teacher Affect and Energy during the Lesson domains, teachers must meet a certain percentage (e.g., "Teacher demonstrates genuine and appropriate affect and energy at least 90% of the time") to score four points.

The coach also provides scores for seven key domains of the Game: (a) Preparing the Students for the Game, (b) Choice of Activity, (c) Timer, (d) Teams, (e) Response to Spleems, (f) Prizes, and (g) After Game/Reviewing Spleems. Similar to the Lessons, each domain of the Game rubric is scored by a zero- to four-point response. For example, for the Preparing the Students for the Game domain, to receive the highest score (four points), teachers must get or have the students attention, give clear/concise directions, identify Spleems, set the timer in view, tell the students how long the Game will be played , and announce the start of the Game. If teachers miss one or more of these items, their score decreases. Each domain of the rubric is set up similarly; teachers have to go through all the key steps of the Game to gain credit for those items and score higher on each domain.

Finally, provide ratings for the other program components: (a) PATHS to PAX GBG Modeling and Generalization (i.e., language, cues, Tootle Notes, Kid of the Day, additional elements, Lesson concepts, student social–emotional competence), (b) PATHS to PAX GBG Game Observation (i.e., system for tracking Spleems), and (c) General Teaching Style and Behavior (i.e., openness to consultation, ability to solve problems, level of punitive discipline, interpersonal style, and classroom management and discipline skills). As with the Lessons and Games, the coach uses a zero- to four-point scale to rate teachers on these key elements.

Along with completing the Good Behavior Game Rubric Rating Form (Appendix N) during the observation, the coach also completes the Good Behavior Game Modeling Checklist (Appendix A) by checking off implementation steps and making notes in the margin to highlight teacher implementation strengths and areas for improvement. In addition, the coach should prepare a Tootle Note offering written praise for implementing key elements of the program successfully. Ideally, the Tootle should highlight specific goals the teacher has accomplished or is improving on (e.g., "Teacher is trying to use the harmonica to gain attention more successfully"). The individual ratings from the Good Behavior Game Implementation Rubric (Appendix M) are not shared with teachers. However, the coach can provide teachers with a copy of the Good Behavior Game Modeling Checklist (Appendix A) and Tootle Note, using these documents to facilitate a conversation involving feedback. In addition, the coach can deliver feedback by providing praise for successful implementation, eliciting the teacher's perspective of what went well or not so well, offering rationales and feedback on elements where the teacher could improve, and setting goals when necessary (see the discussion on feedback later in this chapter).

If time does not permit an immediate and in-depth feedback session, the coach should provide brief feedback by thanking the teacher for allowing the coach to observe, providing praise, and conducting a brief (e.g., two-minute) discussion of the Good Behavior Game Modeling Checklist (Appendix A)as well as any additional points regarding Game and

Lesson implementation. Last, schedule a more convenient time to meet with the teacher to give more detailed feedback.

During each classroom visit, the coach will also want to update a Lesson Log (Appendix O) (discussed later in this chapter) and collect any completed Game Scoreboards (Appendix P) from the teacher to help inform assessment of implementation consistency. For teachers who are implementing the program inconsistently or who are implementing the program at a lower quality, an Action Plan is developed to enhance these goals further and to aid in increasing quality implementation (see Chapter 4).

Phase 3: Consolidate

During Phase 1, the coach's efforts are focused on setting the stage for successful implementation. This involves coteaching Lessons and observing a small set of program components weekly. During Phase 2, the focus is on using active learning strategies to elevate teacher skills to an effective level using modeling, an elaborate observation rubric, and weekly feedback. During Phase 3, the coach shifts his or her attention to helping teachers maintain an effective level of proficiency and to supporting teachers who are experiencing implementation challenges.

Weekly, Ongoing throughout the School Year
Maintain Implementation and Address Minor Challenges

During this phase of coaching, your schedule of observations likely starts to thin out. You'll notice that some teachers have picked up the concepts of the program quickly and are enthusiastic about implementing the program. These teachers may need only the observations and feedback from Phase 2 to solidify their skills to a point where you can simply monitor their implementation. Each teacher's rubric ratings can be informative in this regard. Specifically, teachers who have achieved a rating of three points or more in each dimension are considered to have obtained an adequate level of skill.

For these teachers, the focus is on maintaining adequate frequency and quality of implementation. This requires a weekly meeting with these teachers to discuss how well the program is working in their classroom. The coach's overall goal is to check in and address any minor barriers to implementation.

First, ask teachers which Lessons they have completed and record this information in your Lesson Log. If these teachers are on schedule with the Lessons, praise their efforts. If they have fallen behind with Lesson delivery, create a collaborative plan for getting back on track. By identifying barriers, the coach and teacher can identify potential strategies for overcoming these obstacles (discussed later in this chapter; see Chapter 4 for particular strategies).

Ask teachers for their overall impressions of how the Lessons are going. For example, do they feel comfortable delivering them? Do they have enough time to complete each Lesson? Are the Lesson guides clear? Also inquire about student responses to the Lessons. Do students appear to enjoy the Lessons? Can teachers and students generalize the content to situations that arise in the classroom?

Find out how the Game is going as well. Collect Game Scoreboards (Appendix P) and check to see how frequently teachers are playing the Game. Discuss any obstacles that get in the way of teachers playing the Game two to three times per day, and identify potential strategies for increasing the number of Games played. Ask teachers for their perceptions of how the Game is going when they play. If it is going well, review potential pitfalls (discussed later in this chapter) and rationales for any components teachers omit routinely (based on recent coach observations).

If the Game does not seem to be effective at increasing students' on-task behaviors, review Ten Easy Steps for Playing a Successful Game (Appendix I) with teachers to ensure all steps are covered each time they play the Game. If you identify a step that is missed, review the rationale for that step and encourage teachers to adhere to the ten steps found in Appendix I so you both can monitor whether the Game is effective. If it appears teachers are covering all of steps each time they play the Game (or that following all the steps does not result in progress), consider whether the Game is working for all students. If the Game is not effective for a few students, the coach and teacher can work together to develop strategies about how to address student behavioral challenges.

These guidelines are offered as a framework for weekly check-ins with teachers demonstrating consistent and high-quality implementation. It is normal for teachers to lapse a little in their implementation during transitional times during the school year (e.g., holidays, standardized testing). When you notice a lapse, often a meeting can identify barriers and solutions to bring implementation back up to an effective level. You might even anticipate a lapse during certain times and schedule classroom observations and feedback sessions to help support implementation before it drops too low. These strategies are often effective at increasing teacher implementation. However, teachers who have not yet demonstrated an adequate level of program implementation skills (i.e., less than three points in rubric ratings) may continue to need observations and feedback over a longer period of time before they reach the desired skill level. Some teachers may even need additional supports to improve their implementation (see Chapter 4).

Coaching Session Structure

As emphasized throughout this chapter, regular coaching sessions are essential to teacher skill development and consistent program implementation. It is helpful to establish a consistent weekly coaching visit with each teacher. In the beginning, these discussions may last approximately 20 minutes, but will likely become shorter over time. To maximize the effectiveness of coaching sessions, it is helpful to follow a goal-oriented structure:

1. *Provide a warm-up to the coaching session.* To put teachers at ease, spend a few minutes greeting and chatting with them about neutral topics (e.g., weather, holidays, sporting events) and how things are going before discussing program issues and providing feedback.
2. *Provide praise.* Find something for which to praise the teacher. Ideally, this would be something the coach observed the teacher doing related to the program or something positive in the classroom environment. In rare situations, the coach may have difficulty identifying something to praise. In these cases, it is important to identify something worthy of positive reinforcement, such as the teacher's willingness to meet with you. Be sure to be genuine and specific with praise.

3. *Elicit teachers' perspective.* Rather than jump right in to providing feedback, find out how teachers think the PAX GBG is going in their classroom. However, instead of asking a general question, such as "How are things going?," which often elicits concerns or vague responses (e.g., "Fine"), ask teachers specifically about what is going well. Then, ask teachers about what is not going so well or could be improved. This sets the tone for a positive coaching interaction by providing teachers the opportunity to reflect on their specific strengths and improvements, and for the coach to provide positive reinforcement. If teachers have difficulty identifying strengths, the coach should be able to identify several positive things to point out. If teachers are unsure about areas for improvement, the coach may suggest one for a collaborative discussion (e.g., "Did you notice that not all of the students sat back in their seats after the Granny Wacky Prize was over? What do you think about talking more about improving that?").

COMMUNICATE!

Coach: Hello, Mrs. Smith, how are you today?

Teacher: I'm fine. How about yourself?

Coach: I'm doing well. I just wish it wasn't so hot! I'm heading to the Orioles game tonight and it's going to be hot sitting in the stadium. Are you an Orioles fan? **(Warm-up)**

Teacher: Of course! We don't go to many games though—mostly just watch on television.

Coach: Ah, I'm going to be wishing I was watching the game from my air-conditioned living room this evening I bet! Speaking of games and teams, I noticed you changed the team names in your classroom and hung team signs from the ceiling. They look great! **(Praise)**

Teacher: Thanks. I thought it would be fun to change things up a little bit.

Coach: You're absolutely right! It helps keep students interested in the Game when you change things around. What are your thoughts about what's going well with the Game right now? **(Elicit teacher perspective about strengths)**

Teacher: Well, the teams are winning most of the Games, so we've increased the length of the time we play. That's been making it a little bit harder, but the students are still doing really well.

Coach: Great! That's exactly how it should be going. **(Praise)** Over time, the Game gets longer and hopefully the students get better at PAX and inhibiting Spleems. In your view, what can still be improved? **(Elicit teacher perspective about areas for improvement)**

Teacher: There is still a lot of disruptive behavior during transitions and sometimes during instruction when we are not playing the Game. And one of my students is really not responding to the Game at all.

In this brief exchange, the coach sets the stage for positive interactions by being warm and friendly and by providing praise. By eliciting the teacher's perspective, the coach provides the opportunity for the teacher to reflect on her classroom, rather than jumping in and pointing out strengths and areas for improvement in an expert fashion. At this point, the teacher has provided the coach with a snapshot of how things are going in the classroom.

4. *Express empathy.* Keeping in mind the collaborative approach, it's important to express empathy and validate teachers' perspectives when addressing areas for improvement so they feels understood and supported. There are a few strategies you can use to express empathy. Reflective listening involves rephrasing the teacher's concerns to express understanding (e.g., "So it sounds like you get really frustrated when your student disrupts the rest of the class. I can see why you would feel that way."). You might share some of your own experiences in similar situations in the classroom (e.g., "When I was a teacher that was the most challenging situation for me to handle, too. I became really frustrated when that happened."). Finally, normalizing the situation based on the experiences of other teachers can also go a long way to validating the teacher's concerns (e.g., "So many teachers I work with say the same thing. You would be amazed!").

5. *Narrow the focus.* In general, it is helpful to identify just one or two concerns to address. It can be overwhelming for teachers to be presented with multiple suggestions for improvement, with the end result that they have difficulty implementing any of the multiple strategies effectively. Thus, you may need to help "chunk" teachers' goals (e.g., establish weekly, monthly, year-long goals) so they are realistic and attainable.

 COMMUNICATE!

Coach: It sounds like you have success when you are playing the Game but there are some other times that students are disruptive, and that's usually when you are not playing the Game. And then there is one student who is disruptive more than most students. **(Express empathy through reflection)** I think what you're describing is usually the way it goes. A teacher introduces the Game and it works well when they play but it's not really generalizing yet to times when they are not playing. And most teachers have a student who appears to not respond to the Game. **(Express empathy through normalization)** Together, I think we can come up with a plan of action. If you think about the two issues of your student not responding and the level of disruptive behavior during your instruction time, which of these do you think you'd most like to work on over the next week? **(Collaboration, narrow the focus)**

Continuing the example, the coach did all of the talking, but did so in a way to summarize and validate the teacher's experiences. The coach also offered hope by way of her optimism about developing a plan. Finally, she also demonstrated collaboration by inviting the teacher to select the goal.

6. *Gather information about what has been tried.* Ask teachers what has been tried (e.g., "Have you been able to try anything that you thought might work in this situation?") Asking teachers what they have tried provides information about their approach to and skill level in handling student misbehavior. For example, do they have a lot of tools in their toolkit or do they use the same tool repeatedly for every problem (e.g., a hammer for hitting nails and cutting wood). A conversation about what has been tried naturally leads to a conversation about what to try next.

7. *Identify potential solutions.* A collaborative, systematic problem-solving method can help teachers identify and evaluate potential solutions with your assistance. Brainstorming multiple solutions to a problem gives teachers hope and helps them feel more in control over the situation, as opposed to feeling helpless. There are four steps to selecting a potential solution:

   - Identify the problematic situation clearly (e.g., "Students become too loud and disruptive during Granny's Wacky Prizes").
   - Brainstorm possible solutions without evaluating them (e.g., "Come up with prizes that are silent" or "End the prize immediately if students become disruptive" or "Count Spleems toward the next Game if students become disruptive"). This avoids the trap of "nothing will work" that some teachers may feel when they are stressed or frustrated. Try to come up with a few possible solutions that are humorous or not at all feasible (e.g., "Hand out earplugs for others to use when the class engages in prizes") to keep things light and to demonstrate the process of brainstorming.
   - Discuss potential positive and negative outcomes of each solution to demonstrate that there are often pros and cons to each solution. In the collaborative model, teachers are given clear explanations for any concept, idea, or strategy suggested. Explaining the components of the program increases teachers' knowledge base and their confidence in selecting and implementing a strategy that has a high probability of working in the classroom. In this step, you may have to help teachers think about why a solution that looks good on paper might not work in the classroom (e.g., "I like your idea of giving your disruptive student more positive reinforcement for appropriate behavior. I agree with you that if he sat down, you'd be able to praise him more frequently. Right now it seems that sitting down is challenging for him. Are there other things that he does that you could praise him for so that we can accomplish the same goal of giving him more positive reinforcement?").
   - Select a solution to try.

8. *Anticipate challenges.* It may be helpful to suggest to teachers who are struggling with basic management to think through what could possibly "go wrong" and address it before

it occurs. For example, before students start their math assignment, the teacher could say, "If you don't have crayons in your desk, please share with your neighbor. No one should be out of their seat going to get crayons. If I see this, it will count as a Spleem for your team." Anticipating common issues and making expectations clear alleviate the majority of problems. However, if the situation does occur, the teacher does not have to react harshly; everyone (including the teacher) already knows what the consequence will be. The coach can model this strategy with *every* teacher during the initial Game modeling. If teachers don't mention noticing this during the debriefing session, make sure to discuss it with them.

 COMMUNICATE!

Coach: **(Summarizing steps 6 and 7)** We've been discussing that you'd like to work on some behavior management strategies for one student in particular. We've discussed a number of things that you have tried already as well as some potential solutions. We discussed the situation of having this student be on his own team, but you mentioned that he really loses interest in the Game when that happens. So, right now we're considering giving him the job of holding the timer during the Game and potentially having a much shorter Game for him so he can be successful. Can you think of anything that might not work out with these two solutions? **(Anticipate challenges)**

Teacher: With regard to being the timekeeper, I could picture him being excited at first, but then losing interest in the job over time. So, it might work for a Game or two, but maybe not for the entire week.

Coach: Yes, that's a possibility. If we believe that he'll be motivated by the Game after he's earned a prize a few times, then it's okay if he loses interest in being the timekeeper. We're really just using this strategy to help him feel important and as an opportunity for you to give him praise during the Game. **(Rationale)**

Teacher: Right. So I guess the same thing goes for the shortened Game. If he's successful, he'll want to play more. If I shorten the Game for him, then he'll be successful for his short Game even though he might Spleem while the rest of the students are still playing, but eventually he'll catch up.

Coach: Right. The idea is that we're structuring the Game in a way that increases the likelihood that he will earn a prize. These strategies aren't meant to be used for the rest of the year, but only for a short time until he can be successful on his own. It's kind of like an experiment right now. We have a hunch that he could be successful with some supports during the Game. We've identified two strategies we're going to try and we'll see how it goes. If they are successful, that's great, and we'll work out a plan to fade them out over time. If they are not successful, we'll figure out why not and tweak our plan. **(Collaboration, rationale)**

In this exchange, the coach and teacher discussed the selected solutions. The coach demonstrates collaboration by eliciting the teacher's thoughts about potential challenges. She provided rationales for the solutions and described the "big picture" about their approach to addressing the disruptive behaviors of the identified student. The coach ends the coaching session by summarizing, setting goals, eliciting feedback, and ending on a positive note:

9. *Summarize and set goals.* Another aspect of the collaborative coaching role is to review and summarize. The coach should end each meeting with a summary of the major points of discussion from the meeting and then set goals collaboratively or give assignments for the next session. Giving assignments sounds like a more traditional teaching role, but it actually fits well into the collaborative model because it is through practice/repetition and feedback that teachers become more effective and empowered, and less dependent. It is also important that teachers share with you real-life experiences of trying out their new skills so that any discussion, feedback, and problem solving can be meaningful and practical. Ideally, after your discussion, teachers would identify an area on which they would like to work before your next meeting and then the two of you would develop concrete goals for practice (e.g., "We've spent some time talking about catching certain students being good. What do you think would be a reasonable and manageable goal for praising your student? . . . Okay, so the next time we meet, I'll ask you how it's been going with regard to praising him."). In addition to goals, it is helpful for you and the teachers to discuss and solve any barrier problems that might interfere with goal attainment (e.g., "You've set the goal of playing the Game three times a day. Sometimes things come up that might get in the way of playing the Game frequently. What things do you think might get in the way for you?"). After setting these goals, express confidence in the teacher's ability to use the skills effectively.

10. *Request feedback.* To demonstrate a collaborative approach further, it may be helpful for the coach to summarize the session and ask for teacher feedback to identify any potential concerns or resistance teachers may experience. For example, "We've been discussing how to manage disruptive behavior in your classroom, and our goal was to identify one or two strategies that we think might have the best chance at reducing this student's disruptive behavior while not interfering so much with your teaching. Was I helpful in that regard or do we need to flush this out a bit more?"

11. *End on a positive note.* In addition to improving teacher implementation, the overarching goal of each coaching session is to ensure teachers are receptive to meeting with the coach again; thus, it is helpful for the coach to end on a positive note. This can be accomplished by providing verbal praise or a written Tootle Note (e.g., "You're doing a great job using the harmonica. Keep up the good work!"), thanking teachers for their efforts (e.g., "I'm really impressed with how frequently you are playing the Game. Thank you for all of the effort you are putting into the program."), providing encouragement (e.g., "I think you came up with some great strategies today and I am hopeful we'll see improvement in your student's behavior soon."), using humor, or commenting on something personal mentioned during a previous session, such as asking about a child's basketball game or an upcoming vacation.

We discussed that the coach's role is to support teachers and help motivate and encourage them to implement the program with fidelity. The coach serves as a cheerleader (e.g., "You can do it!") and partner ("Let's work on this together!"). In addition, by modeling the various components and skills (e.g., problem-solving process), the coach enhances the effective things teachers already do and provides teachers in challenging classrooms with hope that they can effect change in the culture of their classroom and make a difference in the lives of their students.

The Nuts and Bolts of Data Collection, Feedback, and Reinforcement

Data collection is an integral part of the coaching model. Data provide coaches with a baseline assessment of teachers' skill level as well as a method for repeated assessment of skill and implementation. This chapter describes four main sources of data—Lesson Logs, GBG Scoreboard Logs, Observation Rubrics, and Coaching Logs—that provide the basis for performance feedback to teachers and the foundation on which coaching decisions are made (see Chapter 4 for more on the integration of data and coach decision making). In addition, later in this chapter the various strategies by which you can use positive reinforcement to shape and reward teacher implementation are discussed.

Data Collection

Lesson Logs

The Lesson Log (Appendix O) is a spreadsheet that lists all the teachers and all the Lessons in the curriculum for the entire year. Using the Lesson Log, the coach can record the month and year that each Lesson was taught by each teacher. This document provides a snapshot of where each class stands with Lesson implementation. It is especially useful for identifying at a glance which teacher, or grade level, has fallen behind with implementation and may need additional help or support. A sample is provided here:

	L1	L2	L3	L4	L5	L6	L7	L8	L9	L10	L11	L12	L13
Ms. Afton	9/11	9/11	9/11	9/11	10/11	10/11	10/11	10/11	11/11	11/11	11/11		
Mr. Brown	9/11	9/11	9/11	10/11	10/11	10/11	X	10/11	11/11				
Ms. Colt	9/11	9/11	9/11	9/11	9/11	10/11	10/11	10/11	10/11	11/11	11/11	11/11	11/11

To maintain an accurate Lesson Log, it is essential that the coach ask each teacher for an update on a weekly basis and note the information immediately in the Lesson Log. In addition, the coach should also document in the Lesson Log any time he or she observes a Lesson being implemented by the teacher.

It is helpful to identify exactly which Lessons should be taught during the month by looking at the pacing guide. It is expected that teachers teach two Lessons per week—approximately eight per month. The number may vary slightly if there is a short month because of a holiday or school break. Referencing the pacing guide helps the coach identify quickly any teacher who has fallen behind. If a teacher has fallen more than two weeks behind, it may be helpful to create a revised pacing guide, outlining exactly how this teacher can catch up to complete all grade-level Lessons by the end of the year. In addition, a quick glance at the Lesson Log can help a coach identify which teachers are on pace, or even ahead, with teaching Lessons. One suggestion is to reward these teachers periodically with some sort of public recognition or small incentive (positive reinforcement is discussed later in the chapter).

Game Scoreboard

The Game Scoreboard (Appendix P) is used by each classroom teacher to record three pieces of information: (a) the number of Games played each day, (b) the duration of each Game, and (c) the number of Spleems each team received during each Game. Each Scoreboard has room for five days of the week so that each week's Game data can be recorded on one sheet. Use the Game Scoreboard Log (Appendix Q) to record the number of Games each teacher has recorded on their Game Scoreboards for the week, thereby providing a snapshot of teacher implementation with regard to Games throughout the year.

During a regular day of instruction, teachers are encouraged to play at least three Games per day. There is also space for the teacher to play a secret Game and record that data as well. At the top of the Game Scoreboard Log (Appendix Q), there is an item that lists the optimal number of Games that could possibly have been played in total for each week. For example, during a regular five-day week, the optimal amount of Games is 15 for that week if the teacher plays three Games each day. On a day when there is an early dismissal or late arrival, adjustments must be made to the number of optimal Games for that day and to the optimal Games for the week to accommodate the difference in instructional time teachers have with their students. The purpose of having the number of optimal Games listed for each week is for the coach to compare that number with how many Games each of the teachers is actually playing.

It is up to the coach to establish a system for collecting GBG Scoreboards (Appendix P) from each teacher in a timely manner, and different teachers may have different preferences. For example, some teachers prefer to place their Scoreboard from the previous week in the same location each Monday so the coach can pick it up at any time that day without disrupting the class. In other cases, the coach may have to ask teachers for their Scoreboard each week. At the beginning of the year, some teachers may wait to be asked for their Scoreboards to see if the coach really collects them, before putting the effort into having them ready each week. Usually, when teachers learn they will be asked for their Scoreboards every week, they will have it ready when you visit them each week to collect the data. Therefore, it is important the coach sets this expectation and is consistent with collecting Scoreboards from the first week of implementation so that teachers get in the routine of completing them.

It is important to collect each teacher's Game Scoreboard (Appendix P) and fill in the Game Scoreboard Log (Appendix Q) as the forms are collected on a weekly basis. The Scoreboard data can be used to help come up with a plan for a teacher who may need some extra help implementing the Game. If a teacher plays the Game three times per day but still has problems with discipline and time on task with his/her students, these data may indicate there is something wrong with the implementation of the actual Game itself. On the other hand, if a teacher does not play the Game regularly but complains about discipline in the classroom, you can use the Game data to encourage these teachers to play more Games and compare any differences in student behavior when the Game is played regularly. The Scoreboards also give detailed information about whether teams are winning 80% of the time, which is an indicator the teacher should increase the length (i.e., minutes) of the Game. It is also possible that one team is always losing the Game, which may be a good time to rotate teams and have students on different teams. These data are also used to determine the winners in the grade-level competitions between teachers, which is another way to encourage more frequent Game playing (grade-level competitions are discussed later in this chapter).

Rubrics

Although the Lesson Log (Appendix O) and the Game Scoreboard Log (Appendix Q) provide a way for you to keep track of implementation *frequency*, the Good Behavior Game Implementation Rubric (Appendix M) provides a method for assessing implementation *quality*. It involves in-class observation of the teacher implementing the Game and a Lesson, and rating the teacher's skill across a number of domains. Because rubric procedures were discussed in detail earlier in this chapter, they will not be covered here; however, the rubric is mentioned here because of its relevance to feedback regarding teacher implementation.

Coaching Logs

In addition to collecting data about teacher implementation, the coach should maintain data on the frequency, duration, and nature (e.g., check-ins, modeling, technical assistance, intervention delivery, needs assessment, relationship building, incentive delivery) of each coaching contact with each teacher (Appendix R). Each contact that involves some form of coaching support or incentive should be noted on the Coaching Log (Appendix R), even if the contact is short (e.g., five minutes). Examples of contacts not considered coaching are discussions about materials or scheduling meetings; however, even a three-minute conversation can be considered coaching if the coach explained something to a teacher or answered a question. Over time, the Coaching Log provides a method for tracking coaching strategies and activities. In the case of high-implementing teachers, the Coaching Log might prompt the coach to observe a teacher with whom you have only done check-ins. In the case of low-implementing teachers, the Coaching Log might suggest it is time to try some new strategies to enhance teacher implementation.

Performance Feedback

As discussed earlier in this chapter, in "Coaching Session Structure," regular coaching sessions are integral to teacher skill development. In particular, performance feedback during these sessions can provide teachers with specific information about the quality of their implementation, and can facilitate goal setting. Although it may be difficult for you to talk at length with a teacher after an observation, the timely scheduling of a detailed feedback session is important to enhance the effectiveness of the information.

Feedback sessions follow the same structure as the general coaching sessions discussed earlier:

1. *Provide a warm-up to the coaching session.* To put the teacher at ease, spend a few minutes greeting and chatting with him or her about neutral topics (e.g., weather, holidays, sporting events) before discussing program issues and providing feedback.

2. *Ask for the teacher's perspective regarding the observed PATHS to PAX GBG component.* This can be accomplished by asking the teacher an open-ended question, such as "How do you think the Game went?" If the teacher did not implement with a high level of skill, it may be helpful initially to direct the discussion toward implementation strengths (e.g., "What's your perspective on what went well during the Lesson?").

3. *Reinforce the positives.* Praise the teacher for any strengths he or she identifies and expand when appropriate (e.g., "Yes, I thought you did a nice job guiding the students on the behaviors to work on next time [praise]. I especially liked how you related those behaviors to helping everyone be more productive [expansion]."). If the teacher has difficulty identifying positives, be prepared to point out teacher implementation strengths.

4. *Identify areas for improvement.* Revisit any areas for improvement brought up by the teacher and ask for the teacher's perspective about what transpired (e.g., "You mentioned that you thought the prize got out of control. What are your thoughts about why that happened?"). If a teacher does not indicate any areas for improvement spontaneously, it may be helpful to ask, "In your view, what can still be improved?" If the teacher is unsure, you might suggest collaboratively an area of improvement for discussion (e.g., "Did you notice that not all the students looked at you when you blew the harmonica?").

5. *Provide constructive feedback.* Feedback is best conveyed by identifying strengths, providing a rationale, and then identifying a way to improve. For example, "I really like the way you review Spleems at the end of each Game. It seems to me that if you reviewed the most recent Spleems at the beginning of each Game, it would help your students remember the behaviors they need to work on." Explaining the components of the program increases teachers' knowledge base and their confidence in being able to implement the suggestions provided during the feedback session.

6. *Summarize and set goals.* Goal setting helps provide continuity across coaching sessions and enhances teacher implementation. Set goals collaboratively with teachers to increase their commitment to practicing these skills (e.g., "We've spent some time talking about catching certain students being good. What do you think would be a reasonable and manageable goal for praising these students? [Teacher: "Three times after lunch."] Okay, so the next time we meet, I'll ask you how it's been going with regard to praising your students."). In addition to goals, it is helpful to discuss and resolve any barriers that might interfere with goal attainment (e.g., "You've set the goal of praising Andrew three times after lunch. Just so we can think this through, is there anything that might get in the way of that?").

After setting these goals, check in with teachers about progress toward established goals, provide lots of positive reinforcement for progress, and resolve any obstacles that appear to have gotten in the way of teachers achieving stated goals. It is particularly important to express confidence in the teacher's ability to use skills effectively!

7. *End on a positive note.* Thank the teacher once again for allowing you to observe, provide praise for teacher implementation, and provide encouragement and expectations of success (e.g., "I am looking forward to returning next week to see how Andrew responded to your praise! I am hopeful he'll respond well to your attention.").

Positive Reinforcement

Data collection provides the coach with a snapshot of teacher implementation; performance feedback provides a way to exchange information with teachers about what works and does not work in the classroom. How do you make program implementation fun for teachers? With positive reinforcement! *Positive reinforcement refers to providing verbal or written praise or a reward for teacher implementation.* Not only does it make program implementation fun for teachers, it serves as a powerful motivator for higher quality implementation when used strategically, and it is a primary component of the program that teachers use with students. *Keep in mind that behaviors that get reinforced get repeated.* Positive reinforcement is used in a variety of ways to reinforce and reward appropriate implementation of the PAX GBG: (a) individually for teachers and staff, (b) as positive competitions among staff members, and (c) as schoolwide recognition.

Individual Reinforcement for Teachers and Staff

During the beginning phases of implementation of a new program in which there is some teacher buy-in but you still need more, positive reinforcement can be a great way to get teachers on board with the program and set a positive tone. Carry a variety of prizes in a bag, along with the PAX General Incentive Checklist (Appendix S) so rewards can be given out whenever you observe authentic implementation of program elements (e.g., harmonica, Kid of the Day). For example, you might allow teachers to choose from a collection of rewards that range from school supplies for the classroom to $5 gift cards for the teacher.

Identify specific teacher reinforcers that focus on particular program elements (e.g., classroom environment, Kid of the Day, Tootle Board) several times throughout the first few months of implementation, with the frequency decreasing as time goes on. Provide teachers with a flyer of information specifying the target element and target date, such as a flyer identifying key components of the classroom environment (Guidelines for Creating a PAX Classroom Environment [Appendix T]) with the date when you will be circulating throughout classrooms to see if environmental cues (e.g., posters, desk signs) are being used and are hung on the walls, and insinuate that the use of these cues "might" (hint, hint) be worthy of a prize. Review the specific elements listed in the flyer with each teacher as it is handed out and point out specific items that are missing from each classroom. When the target date arrives, visit each classroom and complete a Classroom Environment Checklist (Appendix U) regarding the classroom environment components. Teachers who have all the components receive a Tootle Note and a prize. Teachers who do not have all the components are given a feedback sheet with a note attached stating you will return the following week to check again. Repeat this process as necessary to support teacher success. In some instances, teachers may take 2 to 4 weeks before they earn their Tootle and prize.

Game incentives are intended to challenge teachers to play a certain number of Games during a preestablished time period and, for all who succeed, they receive a special reward. Provide teachers with a flyer (Program New Additions Flyer [Appendix V]) indicating the target number of Games to play to win a specific prize (e.g., water bottle, lunch bag, T-shirt). Prizes are identified up front and teachers are shown an example (e.g., the coach might wear the T-shirt when introducing the T-shirt contest). A good place to start with the individual competition is to have the first competition reflect 80% of the optimal number of Games during a given time period. For example, if, during a certain few weeks, the optimal number of Games played is 45 based on teachers playing three Games per day, then the expectation for the prize is that they play 36 Games during those weeks. This will help teachers develop the habit of playing regularly. A weekly reminder of how many Games each teacher has played toward their individual prize can be given easily to teachers by using the coach's Game Scoreboard Log (Appendix Q) to relay that information. A follow-up flyer should be distributed after the individual competition is complete, announcing all winners after the contest period. Teachers who do not win are given the opportunity to create individualized goals (e.g., play once a day every day for the next two weeks) with the coach to earn the prize.

From time to time, teachers who are low implementers may have a negative reaction to rewards, but it is important for a coach to recognize the value of reinforcers in shaping teacher implementation, particularly when paired with goal setting. For teachers who respond to a coach's offer of an incentive by saying "You are trying to bribe me," a coach might say, "Not at all. I would like to reward you for doing something that is beneficial for students. I know you do a lot of great things in your classroom and I don't have many ways to show my appreciation to teachers. I think it's so valuable that I'd like to give you something in return. What do you think would be reasonable in terms of implementation to earn this reward?"

Competitions among Staff Members

Just as the Game promotes healthy competition among students in a classroom, staff competitions related to program implementation work to engage teachers in a positive and healthy "contest." In an effort to increase the frequency of Games in a classroom, consider introducing the idea of grade-level competitions during the first month of implementation. Each member of the grade-level team that plays the most Games during a specified period of time (usually 4 weeks) receives a $25 gift certificate to a local teacher supply store for their efforts. As the coach, you are able to monitor Game playing through your weekly collection of Scoreboards and therefore can also update all teachers (perhaps visually, through a bulletin board display) with regard to their standings in a competition that challenges each grade-level team to play more Games than their counterparts. At the end of the contest, provide the staff with a flyer announcing the winners of the first competition and encouraging everyone to be involved in the next competition. This flyer can also contain information about how all grade-level team Game playing compared with each other (see Appendix V and Appendix W for flyer examples).

Schoolwide Recognition

Some teachers are less interested in material rewards than they are in receiving public recognition for their efforts. For that reason, a bulletin board placed strategically in a common area (e.g., teacher's lounge, front office, hallway) where teachers and other staff members can recognize each other can be a valuable tool. In the PAX GBG, this is called a *schoolwide Tootle Board*. It is best to place the schoolwide Tootle Board in a location where even students and parents can contribute and write Tootles for staff members. The coach might use a bulletin board that already exists in the building or may purchase one that can be hung securely on an empty wall space or displayed on a sturdy easel. As a coach, you can model positive reinforcement by writing a few new Tootles each week and rotating old Tootles off of the board, making room for new Tootles to be posted. As you rotate old Tootle notes off of the schoolwide Tootle Board, make sure they get returned to the person for whom they were written. Be sure the schoolwide Tootle Board is nicely decorated and eye-catching to those who walk by, and that it meets any standards that have been established in the school for classroom teachers' bulletin boards. The use of a schoolwide Tootle Board should also be approved by school administration.

In addition to the schoolwide Tootle Board, within the first few weeks of implementation, choose a Teacher of the Week each week. Selection of the Teacher of the Week parallels the Kid of the Day in that it is completely random and every teacher will be spotlighted as Teacher of the Week at some point during the year. This teacher is recognized by having a special Tootle note written by the coach and displayed on a section of the schoolwide Tootle Board for the entire week. On the Tootle note there should be remarks regarding the teacher's positive qualities, particularly with regard to program implementation. In some instances, coaches have created a flyer (Teacher Spotlight [Appendix X] or Spring Fever Flyer [Appendix Y]) to distribute schoolwide to recognize and highlight key PATHS to PAX GBG elements used by each Teacher of the Week. It is important to encourage other staff members to help highlight the Teacher of the Week and to make this their "special" week. There are several ways to promote the Teacher of the Week within the building. First, make sure administrators are aware the process has begun and that they know who the spotlighted teacher is each week. Encourage administrators to announce the Teacher of the Week over the intercom at the beginning of each week. Also encourage administrators to write their own Tootle for the spotlighted teacher. In addition, encourage other staff members to write a Tootle specifically about this teacher to post near the Teacher of the Week Tootle (e.g., post blank Tootles by the Teacher of the Week display so other teachers can write a Tootle, or hand out Tootles to teachers and ask them to write a Tootle for the Teacher of the Week). You can try several techniques to get staff to add to the schoolwide Tootle Board. Individual incentives can be provided to the first teacher who posts a Tootle for the Teacher of the Week. You can also appeal to teachers by reminding them that, one day, it will be their turn to be recognized as Teacher of the Week, and that the use of the schoolwide Tootle Board is a great way to model the use of Tootles and positive communication to students. Finally, visit the classroom of the Teacher of the Week and make sure the teacher's students are aware of the recognition. Encourage students to write a Tootle for the teacher as well.

The role of a coach is to support teacher implementation of the program. Data collection is integral to the assessment of teacher implementation. The coaching model includes collection of data across multiple domains (e.g., quantity and quality of Games and Lessons), from multiple informants (e.g., teacher, coach, independent observer), and using multiple methods (e.g., self-report, observation). Through systematic data collection, coaches can provide constructive feedback to teachers, monitor the effectiveness of their coaching strategies, and adjust their strategies to address challenges to teacher implementation. Finally, positive reinforcement provides a means by which to add some fun into program implementation as well as to shape and reward teachers' efforts.

Common Early Implementation Challenges

In this next section, common teacher pitfalls with regard to initial Game and Lesson implementation are presented. Anticipate and prevent these foibles by informing teachers about common errors and their effect on students' behavior and learning, which gives everyone a head start toward achieving implementation and program success.

Setting up the PAX Good Behavior Game
Activity Selection
Choosing an activity for playing the Game will impact the effectiveness of the Game. Initially, it should be played only when the students are working independently. This gives teachers the necessary time needed to practice authentically focusing on counting Spleems without distractions. Eventually, when teachers feel comfortable, the Game can be introduced during teacher-led instructional or transition times.

A common pitfall is a teacher who is eager to use the Game during teacher-led instructional time, jumping right to it when they first introduce the Game in their classroom. If teachers do not take the time to practice counting Spleems accurately, it is unlikely they will become proficient at it. This skill may be challenging for some teachers when they first start playing the Game. It requires teachers' full attention; if they start playing the Game during teacher-led instructional times, it may be difficult for them to dedicate the required attention to counting Spleems. As a result, teachers end up being "loose" with their Spleem counting, missing many throughout the Game (see the "During the Game" section).

In addition, teachers should make sure the activity chosen is authentic and has a clear learning purpose. Sometimes teachers give the students "busy work" or nothing to do while they count Spleems. The goal of the Game is to increase on-task behavior in the classroom. If students do not practice (by playing the Game) this skill of being on-task during the Game, then it is unlikely they will make any improvements in this area.

Game Length

Choosing the right amount of time to play the Game is crucial to its success. The ideal length varies by grade level and by time of year, and for each particular activity. There is no "correct" length of time the Game should be played; it is based on teacher judgment. A key point to remember is that you want the Game to be long enough that it is challenging for the students, but short enough that teams are successful and "win." For example, playing a 2-minute Game for a well-behaved upper grade class does not necessarily pose a challenge for the teams. Conversely, playing a 30-minute Game in a primary grade that has difficulty staying on task is not feasible for the students to experience success if the teacher truly counts Spleems accurately (see the "During the Game" section). Finding the right length for a particular class takes some trial and error. A general rule of thumb is that teams should win about 80% of the time. If all teams win all the Games, then it's not challenging enough. Similarly, if all teams are not winning, there is be no motivation to want to play the Game. *In most cases, teachers start with short (3-minute) Games and then increase the time slowly as the class experiences success.* If students are "off" for some reason (e.g., bad day, difficult/exciting task at hand), then teachers should shorten the length of the Game so the students can experience success. For example, consider a class that is typically playing 12- to 15-minute Games on a regular basis, but it is the day before Winter Break. There is very little instruction going on, leading to a less structured environment in which students have difficulty attending to any given task. Teachers will still want to play the Game, but should recognize the teams may not be successful playing a 12-minute Game. Therefore, on this day, teachers may choose to play 5-minute Games with their class.

Number of Teams

Aim for approximately four to five students on a team. If there are too many students on a team (e.g., boys vs. girls) then it may become difficult for the team to succeed. If there are too few on a team, then the power of working as a team and the peer pressure effect will be reduced. In addition, having too few members on a team will lead to many teams in the classroom, which will make it difficult for teachers to track Spleems accurately during the Game (see "During the Game").

Teams of One

Occasionally, it may be helpful to create a team of one because of a student's special needs and/or problem behavior. This should be a *temporary* placement and it should be done only after the student has had multiple opportunities to be on a team and is unsuccessful. A common pitfall is that teachers may assume, based on past experiences with a child, that a particular child will cause a team to lose and may put these children on their own team immediately, without ever giving them a chance to be part of a team. *Many students who have "difficulties" during the rest of the day will actually respond well to the peer pressure of being on a team.* When students are placed immediately on their own team, teachers are conveying expectations for failure; this strategy reduces the incentive for them to demonstrate positive behavior during the Game. On the rare occasion that a team of one is necessary, the student should know that this placement is not forever; he or she will be given the opportunity to earn his or her way back onto a team.

Definition of Spleems

The ideal definition of a Spleem is anything that gets in the way of students or teachers completing their work. Some Spleems are obvious. Hitting someone is a Spleem. However, some Spleems are a bit confusing. Is talking a Spleem? It depends on the situation. Talking during a math test is a Spleem. Talking during a group project would not be a Spleem, unless the students are talking about a video game and not the group project. In other words, Spleems are *contextual*. Examples of Spleems may include calling-out (not raising your hand), getting out of your seat without permission, talking to peers during individual work, throwing things, physical aggression, and any other off-task behavior.

The confusion sets in when teachers have a set list of Spleems and do not go over expectations before the Game. Talking is sometimes acceptable; other times, it is not. Students need to be reminded verbally of the behavior expectations—what is and is not acceptable—before each Game/Lesson/activity in the classroom. It is important that these behavior expectations and Spleems are posted visually in the classroom and are reviewed frequently with students. Furthermore, remember that Spleems can be modified for particular students. Just as teachers might modify an assignment per an Individualized Education Program, so, too, might they modify tolerance for certain students, thereby not penalizing students for behavior they cannot control.

During the Game
Response to Spleems

The ideal way to respond to a Spleem is by calling out unemotionally the team name for which you are recording the Spleem. It is recommended teachers label the specific behavior of the Spleem. For example, state calmly, "Spleem for Team 2, for not working on the assignment." It is very important to use a calm voice and not yell, because this may lead to arguing and unnecessary confrontation. In addition, announcing the Spleem and moving on quickly with instruction ensures that instructional minutes are not lost.

Sometimes teachers count Spleems without identifying the specific behavior, particularly when the Spleem seems so obvious as to not need an explanation. However, what is obvious to teachers may not be obvious to students. For example, a student on Team 3 may be tapping a pencil repeatedly on her desk. The teacher may say, "Team 3, that is a Spleem," and that student continues to tap the pencil. The teacher then says, "Team 3, you have another Spleem." That student may be looking around and wondering why their team keeps receiving Spleems. This cycle could continue until the team gets four or more Spleems and/or teammates argue with each other to stop Spleeming (which is what we want to avoid). A better way to address the situation would be to state the specific behavior along with noting the Spleem. For example (in a calm voice), say, "Spleem for Team 3, for tapping a pencil." Now the particular student knows exactly what the Spleem was for, without being pointed out individually to the class and he or she can stop the behavior.

Some teachers may want to name individual students when identifying Spleems. This is completely normal because this is the way most people try to correct others; yet, it is problematic because the whole point of the Game is that it is *team* based. When a teacher isolates an individual and labels his or her behavior as bad, confrontation or hurt feelings may follow. Children can get off task quickly when they think they are being picked on. Also, naming a student can lead to arguments and confrontation among the students. This is why Spleems are announced quickly by team name and the specific behavior, and not by individual students. If a student points out which student Spleemed, they would also receive a Spleem. Students are instructed to stay on task and ignore other students that Spleem. Students catch on quickly that any name-calling, tattling, pointing out, and so on, will result in another Spleem for their team, and this behavior will disappear quickly from the classroom.

When counting Spleems, teachers may express frustration, anger, or other negative emotions. It is completely normal for a teacher to have these feelings because teaching is a very challenging job and they have expectations the Game will result in decreased disruptive behavior. However, when teachers express their anger and frustration, it often makes the situation worse because students recognize the teacher's anger and frustration and, most likely, will respond to the teacher with their own feelings of anger and frustration. When the teacher remains calm, the situation is less likely to get out of control. Again, students will learn very quickly that arguing back about a Spleem is another Spleem. This is very clear to students when the teacher remains calm. It's almost as if the teacher is simply keeping score during the Game and arguing has no positive effect (only the negative one of more Spleems).

Tracking Spleems

The ideal way to track Spleems is with a consistent scoring system. Using the Good Behavior Game Scoreboard (Appendix P) or a similar form to track and document Spleems by team provides the consistency needed for tracking implementation. Using sticky notes or scrap paper usually results in inaccurate scorekeeping or teachers may lose the small pieces of paper. The Scoreboard comes in two formats. One is a large poster-size form that can be displayed to the entire class. The large Scoreboard is recommended to be used in the lower grade levels (although it can be used effectively in any grade). The second format is an 8-by-11-inch Scoreboard that teachers can use with a clipboard. The smaller Scoreboard format is recommended to be used for the older grades or when wall space is limited. It is helpful to provide verbal score updates throughout the Game using this smaller version of the Scoreboard (e.g., "Purple team has 3 Spleems so far, blue team has zero Spleems, yellow team has one Spleem").

It is extremely important that teachers record Spleems accurately during the Game. It can be very easy to call out a Spleem and forget to note it on the Scoreboard. It is recommended that teachers find a specific spot on the board to track Spleems, use the large Scoreboard posted on a wall, or use a clipboard with the smaller version of the Scoreboard. Whatever method a teacher chooses, it needs to be consistent so it becomes routine. If the students know the teacher calls out Spleems but doesn't record them, the Spleems lose their effect of monitoring and changing behavior. It would be like keeping score of a basketball game but not counting every basket. The accuracy would not be there, which leads to a diminishing effort by the players (students).

Another common pitfall is giving a team or student a "break" and not recording a Spleem the teacher observed. This does more harm than good in the long term. The goal of the Game is to change behavior and improve on-task behavior. Any kind of break in counting Spleems diminishes the effectiveness of the Game.

In addition, when students are playing the Game and they are not Spleeming, it is time for the teacher to praise appropriate student behavior (e.g., "I love how Team 3 is working so quietly and got started right away!"). If individual students are on task, praise them (e.g., "Thank you, Joseph, for putting your name at the top of your paper as soon as you received it and getting started so quickly!"). *Remember, what gets reinforced gets repeated.*

After the PAX Game

Reviewing Spleems

At the end of the Game (when the timer goes off, but before the prize is awarded) it is important to review the Spleems tracked during the Game. Each team should be informed about how many Spleems their team received, what each Spleem was for (e.g., specific behaviors), and which teams won the Game and gets to participate in the prize. It is also important to summarize the types of Spleems and positive behaviors noted during the Game, then guide students on what to work on for future Games. This increases the long-term effect of the Game. It also helps students to establish a link between their behavior and whether they get to participate in the prize, which leads to improved self-control. For example a teacher might say, "Team 1 you had zero Spleems, did you win the Game? Yes! Team 2 you had two Spleems for talking, did you win the Game? Yes! Team 3 you also had zero Spleems, did you win the Game? Yes! Team 4 you had one Spleem for getting out of your seat without permission, did you win? Yes! Everyone gets to participate in the prize! Next time we play the Game, please remember to raise a quiet hand if you need something and do not talk to your neighbors during independent work."

Sometimes teachers do not review the Spleems at the end of the Game. As stated, it is important to let each team know whether they won the Game and the number of Spleems each team received. Simply stating everyone won or everyone lost is not sufficient. The goal is to reduce the number of Spleems, so letting each team know the number aids teams with trying to improve their score. A key component is also to increase students' awareness about their behavior, and to have a discussion about the specific Spleems observed and how students can improve their on-task behavior for the next Game. It is also helpful to track total Spleems for the week for weekly contests.

Prizes

Types of Prizes

PAX GBG prizes are not tangible and do not need to cost teachers any money. Therefore, teachers do not have to worry about buying toys for a prize box or giving food to students that may have allergies. Overall, the idea is to have a very quick and fun "brain break" from instruction, and get back to work quickly. Many of the prizes are opportunities for students to "get the wiggles out" and have some physical activity throughout the school day. Examples of prizes include tapping a pencil, writing a note to a neighbor, doing jumping jacks, singing or dancing to a song, sitting under the desk, or sitting backward in a chair (see Appendix Z and Appendix AA for PAX GBG Prize Lists).

Length

Prizes should be short and should reflect how long the Game was played. For example, a longer Game (e.g., 10–20 minutes) might warrant a prize that is a little longer (e.g., 20 seconds–2 minutes), but a shorter Game (e.g., 5 minutes or less) should be rewarded with a shorter prize (e.g., 10–20 seconds). When prizes are too long and/or do not reflect the Game played, then it is not as successful and the students may expect longer and longer prizes for shorter amounts of Game time. Furthermore, sometimes the prize is too long and students actually become bored with doing the prize, which lessens the impact of a fun prize and winning the Game.

Activity Level

When giving a prize, teachers should be careful of the activity level of the prize. There are some prizes for which the activity is quiet and calm, then there are some prizes that are louder and more active. Teachers should prepare for this and plan for when these more active prizes are appropriate. For instance, if teachers are playing the Game in the middle of a math Lesson and the Game ends, this may be a more appropriate time for a calmer prize so that students are able to return to the math Lesson more easily. The teacher will still want to choose a prize randomly from the prize box, however since students can not see what is written for the prize the teacher may secretly "choose" and announce a more calm prize to students even if they actually pull out a more active prize (see "Choosing a Prize"). If teachers choose to do an active prize, they have to prepare the students to complete the prize successfully while having fun (see "Stating Expectations"). After a more active prize is complete, the teacher may also want to use PAX Quiet to refocus the students and to give the next direction, or the teacher may want to go through the control signals to help students calm down from all the excitement of the prize.

Stating Expectations

When a prize is chosen randomly, teachers will want to preteach the expectations for the prize so students know exactly what is required of them and how they can have fun with the prize while being safe in the classroom. Teachers should think of possible scenarios that could go wrong with the prize (e.g., students running instead of walking, students yelling or talking too loud) and preteach these expectations. Teachers should also remind students that if they cannot handle the prize, then they will have to remove this prize from the prize box until they can participate in the prize successfully and safely. Teachers will also want to prepare students to be able to hear the timer that signals the end of the prize. Teachers may want to remind students that they will blow the harmonica and put up the quiet sign as the timer goes off to signal the end of the prize and to regain attention. When this happens, if the students are out of their seats or making loud noises/talking/laughing, they are to stop and return to their seats safely and quietly. If students are unable to follow these directions after the prize is complete, then the teacher will have to remove this prize from the prize box. Teachers may also want to model the prize before starting it, or have the Kid of the Day model the prize while going over the expectations. After a prize has been chosen multiple times, this process will take much less time, but it is important to spend the time in the beginning to set up a prize safely and successfully.

Timing

Prizes should be delivered *immediately* after the end of the Game and the review of Spleems. This is important so students realize they received a prize for their hard work during the Game, and teachers are accountable for delivering the prize promised to them. Teachers should not wait until later to deliver the prize because they may forget to deliver it. The delay in gratification may decrease students' motivation to play the Game successfully in the future, if they know they may or may not receive the prize immediately after a Game win. For younger students, it is especially important to tie the reward immediately to the positive behavior observed. They may not be able to connect the reward to the positive behavior if it is delivered hours after the Game is completed. The only time a prize should be delayed is if the teacher is in the middle of a Lesson/discussion and wants to complete the thought before delivering the prize, or if an unforeseen circumstance gets in the way of completing the prize immediately (e.g., fire drill, lunchtime). In the first case, if teachers are in the middle of a Lesson/discussion, they may delay the prize until the end of the Lesson/discussion, but they must tell students their plan to award the prize and then follow through as soon as possible thereafter. If something unforeseen gets in the way of delivering the prize, teachers should plan when to deliver the prize and make the students aware of the plan. If possible, teachers can choose a prize the students can do in line or as they leave the class (in the case of going to lunch, not during a fire drill!).

Choosing a Prize

When choosing a prize, teachers will always want to choose a random prize from the prize box. This ensures the prize was not chosen by the teacher, and the element of surprise is greater and in turn makes the prize more enjoyable and fun. If the teachers choose the prize, then students may not be as excited to do the prize or they may not like the prize because it is what the teacher wants, not a surprise for the class. Teachers always have the option of "changing" the prize they pull from the prize box without students knowing. For example, if the teacher chooses Simon Says and there is not enough time before lunch to implement this prize, then the teacher should think of a backup, quick prize to use in such instances. Teachers should pretend that a calmer, quieter, and quicker prize was just pulled from the prize box, and play that prize instead. The students will still think it was random and will enjoy it much more than if the teacher chose the prize and made the students aware of it. Teachers will also want to review all prizes before putting them in the prize box. If they do not like a prize or do not know how to do the prize, then these prizes should be left out of the box.

Undesirable Prizes

When the prize is chosen, if the students groan, this is a hint to teachers that this prize may need to be switched out of the box and the prizes need to be refreshed (add more, switch prizes). Teachers should still deliver the prize; however, they should make it clear the prize will be taken out of the box and new prizes will be put in its place. This will create more excitement for future Games and prizes, and helps students realize their concerns ("groans") were heard. Students can also be told they do not have to participate in the prize if they do not wish to do so. Another variation that can increase enjoyment of the prize is to offer larger prizes on a weekly basis (e.g., win three Games during the week and students can have10 minutes of extra free play, watch a movie on Friday, or spend a longer time at the computer). Finally, having the teacher participate in the prize alongside the students often increases the excitement of the prize as well!

When a Team Loses

Teachers should always be prepared for a team to lose the Game and to plan ahead for how best to handle the prize. The most effective thing to do is to congratulate the winning teams and remind the losing teams they will have another chance to play the Game and win later that day (or the next day, if it's at the end of the day). Teachers can then set up the rules for the prize as they normally would, and deliver the prize to the winning teams. If teachers think the losing team will participate in the prize, they may want to stand by the losing team and praise those team members who do not participate and ignore those who do. Often, proximity (e.g., standing next to the losing team) is enough to make sure the losing team does not participate. Sometimes it takes a little preprize setup, such as telling the losing team members that if they participate they will receive a consequence (worst-case scenario). After the prize is complete, teachers should praise the winning teams for doing well with the prize and praise the losing teams for being such great sports (if they, in fact, met the teacher's expectations of not participating in the prize). This will help to create a positive experience during the next prize and will give credit to those who lost the Game, but demonstrated good self-control and acted in a positive manner.

Lessons

Preparation

Preparing to teach a good PATHS to PAX Lesson may only take 10 to 15 minutes, depending on the skill level of the teachers and their familiarity with the topics being addressed. To prepare appropriately, teachers should read through the Lesson thoroughly, including the supplemental activities and additional suggestions provided at the end of the Lesson. Materials should be found and prepared as necessary so that using them during the Lesson is not a distraction. If teachers do not prepare, then they may end up reading the Lesson word for word as it is written. Although the Lessons are scripted so anyone can teach them, the idea is that teachers make the Lesson their own and modify the "script" to make it natural. This increases student engagement and interest. Being knowledgeable about the Lesson also adds a genuine aspect to the topics being discussed and helps teachers emphasize Lesson objectives. Because the topics can sometimes be of a personal nature, if teachers can come up with examples they have actually experienced in their own life related to the Lesson topic, then the Lesson will be more meaningful to both the teachers and students. For example, if the Lesson is about frustration, teachers could share a time when they felt frustrated, then encourage a few students to share with the class what makes them frustrated.

Student Engagement

Any Lesson that involves students and keeps them engaged is going to be more successful at meeting stated objectives and keeping students interested. Student engagement is measured by looking at the expressions on students' faces and observing the number of questions they ask. When teachers deliver their Lesson in a monotone, students lose interest and become bored quickly with the material being covered. In addition, if a teacher talks *at* students instead of involving them actively, they will learn to not enjoy the Lessons. When students are bored or disengaged, unwanted and disruptive behaviors may increase and cause unnecessary stress in a classroom. Skilled teachers take ownership of a Lesson and its objectives just as they do with any academic Lesson.

If the coach suspects teachers are having difficulty with student engagement, ask them, "How do you think the Lesson went?" to determine their level of awareness regarding student engagement. From that point, the coach can work with the teacher to develop a plan to increase student engagement during the Lessons.

Strategies to Enhance Student Engagement

1. Have teachers vary their nonverbal cues of emotion (e.g., tone of voice, facial expressions, body posture).
2. Use appropriate self-disclosure of examples from the teacher's own personal life.
3. Ask students to share examples from their own lives or from pop culture/media.
4. Provide more opportunities for students to ask questions and provide their opinions.
5. Make connections between Lesson concepts and the academic curriculum.
6. Have students "turn and talk" to a partner.
7. Play games or read books that connect to the Lessons (multiple ideas are provided in the curriculum binder).
8. Have students act out or role-play concepts and skills.
9. Provide students with opportunities to complete activities, write, or draw pictures about the Lesson topics.
10. Play the Game during the Lesson.

Pacing

A Lesson should be long enough to achieve the stated objectives and short enough to keep students engaged and interested. The ideal length of a Lesson is 20 to 30 minutes. A common pitfall is that teachers sometimes extend the Lesson beyond the ideal 20 to 30 minutes, thinking this will help cover the objective more thoroughly. What happens in this situation is that students often become bored; multiple examples may be given that seem to restate the objective repeatedly. In addition, it is difficult for many students to sit for that long without taking a break or doing another activity. When a concept is understood by students, teachers should feel free to move on. Not all examples or supplemental activities listed in a Lesson have to be used. Teachers may want to use a timer to keep track of their pacing.

Generalization

Generalization involves the reference or use of program concepts in daily classroom life, particularly outside the times when the program material is being delivered. Sometimes when a new curriculum is introduced into a classroom, teachers are uncomfortable with it and may only address the ideas and concepts presented in the curriculum during the specified time allotted for implementation. When this happens, the concepts may be discussed only for a total of 40 minutes each week. Because PATHS to PAX GBG is designed to help students learn how to deal with and recognize their emotions, including times when their emotions may get in the way of learning, generalization throughout the school day is essential. Because emotion knowledge and regulation is a constant for all, bringing the concepts learned within the program into "everyday" activities helps students to be more effective at using the skills taught in the curriculum. Making connections between the Lesson topics and the academic curriculum, as well as using teachable moments throughout the school day, are very efficient ways for teachers to use their time, and these strategies create a more meaningful experience for students. Making connections between PATHS to PAX GBG and the academic curriculum throughout the day provides students repeated practice of concepts and skills. This is similar to effective teaching approaches, such as those used when teaching a student how to read. Teachers continuously practice, point out key words, ask questions, and prompt children to read things throughout the day to enhance their ability to read. They would not just begin teaching children to read and then never go back to the key elements or practice throughout the day. If program concepts and ideas are not generalized throughout the day and at times when the skills are needed to help students control their emotions, then disruptions will increase and unwanted reactions to intense emotions will be more likely to occur.

To increase generalization of the program throughout the school day, work with teachers to review past and to brainstorm possible future *teachable moments* to reinforce the skills taught during the Lessons. Some examples of generalization include praising students who share materials after a Lesson on sharing was taught that week, or encouraging students to use problem-solving strategies when they have a conflict with peers or a difficult decision to make in the classroom. Having the PATHS to PAX GBG posters hanging visibly in the classroom and throughout the building in the hallways, bathrooms, cafeteria, and resource rooms also helps with generalization. Another example of generalization is to encourage students who are sent to the office or to an in-school suspension room to write about how they could use program strategies in the future to handle situations differently (e.g., using the turtle technique or control signals to use deep breathing to calm down) . Last, to promote generalization, the Game can be played in different settings (e.g., during transitions, in the hallways, on the carpet, at students' desks, in the cafeteria, during resource classes). As always, it is important to find ways to reinforce the teacher for program elements currently in place and any attempts at generalization.

In this last section we discussed some of the most common mistakes teachers make with the Games and Lessons. By anticipating these mistakes, the coach can use discussion, modeling, observation, and feedback to help teachers avoid these pitfalls to experience implementation success. In the next section, common coaching pitfalls are discussed, such as getting down to business too quickly, follow-through, involvement in gossip or school politics, sharing teacher information with school administrators, organization, and difficulties with the role of expert. The goal is to share these pitfalls with our coaches so they can be aware, save time, and avoid making these common mistakes.

Common Coaching Pitfalls

This next section presents a set of Lessons related to coaching foibles. Although the information presented in this manual provides the foundation for effective coaching, it is unreasonable to think a coach will absorb all the information and never make a mistake. Just as it is helpful to be aware and anticipate common teacher implementation challenges, so, too, is it important to be familiar with common early coaching pitfalls, their associated problems, and steps you can take to avoid them.

Coaching Relationship
Acting Like an Outsider

Sometimes a new coach might not feel like part of the school staff, but more like an "outsider" who visits the school to conduct observations. This can be problematic if a coach is perceived as an outsider because teachers may not be as invested in the program or the overall coaching process if they do not have a good relationship with the coach.

The most important thing to do to gain credibility and be viewed as part of the school team is to spend more time in the school. It may be challenging for the coach to find extra time to try some of these strategies; however, you may find you are already doing some of these things. A coach may want to have a more strategic approach to time management and make more time in his or her schedule to be at the school. For example, the coach could stay at the school to complete paperwork (after observations) on a bench in the hallway or may bring lunch and eat in the teacher's lounge. Spending time informally in the hallways, office, and teacher's lounge provides the opportunity for school staff to get to know you as a person as well as see you as a resource.

To "join" the school staff, the coach should learn the names of people who are often at the school (e.g., paraprofessionals, parent volunteers, janitor) and smile and greet people in the hallway. Look for small ways to be helpful while in the building, such as making copies or assisting teachers in their classrooms when invited. Other examples involve stepping in to help teachers in times of crisis, including helping a teacher if a fight breaks out in the classroom during an observation or taking over the class if one of the students has a medical emergency.

Despite your best efforts, at times coach and teacher will not have an immediate connection. Naturally, the coach should find some sort of connection with the teacher, but sometimes you may try too hard (e.g., making comparisons to his or her own teaching experiences that are not true, praising efforts that are not there). This can be problematic if the teacher "sees through" these efforts and does not believe the coach is being genuine. When faced with this situation, the best approach is simply to spend time in the teacher's classroom. Eventually, a natural connection will most likely be made as the coach and teacher get to know one another.

Getting Down to Business Too Quickly

Sometimes coaches may not take the time to build rapport with teachers and may try to "get to business" too quickly. For example, the coach may come into the classroom, sit down at the table, and start talking about the agenda items for the coaching meeting without first greeting the teachers or asking about their day. This is challenging because the coach may feel pressure to talk about a lot of things during a short period of time (e.g., teacher's planning period when the teacher also has several other things to do during this time). However, it can be problematic if the coach does not take a few minutes each session to build rapport with the teacher. If the teacher does not trust the coach or there is no rapport between the two, it can be detrimental to the overall progress of the coaching process.

To avoid this situation, have a balance of talking about coaching issues and spending a few minutes at the beginning of each session to build rapport. These strategies have been discussed in other sections of the book (e.g., asking teachers about their weekend or a recent vacation, or listening to them as they share information about their child's most recent accomplishment). Although there may be times, because of time constraints, the coaching meeting is all business and there is not much time to ask acceptable personal questions, be careful not to make a habit of jumping into coaching too quickly so you do not affect the overall coaching relationship. In other words, the coach should send a clear message to teachers that he or she is not there just to collect data and leave; the coach genuinely wants to help teachers improve their classroom climate. When teachers notice the coach is genuine, they are more likely to be cooperative and listen to suggestions about ways they can increase program implementation.

In addition, if the coach is not sure about teachers' buy-in to the program it may be helpful to reflect on the amount of time you have spent building rapport with the teachers and brainstorm ideas for how to improve the relationship (e.g., plan to ask about the picture on his desk of him skydiving, bring them their favorite soda).

Following Through

Even with the best intentions, sometimes promises can be forgotten. Most coaches want to help each teacher to be successful with PATHS to PAX GBG because they can empathize with some of the challenges of being a teacher, combined with the challenge of learning a new program. When teachers ask the coach for help, it is important to take the opportunity to offer any support possible; however, offering support and then being unable to follow through can end up hurting the coach–teacher relationship. As a result, teachers may be less motivated to attempt implementation on their own because they interpret the lack of follow-through as a sign that the program is not truly important in their classroom. What can be problematic about offering support is that, often, the coach truly does not have the time or resources to offer *all* the needed support to teachers. One way to avoid this issue is to empathize with the teacher, then set up a meeting when the two of you can take a look at the situation and brainstorm some ideas together. Taking a step back and thinking about this particular situation in the context of all the other tasks and support you want to provide to this teacher as well as the other teachers in the school can help you organize and manage your resources more efficiently. Often, teachers appreciate the coach's time and willingness to meet to help solve problems. This is a great way for the coach to listen to the teacher and build rapport.

Expanding Boundaries beyond the Responsibilities of a Coach

Boundary issues relate to the blurring of the roles and responsibilities of the coach as a professional who is supporting teacher implementation of the program. One of the coach's primary goals is to make teachers feel comfortable and to build a working relationship with them. However, there are times when this can be misinterpreted by the teachers. For instance, if a teacher craves attention or friendship, he or she can misinterpret the coach's responsiveness as an invitation for friendship rather than as a working relationship. This can be a problem if the teacher's primary interactions with the coach become unrelated to the program and the teacher begins to view you primarily as a friend (e.g., always wanting to share personal experiences or issues). If you find yourself in this situation, see if there is an opportunity to validate the teacher's feelings and redirect the teacher back to the discussion (e.g., "It sounds like you had a really nice weekend! I am looking at the clock and we only have a few more minutes before the students get back from resource, so let's see what we have next on our agenda for today."). It is important to note there certainly may be cases when the coach and a teacher do form (or already have) a genuine friendship, and this would be problematic only if it interferes with the coach–teacher relationship (e.g., interactions during coaching sessions that are unrelated to program implementation). This can be avoided by keeping in mind that it is the coach's responsibility to maintain a professional working relationship at school and to set the tone for meetings with teachers. Time spent with teachers during the school day should focus mainly on program implementation, with only brief acknowledgments paid to personal issues.

Similarly, teachers may use a coaching session to express frustration or distress about school administration, parent involvement, or personal problems (e.g., marital conflict, health problems, fatigue/stress). It is natural for the coach to listen and sympathize because the teacher is going through a difficult time; however, it can be problematic if the majority of the coaching session is spent focusing on the stressors. *It can be especially problematic if this becomes a habit and the coaching session is used repeatedly as a time when teachers vent about the stressors in their life.* The relationship can quickly become more of a therapist–patient bond, leaving little room for coach–teacher collaboration. Like the situation described earlier, if you are faced with this situation, validate the teacher's feelings and redirect the teacher back to the discussion by saying something such as, "That sounds frustrating, I'm sure it's hard to focus on teaching when you are experiencing that type of situation at home. You might find that focusing on Tootling with your students first thing in the morning can help take your mind off of things at home and prepare for the school for the school day ahead."

Moreover, the coach may not want to ask open-ended questions or do things that would encourage the teacher to continue talking about the personal topic. Keep the sessions focused by always using an agenda to guide the meeting. The coach may find it helpful to e-mail teachers before meetings to remind them about the meeting and let them know he or she is excited to talk with them about new prizes they can use in their classroom and the Kid of the Day (list specific agenda items). Furthermore, during the meeting the coach may need to redirect teachers to the coaching content. It is important to be firm but also polite and respectful in the meetings (e.g., "I am so sorry but I am looking at the time and I want to be sure we spend some time talking about prizes today"). The coach can still express support by sending teachers an e-mail or card to let them know he or she is thinking about them, or bring a small treat (e.g., chocolate) to the next meeting to acknowledge their difficulties.

Being Involved in Gossip or School Politics

More worrisome is when teachers vent feelings or provide personal information about colleagues or administrators. Even if teachers express valid concerns or views that are shared by the coach, being involved in gossip or expressing an opinion about other teachers is problematic, because it can undermine the trust of the individuals being talked about as well as the teachers who are talking about other staff members. This has the potential to create a negative environment that can interfere with the coaching relationship. As a coach, if you are confronted by gossip, see if there is an opportunity to validate the teacher's feelings without directly commenting (e.g., "It sounds like you are frustrated by this challenging work situation") and redirect the teacher back to the discussion (e.g., "I know it can be difficult to think about other things when we're dealing with workplace issues, but I have found that focusing on my own classroom can sometimes help refocus my energy onto positive things."). There are steps you can take to demonstrate professionalism with regard to gossip, such as never divulging your thoughts and opinions about teachers to each other, including inadvertently letting one teacher know how you feel about another teacher with regard to (a) skill level (e.g., "You do a much better job playing the Game than Mr. Sanders"), (b) classroom management skills, and (c) personal opinions.

Sharing Teacher Information with School Administrators

Typically, coaches offer general information regarding teacher implementation to school administrators. However, there are times when administrators will ask for more specific information. Providing such information is certain to have a detrimental effect on the coach–teacher relationship and it is the coach's responsibility to protect this relationship by providing general information only. This situation is best handled simply by reminding the administrator that to foster a collaborative relationship with teachers, it is important to talk only broadly about implementation. Offer to complete a walkthrough with the administrator to point out positive aspects of implementation. Remind administrators they have access to the Administrator Classroom Environment Checklist (Appendix BB) and they can use it to make their own judgment of a teacher's implementation level.

Despite the coach's efforts to avoid providing evaluative information to administrators about teacher implementation, there are times when teachers may perceive the coach as part of the administrative team (e.g., walking around the building with the principal, asking teachers for data). It is essential the coach recognizes this and takes action to ensure teachers understand the coach is *not* in an evaluative position in the school; otherwise, it will become very difficult to have a collaborative relationship with teachers as a result of a lack of trust (e.g., a teacher fearing the coach reports back to the administrator). In most cases, a misunderstanding like this can be avoided simply by making your actions in a building public knowledge. This can be done through conversations, e-mails, or fliers placed in mailboxes (e.g., "I will be touring the building with the principal tomorrow. No need to worry; we are not evaluating your performance. I'm doing this to point out all the positive things happening here.").

Prioritizing School Needs above Program Needs

Finally, in some cases, a coach's willingness to help out in the school can lead to administrators having unrealistic expectations of the coach's role in the building. This can be problematic if the expectations begin to interfere with a coach's ability to get effective coaching completed (e.g., too much time is spent on helping and not enough time spent coaching). In these situations, it is helpful for the coach to convey a sense of wanting to provide assistance while providing a reminder of the coaching priorities (e.g., "I'd love to help out with lunch duty in the cafeteria, but I have a meeting scheduled with Mrs. Smith during lunch."). Finding a way to offer assistance on a smaller scale may help address the administrator's need while maintaining the coaching priorities (e.g., "How about I help the teachers start a Game during the transition out of the cafeteria back to the classroom after my meeting?"). Often, administrators are very understanding when the coach reminds them they have other responsibilities or deadlines.

Organization
Time Management

As a coach, you may sometimes find it overwhelming to manage multiple roles—modeling, observing, building relationships with the school staff, completing paperwork, attending meetings, and so on. There might even be times when you volunteer to take on activities outside of typical coaching duties in an effort to strengthen relationships at a school (e.g., helping with an assembly, stepping in for lunch duty when the school is short staffed). There may be a few teachers or schools that monopolize your time by asking for additional modeling or support. Also, some teachers or schools may ask you repeatedly to do things outside your coaching role (e.g., lunch duty, substitute teaching). Although it is recommended the coach help out at the school to "join" the staff and gain their acceptance, you need to be careful to manage your time in a way that allows you to take care of coaching priorities. Giving your time freely can be problematic if it takes away time that could be spent coaching teachers.

There are several things you can do to improve time management and use your time most efficiently. When faced with a situation in which someone requests assistance outside of your coaching responsibilities, remind administrators of the primary reason you are there: to coach and improve teacher program implementation. This should be done in a gentle but firm enough way so there is no room for misinterpretation (e.g., "I'd love to help out in the cafeteria today, but I am scheduled to be in third grade to assist with a Lesson. With all of my coaching responsibilities, I'm not going to be able to help out with cafeteria staffing needs today.")

In addition, the coach may want to assign a specific day (or two) of the week to each school. If this is the case, minimize visiting the school (e.g., delivering materials, scheduling observations or modeling) when it is not the assigned day, to reduce traveling back and forth between schools. On the school's assigned day, a schedule can be developed collaboratively with teachers to visit classrooms and assist with or observe program implementation. Depending on other responsibilities, it may be necessary to reserve time for planning, paperwork, and coach supervision meetings. If time is not scheduled for planning and paperwork, you may not be able to complete it during regular work hours. It is a good idea always to have some work with you in case a teacher cancels or there is some unexpected downtime at a school. Create a running to-do list when visiting schools to help stay organized for the next visit (e.g., plan to coteach with Mrs. Morgan, bring Mr. Roberts a harmonica, remind Ms. Moore about the observation). Last, it may be helpful to schedule a planning time at the start or end of each day to get organized, gather materials for the next day, and create a detailed schedule of what needs to be done the following day.

Falling Behind with Data Collection

One coaching pitfall is not keeping up to date with data. It is very easy to put off data collection and think you'll get to it later. The problem with this is that details can be forgotten and then are not recorded. Key information that could make the difference in helping a teacher be successful can be lost if a coach's records are not accurate and noted timely. Use data sheets that are easily accessible whenever you visit teachers. Moreover, whenever possible, track data immediately after interactions with teachers so you don't forget the details. Sometimes, situations don't allow you to immediately record data and important information that can be used to guide your coaching of teachers. In these instances, it's important to leave some time at the end of the day to record data accurately. Taking notes and tracking data should be a regular routine after each school visit. By dedicating just 10 to 15 minutes at the end of each day to record all needed information, you will keep track of details that might otherwise be forgotten.

Difficulties in the Role of the Expert

Acting as an Expert

Sometimes when coaching teachers, despite good intentions, it is possible to come across as a know-it-all. This can be a major problem for the coach–teacher relationship and may cause a great deal of resentment from teachers. Although you are only trying to help, stressed-out or angry teachers may perceive any constructive criticism as judgmental or even threatening. As the coach, it is important not to overwhelm the teacher with a "laundry list" of criticisms and to avoid using an "I'm just going to give you advice" style of coaching. *Often, the coach can learn more by listening to teachers rather than telling them something.* The goal is to strive for a balance of having credibility as a coach but not coming across as an expert or evaluator. The coach should acknowledge and respect that teachers are the expert in their classroom, and the coach's expertise (e.g., with the program, teaching experience, observation of multiple teachers and seeing best teaching practices that can be shared) can create a wonderful partnership that can enhance the classroom environment to facilitate students' learning.

Expecting Teacher Prioritization of the Program

It is easy to forget that the program is not every teacher's number one priority, especially given that it *is* the first priority of a coach. Instead, teachers' top priority is to educate their students. They often have to balance requirements from administrators, suggestions from parents, and feedback from mentor teachers. Although using PATHS to PAX GBG helps to make educating children a little easier, it isn't always used as frequently as needed for teachers to experience the positive outcomes. Of course, the more a teacher uses the concepts from the program, the more effective it is. Patience and understanding are necessary here. *Teachers are under a tremendous amount of stress.* High-stakes testing, merit-based pay, lack of resources, and so on, all contribute to high anxiety for some teachers and may interfere with their willingness or ability to implement the program. Remembering this will help a coach maintain patience and consistent support and availability with teachers who are trying to juggle a number of competing demands.

Expecting Perfection

As the coach and expert in the PATHS to PAX GBG program, it can be easy to become frustrated and impatient with teachers who appear unable or unmotivated to implement program components correctly. Even some of the parts of the program that seem like the simplest pieces to implement may be challenging for some teachers. If teachers sense your frustration with them, they may resent your perceived lack of support and may avoid you. *Real results take time, and some teachers need extra space to help themselves feel more comfortable with the program and to attempt to make it something that fits well in their classroom.* Although some teachers run with the program immediately after they are trained, others may take several weeks or more to get it going in their classroom. It can be helpful to break up the program into very small steps for some teachers who express they find the whole thing overwhelming or too involved. It is important to remember every teacher is individual in their abilities and experiences, and some teachers require more patience than others.

Working Alone

Most of the time, coaching teachers takes place as a solo venture. You visit several schools and develop relationships with teachers. You collaborate with individual teachers about how to implement the program in their classroom. Therefore, you can get used to doing a lot of things single-handedly. However, often it is helpful for a coach to enlist the assistance of colleagues when dealing with teacher implementation challenges or other novel situations. You may encounter a situation with a teacher that another coach or supervisor has already experienced; yet, without taking the time to collaborate with other coaches, you may miss out on learning what techniques others have tried and how successful those techniques were. Some coaches worry that if they ask for others to give their opinion on something, it makes them appear not able to handle certain situations. However, it reflects well on a coach's desire to develop professionally when challenging situations are discussed with others, and it provides an opportunity for shared experiences and knowledge that has the potential to benefit all those involved (for more information on coaching supervision, see Chapter 6).

Low Program Implementation

There are different degrees of low-implementing teachers. There are teachers who are high-quality teachers, who are able to implement the program successfully, but they are not doing so consistently; some don't implement the program at all. There are also teachers who are middle-quality teachers who may or may not be implementing the program, but need some assistance and support. And finally, there are low-quality teachers, who may or may not be implementing the program, but need a lot of assistance. For example, these teachers may need additional support with classroom/behavior management, organization, time management, and/or instructional support. The coach's job is to work with all levels of teachers and encourage them to implement the program while offering the "right" amount of assistance.

Offering Too Much Assistance

There will likely be times when you will struggle with how much assistance to offer teachers to get them on track. Offering too much assistance may enable them to rely on you to complete what needs to be done; offering too little assistance can leave teachers feeling isolated and overwhelmed. The key is to provide a balance between offering help and "pushing" or encouraging teachers to do some of the work.

The best strategy is to offer some help while finding a middle ground with teachers (e.g., "How about we share some of the work. If you can teach Lesson 30 on Tuesday, I'll teach Lesson 31 on Thursday? Does this work for you?"). If the teacher is a high-quality teacher and is able to teach the Lessons successfully, but just can't find the time or doesn't want to find the time to teach them, then you may offer this time when you are teaching as free time for the teacher. If the teacher is a mid- to low-quality teacher, then this is also a great opportunity for the coach to teach the Lesson and model key elements of the program and general teaching strategies while the teacher observes. The coach should not offer to teach all Lessons unless there are unique circumstances (e.g., teacher is out for an extended period of time). Offer to help, but encourage teachers to implement the program and generalize the ideas in their day-to-day teaching. The coach may also offer to help with planning the Lesson to ensure teachers follow through with teaching the Lesson, and then the coach will want either to observe this Lesson or check in later during the week to make sure the Lesson was taught. An incentive can be offered to get teachers to follow through and to reinforce desired behavior.

Also, if teachers are able to play the Game successfully but are not doing so consistently, then you might want to spend some time in the classroom and prompt Game-playing opportunities. If teachers struggle with the elements of the Game, then you may want to spend some time in the classroom prompting Game opportunities, helping out with playing the Game, or even playing the Game while the teacher is instructing. This offers a chance to model the Game, show the teacher that it can be played easily during regular instruction, and provide key times to play the Game in the class (e.g., right after lunch, during an independent activity). Collaboratively, the coach and teacher can plan times when the Game can be played during the day, then you can check in on the teacher and reward him or her if the Game is being played during these times or if the teacher is increasing the consistency of playing the Game in the classroom.

You can also offer to help out with things such as creating a Tootle Board, changing the Tootles on the Tootle Board, creating PAX Stix, and so on. However, first encourage teachers to try these things on their own while providing incentives, before offering to do these things for the teacher (e.g., "I noticed you have your Tootle Banner up, but there are no Tootles on your Tootle Board. If you can get some Tootles up there by the end of the week, then I'll stop by with a reward for your efforts.") Sometimes these actions affect the coach–teacher relationship positively and help teachers get started—especially if the coach actually initiates certain ongoing tasks (e.g., changing Tootles on the Tootle Board). Other times, it enables teachers to depend on the coach more to do these things. It is up to you to use your best judgment on how much assistance to offer before encouraging teachers to do these things on their own.

Being Too Lenient

There are other times when you may fall into the trap of being too lenient with a teacher and allowing too many excuses for why implementation is not occurring. Some teachers will make many excuses regarding why the program doesn't work, why it doesn't follow their ideals of teaching, or why they don't have time to fit the Lessons or Games into their day. This can become a problem because some of these excuses may be valid; but, if made week after week, it becomes more and more difficult to get teachers onboard and caught up. You should be understanding and listen to these teachers' concerns, while offering help to get the program started. If teachers continue to be resistant and still make excuses as to why they cannot implement the program, then you need to challenge these teachers and remind them this is a schoolwide program, then brainstorm ways to increase implementation in the classroom (e.g., "It sounds like finding the time to fit the program into your day is becoming more and more difficult to do, especially around state testing in the Spring. How about we try to come up with some possibilities of when you could play a Game while preparing your students for these exams?") Again, it's the balance between being understanding and encouraging teachers to do what is required of them in implementing the program. Remember, tackle these problems sooner rather than later to keep teachers on track with teaching the Lessons and implementing key elements of the program. As a coach, offer suggestions, help out, and set goals with teachers, then reward them as they accomplish the identified goals.

Losing Hope That the Program Will Work

Another common concern for coaches is whether the program will even work in a challenging classroom and/or school, which often leads to loss of hope and the potential for a coach to give up on a teacher or school. It is both draining, both physically and emotionally, to work with teachers who are negative about the program or who have a very low teaching skill level. It can be a struggle to deal with how much support to provide these teachers, especially if the goal of the coach is to get the teacher to implement the program successfully and not to help a teacher teach a class. However, there are times when the coach has to start at Step 1 and work on instructional or classroom/behavior management skills before tackling key elements of the program. Things such as making sure materials are organized and ready for the day, developing a plan for the day, and planning for transition times are key. Gradually, you can work on adding program elements such as using the timer during Lessons. The key is to take baby steps and try to get the teacher to implement the program while working on the quality of implementation. It will be helpful to model teaching a Lesson and playing a Game while the teacher is observing and participating with a small task. Try to remain optimistic and not give up hope on a teacher or a school regardless of how challenging the situation is! If teachers learn to implement one element of the program successfully or pick up on some general teaching skills (e.g., praising positive behavior, ignoring minor negative behaviors), then your efforts will be worth the time and energy you put into them. Being a constant support and encouragement in the classroom can help the teacher and students in that class.

Not Setting Explicit Goals with Teachers

It is very important, to set explicit goals with teachers. Failing to set explicit goals with teachers may lead to feelings of failure and loss of hope for the program to work in the classroom. *Setting goals helps set up teachers to succeed, even if they reach a small goal in a minor part of the program.* Set specific, short-term goals with teachers and check in on progress every week (possibly even daily, depending on the goal). At the start of implementation, help teachers establish small goals around classroom setup, possibly offering some assistance. These goals can be linked to the beginning Lessons and lead up to playing the Game. When the Game is introduced, model the Game and, if needed, work with teachers on breaking up the Game into segments that are understood more easily and for which goals can be set. For example, if a teacher is having a difficult time introducing the prize after the Game, model prize setup and delivery, then have the teacher try setting up the next prize while you observe. Then, set a goal collaboratively with the teacher for the teacher to practice setting up expectations before the prize and delivering the prize during the week. Check up on the teacher at the end of the week and observe a Game including awarding of the prize. If the teacher appears to understand all concepts of the program and is just not implementing them because of time or other constraints, then set goals with this teacher specifically around finding the time to implement the program. For example, if the teacher is behind on Lessons, review the pacing guide with the teacher, come up with a revised pacing guide, and set a goal for the week. At the end of the week, check in to make sure the plan or goal was accomplished. You can also offer incentives to all teachers who meet their goals—even if it is a small goal—to help increase the likelihood the teacher will continue to work on the goals and implement the program. *Celebrate small successes and progress!*

Avoiding Challenging Situations

It is very difficult to work with teachers whose priorities do not include the program or around whom you feel uncomfortable. The first thing to remember is to try to remain positive and be as understanding, friendly, and caring as possible with *all* teachers. It may take more time for teachers to see you really care and are a valuable resource. As easy as it would be to avoid these teachers, try to keep consistent contact. This helps them see that the program is being implemented schoolwide, and that it is the coach's job to check in with all teachers and offer assistance to them when they are implementing the program. For a more extensive description of strategies for working effectively with teachers with whom you have difficulty making progress, see Chapter 4.

Focusing All Coaching Efforts on Low-Implementing Teachers

As mentioned, when teachers first begin implementing the program, you may find that some teachers "run with it" immediately. However, it is still important to continue to complete the first few weeks of modeling, observing, and planning with these teachers. Because of their momentum and enthusiasm in the beginning, you might get comfortable with these teachers and almost "forget" to check-in on them as time goes on. When it is time to update your data, you may realize certain teachers haven't been visited or there have not been any meaningful interactions with them in quite some time. When going to check in with these teachers again, it may become evident they have *not* been implementing the program. Suddenly, teachers who were doing an excellent job implementing the program at the beginning of the year turn out to be teachers with whom you need to spend a lot of extra time, helping them get caught up. One way to avoid this situation is to make sure to check in with all teachers regularly during their scheduled Lesson times on a weekly basis, and meet with all teachers to inquire about any classroom challenges related to the program. Heeding these strategies will serve you well. *It's a lot more difficult to remotivate teachers than it is to keep their momentum going!*

Chapter 3 Reflection Questions

- What are the three phases of coaching activities discussed in this chapter?

- What are some ways you can "connect" and build rapport with teachers?

- Why is it important to identify teacher strengths at the beginning of a coaching session?

- Why is data collection an integral part of coaching? What data will you be collecting from teachers?

- Are there any coaching pitfalls you think will be challenging to avoid in your work with teachers? What can you do to be aware of and to avoid these pitfalls?

Indicated Coaching Model

The Universal Coaching Model described in Chapter 3 may not be sufficient to improve program implementation for every teacher. Therefore, an Indicated Coaching Model was developed that outlines specific procedures and strategies for working with teachers who need additional support. The Indicated Coaching Model espouses the same principles of engagement, collaboration, feedback, and reinforcement reflected in the Universal Coaching Model; however, the Indicated Coaching Model is influenced even more heavily by behavioral assessment, principles, and strategies than the Universal Coaching Model, as discussed in the pages that follow.

Objectives

- Understand the process for collecting and using data to develop a plan for supporting teacher implementation.
- Learn how to identify barriers and facilitators of implementation.
- Develop proficiency in devising hypotheses about which factors to target when supporting teacher implementation.

Behavioral Assessment and Coaching Plan Formulation

A process was established that is grounded in behavioral assessment by which information was gathered on teacher implementation. Then, a hypothesized working model of the teacher's behavior was developed that led to creating a plan for addressing factors hypothesized to influence teacher implementation. Finally, assessment procedures and timelines to measure teacher progress were developed. This process is outlined in the Teacher Implementation Support Planning Checklist (TISPC) in Table 4.1. The product of this process is the Coach Action Plan (CAP; Appendix CC), a dynamic document that specifies coach strategies to support teacher implementation.

TABLE 4.1 Teacher Implementation Support Planning Checklist

	ASSESS	
1. Collect information.	1. Collect structured observation data. 2. Collect informal data through observation, discussion with teacher, teacher questionnaires, and so on.	Materials: • Rubric notes and scores • Lesson Logs • Game Scoreboards • Coach notes
2. Identify teacher strengths.	1. What are the teacher's strengths with regard to personal and professional characteristics and program implementation?	Materials: • Coach Action Plan
3. Identify teacher implementation challenges.	1. Define the teacher's implementation challenges in behavioral terms. 2. Develop hypotheses, considering the influence of the following factors: ▪ Rapport with coach ▪ General teaching skills ▪ Engagement in the program ▪ Understanding of program components ▪ Quality of program skills ▪ Motivation ▪ Ability to manage personal stress ▪ Classroom composition ▪ Administrative context 3. Identify and prioritize hypothesized factors for intervention.	Materials: • Coach Action Plan
4. Identify strategies that have been tried.	1. What strategies have been tried and what have been the outcomes?	
	PLAN	
1. Identify behavioral goals.	1. Identify long-term behavioral goals. 2. Develop smaller, short-term specific weekly behavioral goals.	Materials: • Coach Action Plan
2. Identify strategies.	1. Prioritize and select strategies that address implementation challenges and correspond to hypotheses.	
3. Identify assessment procedures, progress indicators, and timeline.	1. Indicate how will you assess teacher progress. 2. Note the progress you expect to see and the timeframe in which you want to see it.	Materials: • Coach Action Plan
	DO	
1. Implement the Coach Action Plan.	1. Begin implementing one to two strategies associated with short-term goals.	Materials: • Coach Action Plan • Coach Activities Log (to track strategies)
	EVALUATE	
1. Evaluate and monitor plan effectiveness.	1. Implement assessment procedures and timelines. 2. Review progress and return to earlier steps if needed.	Materials: • Rubric notes and scores • Lesson Logs • Game Scoreboards • Coach notes • Tootles

In this chapter, each step of the TISPC is described and the development of a CAP (Appendix CC) is detailed. In general, this is an "in-house" procedure—meaning, coaches and supervisors collect data, identify challenges, and determine coaching strategies without teachers' involvement. This allows for the open brainstorming and discussion necessary to come up with a coherent plan before sharing data with and involving teachers in the process of improving implementation.

Teacher Implementation Support Planning Checklist

In this section, each step in the TISPC is described. The following example is provided to demonstrate how these steps were implemented by one of the PATHS to PAX GBG coaches with a specific teacher:

> *Mr. F. was an upper elementary teacher with a classroom that had a high rate of disruptive student behavior. There was not much evidence of the program being implemented in his classroom. He frequently remarked about how the kids today don't respect adults and they don't care about their education.*

Step 1: Assess
Collect Information

The assessment process begins with ongoing, multimethod (e.g., observation, teacher report), data collection as described in Chapter 3. Data is gathered formally through structured observation (e.g., Good Behavior Game Implementation Rubric [Appendix M]) and collection of teacher materials (e.g., Game Scoreboard [Appendix P], Lesson Logs [Appendix O]) as well as informally through observation (e.g., coach taking notes while observing a Lesson; coach passing by classroom in hallway and hearing yelling, which may be inconsistent with how the teacher behaves during classroom observations), and discussions with the teacher (e.g., teacher reporting implementation difficulties). This information allows coaches to assess teacher skill and consistency with regard to program implementation. When it is determined a teacher has the skill set but is inconsistent with implementation, the coach makes a plan for encouraging and reinforcing extra practice and increased frequency of implementation, and continues to monitor program implementation by that teacher.

> *Mr. F.'s rubric scores were satisfactory, suggesting he had the skills to play the Game and deliver Lessons; however, he rarely turned in Scoreboards and, although his Lesson Log was on pace, the quality of the Lessons needed to improve. For example, his Lessons were long (45 minutes on average), he did not ask for student participation during the Lessons, and he rarely linked Lesson content to students' everyday lives.*

Identify Teacher Strengths

When it is determined that a teacher lacks the requisite skills for high-quality program implementation or demonstrates behaviors that undermine program concepts (e.g., hostility toward students), then the coach continues to follow the TISPC and begins to create a CAP (Appendix CC). This involves the identification of teacher strengths: personal (e.g., friendly) and professional (e.g., demonstrates high-quality teaching skills), and with regard to program implementation (e.g., uses harmonica on a regular basis). *Identification of strengths allows the coach to build on what the teacher is already doing well, and helps build a positive working relationship between coach and teacher.* In addition, a strengths-based approach is consistent with the principles of the PATHS to PAX GBG program. Although in some instances it may be challenging for a coach to identify teacher strengths, this process is important to help you develop insight about how your own negative reactions to the teacher might interfere with coaching. Similar to how coaches encourage teachers always to find *something positive* to say about students with challenging behavior, you need to strive to find something positive for which to praise teachers genuinely (e.g., colorful bulletin boards, taking time to meet with the coach).

> *Mr. F. often appeared frustrated because he wanted to be a good teacher, but felt powerless to manage student behavior and to change what he perceived as "the way kids are today." As a coach, I appreciated his willingness to share his concerns because these are difficult thoughts and feelings to experience, and even more difficult to share with someone else who might be perceived as an expert in behavior management.*

Identify Teacher Implementation Challenges

Next, the teacher's implementation challenges are defined in observable, measurable, behavioral terms. This means identifying a specific and concrete action as well as indicators of the frequency, intensity, or nature of the behavior. For example, rather than indicate the teacher is "disorganized" during the Lesson, it is much more informative to say the teacher "has not had the opportunity to read/prepare the Lesson ahead of time, does not have necessary materials ready, reads directly from the manual, and often does not emphasize the purpose of the Lesson." Similarly, teacher "hostility" would be specified as "reprimanding students in front of peers using a loud tone of voice and demeaning language (e.g., "You are being stupid") approximately twice an hour." It is important to define teacher behavior in observable, measurable, behavioral terms because observation and measurement are key components of the scientific process as well as the coaching model. These components assist the appraisal of the success of the coaching strategies in improving teacher implementation. Other benefits to operationalizing teachers' behavior include the following:

1. Giving feedback in a nonjudgmental manner (e.g., "I noticed you had to spend a few minutes in the middle of the Lesson to look for materials" is more respectful than saying the teacher is disorganized)

2. Helping the teacher to identify a specific problem and develop specific strategies on which to work to change the behavior (*disorganized* is a vague term and can be an overwhelming problem on which the teacher should work)

After identifying teacher implementation challenges, consider what factors might influence teacher behavior. Coaches should also make an effort to specify these factors (listed in Table 4.1) in observable, measurable behavioral terms. For example, "poor rapport" might be specified as "avoids eye contact with coach, cancels meetings on a weekly basis with coach, and often uses negative tone with coach."

The key to the implementation support process is the development of function-based hypotheses about how these various factors interfere with a teacher's ability to implement the program. Examples of hypotheses include: "If the teacher were less stressed, she would be more engaged in coaching sessions and would use the program tools more regularly" and "If the teacher were less anxious about being evaluated by the coach, she would not cancel coaching sessions and she would allow the coach to observe Lessons more frequently." Certainly, low teacher implementation can be influenced by multiple factors; however, the goal with regard to the hypotheses is to develop a deeper understanding of what might be contributing to the problem, create a list of possible modifiable factors, and prioritize the factors that have the best chance for being modified to improve teacher implementation.

> *From a coach's perspective, Mr. F.'s biggest challenges were his views that the problem was too overwhelming to tackle (thereby resulting in him not implementing much of the program because of the belief it wouldn't work) and that his Lessons were not engaging (e.g., too long, lacked student participation, not linked to everyday life). One hypothesis is that if he could shorten the Lessons, increase student participation in the Lessons, and link the content to real life, he would engage students and thereby decrease disruptive behavior. Increased student engagement might also help him connect with his students and gain perspective on their lives so he would view them in a more positive light.*

Identify Strategies That Have Been Tried

It is important to identify the strategies that have been tried and to evaluate their implementation and outcomes. Did the coach use the strategy consistently to improve teacher implementation? Did the teacher make any progress following the coach's coaching strategy? It may be the case that a relatively low-effort strategy was not implemented consistently; hence, it might be wise to try this strategy again before moving on to a more intensive coaching strategy. It may also be the case that the teacher made small progress following the use of a particular strategy; this may be a time when judgment must be used about whether to continue using this strategy to bring about incremental progress or whether to augment the coaching plan with additional strategies.

> *Because implementation challenges were present for Mr. F. from the beginning, the only real strategies that had been tried were the group training and coach modeling the Game*

in his classroom. Therefore, Mr. F. might respond better to more structured support while he tries implementing program components, particularly because there appears to be a positive relationship with the coach.

Step 2: Plan
Identify Behavioral Goals

After gathering information, as well as creating and prioritizing hypotheses, it is time to artic-ulate a thoughtful plan of action regarding improving teacher implementation. The coach drafts and prioritizes long- and short-term goals to be shared with the teacher for feedback. Long-term goals might include what the coach envisions teacher implementation should look like after a certain period of time (e.g., "Teacher will prepare and deliver Lessons on a weekly basis and have all materials available during the Lesson"). Short-term goals should reflect manageable behavioral improvements (e.g., "Teacher will meet with coach to coplan the Lesson the day before the Lesson" and then, "Teacher will plan and prepare for the Lesson on her own and show the coach her Lesson materials").

> *Possible long-term goals for Mr. F.: (1) increasing positive classroom management strategies and (2) increasing a positive classroom environment. I met with Mr. F. and, building on previous discussions we had shared my experiences as a coach and former teacher. When he confided his anger about his students to me, I expressed empathy and acknowledged that, as a teacher, he has one of the most challenging jobs. I also told him I was impressed at his resilience. I explained that the program offers strategies to help with classroom management and to improve the overall environment, and I asked for his perspective on how things were going with regard to his use of positive behavior management strategies and his classroom environment. He agreed these were things that are important in effective classrooms, but he felt he thought he was failing in both areas. This gave me the opportunity to normalize these challenges again (e.g., "When I was a teacher" and "Lots of other teachers I've coached") as well as to instill hope that things would improve (e.g., "Upper elementary classrooms are challenging and I think you are on your way to developing some skills that will make teaching more enjoyable for you. I am here to support you. I have lots of ideas, so let's put our heads together and figure out where to start."). Mr. F. and I developed short-term goals that included playing the Game more frequently and consistently, and starting to address the classroom environment slowly.*

Identify Strategies

The goal for the coach is to identify and prioritize strategies that address the factors hypoth-esized as interfering with implementation. To determine how to prioritize strategies, first the coach guides the teacher in identifying small, specific goals for the upcoming week that work toward the short- and long-term goals. In other words, the coach helps the teacher "chunk" a big task into smaller tasks to make them more attainable. The coach should suggest goals that give teachers the "biggest bang for their buck." For instance, the goal could meet several of the teacher's short-term goals by increasing one program component (e.g., playing three Games per day). In addition, it is also important the teacher see immediate results, if possible (e.g., by playing the Game three times a day this week there have been fewer student disruptions/office referrals).

> *First, we worked on playing the Game for a shorter amount of time more frequently and consistently. We identified routine times to play the Game (transitions and independent work at first, then during instruction) and also to play whenever behavior problems started to increase. Next, we tackled the classroom environment slowly by doing Tootles only during Mr. F's most difficult time of the day: when students returned from lunch. We made this a daily routine (allowing each student to write two Tootles to whoever they wanted when they came back from lunch). This helped calm down the students and transitioned them to getting ready for the afternoon's instruction. Then, we focused on the Lessons and how they can help with the environment. The Control Signals Poster [a poster with steps to help students calm down] was very effective at peaceful conflict resolution. Mr. F. also started using the Control Signals Poster whenever he felt angry or stressed. Using these opportunities to apply the control signals might serve the dual purposes of reducing his immediate stress as well as modeling appropriate emotion regulation for the students. Some of the other strategies implemented included, tackling student engagement in the Lessons by setting a timer to go off after 20 minutes to signal Mr. F. to wrap up the Lesson, asking for three student volunteers to share their own experiences during the Lesson, and, last, planning ahead of time for how the content might be related to current academic material in their classroom or events in students' real lives.*

Identify Assessment Procedures, Progress Indicators, and Timeline

Establishing procedures for assessing teacher progress involves identifying means (e.g., observation, teacher report, data to be collected) and benchmarks that indicate the teacher is making progress toward the long-term goals (e.g., "Teacher and coach will meet to coplan Lessons before class on a weekly basis for the next 4 weeks. For the 4 weeks following, the coach will check in with the teacher the day before the Lesson to ensure that the teacher has materials ready").

> *Because, initially, the coach was going to be in the classroom, behavioral observation was a key data source, as were Game Scoreboards and teacher self-reports on the days when the coach was not in the classroom. In addition, the coach asked students frequently about their most recent Lesson to get a sense of how involved they were in the Lesson.*

Step 3: Do

Implement Coach Action Plan

During this phase, the coach begins to implement the strategies identified in the CAP (Appendix CC) to achieve short-term goals.

> *Mr. F. and the coach implemented the plan together the first two days while the coach was present to observe. The coach and Mr. F. completed the Ten Easy Steps for Playing a Successful Game together so he could evaluate his own implementation, and they met on a weekly basis to review Game Scoreboards as well as Mr. F.'s impressions of implementation and student behavior.*

Step 4: Evaluate

Evaluate and Monitor Plan Effectiveness

This phase involves repeated assessment of teacher progress and evaluation/review of the effectiveness of the current plan. If progress is apparent, the coach will likely continue to implement strategies to assist the teacher in achieving short- and long-term goals. If progress is not apparent, the coach may need to implement strategies more consistently or intensively, or return to earlier steps and reformulate hypotheses that reflect teacher implementation challenges better.

> *By sharing observational data, it was noted that students looked forward to the Game and that although their behavior was good during the Game, it did not improve outside the Game during the first week. The coach normalized this experience by saying that "consistency is the key to success." Throughout the course of 3 weeks, through observations and data on Spleems from the Scoreboards, there was an improvement in student behavior during the challenging periods of morning arrival and after lunch. Mr. F. was also able to begin to generalize the Lesson material a bit more and used student disruptive behavior as opportunities to revisit Lesson material and encourage the students to use the control signals.*

Coach Action Plan

The process described using the TISPC is based on assessment, planning, and evaluation of the plan. To facilitate planning and evaluation of the plan, a CAP (Appendix CC) is developed for each teacher that outlines the strategies the coach will use to improve teacher implementation of the program. The CAP formalizes in a written document the process described earlier with the TISPC so that coaches and supervisors can review the plan and progress on a weekly basis. Implementation of an individualized CAP (Appendix CC) is guided by three principles:

1. Evidence of the teacher's potential to improve with regard to implementation
2. Data-informed hypothesis development and testing
3. Application of coaching strategies in staged levels, such that the easiest strategies are applied before the coach introduces more complex strategies with the teacher

Coach Action Plan			
Coach:	**School:**	**Teacher:**	**Date:**

1) Data:

Lesson #_____   Games/week_____   Rubric:

Game_____

Lessons/week_____   Avg. Duration_____

Lesson_____

2) Teacher Strengths:

3) Influential Factors:

4) Hypotheses:	5) Goals:	6) Action Steps:	7) Short-term indicators of progress:	8) Assessment:

FIGURE 4.1 Data Collection.

The CAP format and process shares similarities with functional behavioral assessment procedures, such that the goal is to synthesize information to establish working and testable hypotheses about how to improve teacher implementation. The CAP has eight components (Figure 4.1): data collection, teacher strengths, influential factors, hypotheses, goals, action steps, short-term indicators of progress toward goals, and assessment. Each of these components is discussed next.

Data Collection

First, the coach collects data from multiple sources, including structured classroom observations as well as informal data noted during classroom observations, discussions with the teacher, data obtained on the teacher questionnaires, and any other information collected. The coach should also reference all rubric scores and notes, Lesson Logs, and Game Scoreboards. It is important for the coach to take detailed notes (e.g., specific things teachers have said, strategies used, student reactions/engagement) during and after the observations and interactions with teachers so the notes can be reviewed at a later time.

Teacher Strengths

In this section of the CAP, the coach identifies strengths that may be relevant to teacher implementation. Strengths may reflect a teacher's personal (e.g., friendly, warm) or professional (e.g., solid teaching skills) strengths. In addition, strengths related to the students (e.g., children respond well to praise), school/classroom environment (e.g., school staff and students appear to treat each other positively and with respect), and administration (e.g., principal offers support to teachers in nonpunitive way) are also appropriate to note. Even if it is difficult to identify a few strengths for some teachers, the coach needs to highlight at least one area of strength for each teacher.

Influential Factors

This section in the CAP is devoted to factors that interfere with implementation. They may reflect coaching issues (e.g., little rapport with teacher, as indicated by repeated cancellations of meetings with coach), teacher factors (e.g., hostility, as demonstrated by excessive yelling; poor organizational skills, as indicated by repeated instances of teacher misplacing materials), classroom composition (e.g., large number of disruptive students), school environment (e.g., school staff are quick to respond to student misbehavior in punitive ways), and administration (e.g., administrators do not support program as much as they could, principal's lack of participation in program meetings with coach). These factors are generally described in concrete behavioral terms.

Hypotheses

The hypothesis section is the lynchpin of the CAP. Here, the coach uses critical thinking skills to determine how the influential factors interfere with implementation. In other words, the coach identifies the mechanism by which the influential factors disrupt program implementation with the idea that these mechanisms can be modified and, therefore, implementation can be improved. Sample hypotheses include "If the teacher were more engaged in the Game with her students, then students would be more engaged in the Game, thereby making it more effective and increasing the likelihood that the teacher would play the Game" and "If the teacher were better able to plan and prepare, then she would implement the Lessons more consistently."

Goals

Behavioral goals are developed for the teacher—in other words, the areas in which the coach believes the teacher has the potential to improve. Sample goals include "increase teacher's engagement with students" and "increase teacher's consistency with implementing the Lessons." The goal is to have teachers experience small successes, which reinforce them positively to continue to increase program implementation.

Action Steps

The coach identifies specific "next steps" for coaching the teacher toward achieving the stated goals. These next steps should cover the next few coaching sessions, but may need to be revised depending on teacher progress. Action steps might include "initiate discussion about students' positive response to teacher when she participates in Granny's Wacky Prize" or "provide praise and tangible reinforcers when evidence of planned Lesson is observed."

Short-Term Indicators of Progress

Next, the coach identifies steps that indicate the teacher is advancing toward the specified goals. Absence of these indicators might signify lack of progress and suggest the action steps may require modification. Progress indicators might include "Coach observes teacher participate in Granny Wacky Prizes with students," "Majority of students participate in prize when their team wins," and "Coach observes the teacher teaching a Lesson that has obviously been planned for in advance (e.g., materials prepped, teacher knowledgeable about content)."

Assessment

On a regular basis, the coach updates the Assessment section to indicate the teacher's progress. For example: "Baseline (date): when coach 'pops in' during the identified Lesson time the teacher is often not planning on teaching a Lesson that day and makes excuses for why the Lesson is not being taught. Two weeks later (date): During a scheduled observation, teacher had prepared content for the Lesson in advance as demonstrated by her integration of Lesson materials with classroom technology and her decreased reliance on the manual."

CAP Example

To illustrate the process of creating a CAP for a teacher, it is helpful to walk through an example of an actual CAP. (Please note demographic information has been changed for confidentiality purposes.) Ms. S. is a fourth-grade teacher at Bayview Elementary School who exhibited difficulty with implementation of the PATHS to PAX GBG program. The coach assigned to her, Kelly, described the situation as follows:

> On entering Ms. S.'s fourth-grade classroom, it was immediately evident that disruptive behaviors had overpowered any teaching that might be going on and learning was not happening for the majority of students. There was not any evidence of the program being implemented. A few days later, for her first scheduled observation of a Lesson, Ms. S. appeared to have completely forgotten she had agreed to teach Lessons at 9:30 on Tuesdays and Thursdays.
>
> This was Ms. S.'s first year of teaching and, although she was eager to please, she was struggling with classroom management. She expressed on several occasions that the teaching profession was much harder than she ever expected and that she didn't know if it was the right choice for her. Ms. S. had the potential to be a very effective teacher; she cared greatly about her students and wanted them to succeed, but she was clearly lacking the skills to manage a classroom. She had difficulty engaging students in classroom activities, which naturally led to disruptive behavior. Inevitably, she would become frustrated and yell at the students, which in turn would create more disruptive behavior. Two months into the school year, Ms. S. was already very tired and frustrated. She felt that no matter how long and hard she worked, it didn't seem to matter, none of her students listened to her. Ms. S. admitted that when she attended the PATHS to PAX GBG training, she did agree with much of what was said, but couldn't imagine it ever being applied in her classroom; therefore, she tuned out most of the day, just glad to have a break from the students for a few days.

Coach: Kelly	School: Bayview Elementary	Teacher: Ms. S.	Date:

2) Teacher Strengths:

- **Good coach-teacher rapport**
- **Teacher asks coach questions about modeled techniques and is able to demonstrate the techniques with good fidelity when the coach observes and provides immediate feedback**
- **Students eagerly participate in Lessons and demonstrate good behavior during the Game when the coach leads them**
- **Teacher genuinely likes her students and demonstrates warmth and empathy when working with them individually or in small groups**

FIGURE 4.2 Teacher Strengths.

Based on classroom observations, Kelly identified a number of *teacher strengths* in this Situation (Figure 4.2).

Kelly had established good rapport with Ms. S., which provided a solid foundation for additional coaching support. Had this not been the case, increasing a positive rapport would have been one of the first targets (see Chapter 3 for rapport-building strategies). Ms. S. also demonstrated that she was open to learning program components; she allowed Kelly to model techniques and often asked questions about program components. She was able to demonstrate the techniques with good quality when Kelly observed her and gave her immediate feedback. Moreover, there was evidence the techniques worked. The students participated in the Lessons and exhibited appropriate behavior when the coach implemented program components. All in all, Kelly felt confident there were signs the teacher could improve with targeted coaching support.

Based on classroom observations, Lesson Logs, and Game Scoreboards, Kelly also identified a number of *influential factors* that might be related to low program implementation (Figure 4.3).

Coach: Kelly	School: Bayview Elementary	Teacher: Ms. S.	Date:

2) *Teacher Strengths*: Good coach-teacher rapport; Teacher asks coach questions about modeled techniques and can demonstrate techniques; Students eagerly participate in Lessons and demonstrate good behavior during the Game when the coach leads each; Teacher demonstrates warmth and empathy towards students when working with them in small groups.

3) Influential Factors:

- **Teacher stress (1st-year teacher, too much to do)**
- **Poor teacher engagement with students**
- **Poor general teaching skills (lack of meaningful assignments, poor organization)**
- **Poor behavior management skills**
- **Low teacher motivation**

FIGURE 4.3 Influential Factors.

Kelly noted that Ms. S. often reported feeling overwhelmed, as is common among first-year teachers. As mentioned earlier, Ms. S. stated on occasion that teaching might not be the right profession for her. Kelly observed that Ms. S. did not appear to have developed strong relationships with her students, although she displayed appropriate warmth and empathy when working with them individually or in small groups. Compared with other classrooms, Kelly perceived that class time was not enjoyable for the students or the teacher. Ms. S. often seemed unprepared and disorganized. She had difficulty creating meaningful class activities that involved the entire class, which had the unintended effect that, during many assignments, there were a number of students who were not involved directly and were more likely to feel bored and to misbehave. Although she tried to praise her students, Ms. S.'s compliments were generally unenthusiastic. She often raised her voice to correct minor misbehavior and she did not appear to incorporate behavior management strategies other than yelling. Because she rarely participated in any of the program components, Ms. S. had not earned any of the program incentives.

After considering these influential factors, Kelly developed several *hypotheses* that might account for low program implementation (see Figure 4.4).

Because Ms. S. appeared to be experiencing stress comparable with other first-year teachers, Kelly thought organization/preparation skills were a key factor interfering with implementation. Based on her own experience as a teacher and her experience as a coach, Kelly knew that enhanced organizational/preparation skills would not only improve implementation, but also would enhance the effectiveness of Ms. S.'s teaching in general. In addition, it would have the potential to improve classroom structure and decrease disruptive behavior.

Based on her observations and Ms. S.'s reports, it was apparent that Ms. S. was not enjoying her job, did not feel very effective as a teacher, was questioning whether teaching

Coach: Kelly   School: Bayview Elementary   Teacher: Ms. S.   Date:
2) Teacher Strengths: Good coach-teacher rapport; Teacher asks coach questions about modeled techniques and can demonstrate techniques; Students eagerly participate in Lessons and demonstrate good behavior during the Game when the coach leads each; Teacher demonstrates warmth and empathy towards students when working with them in small groups
3) Influential Factors: Teacher stress (1st-year teacher, too much to do); Poor teacher engagement with students; Students do not appear motivated to behave well during the Game; Poor general teaching skills (poor Lesson planning, poor organization); Poor behavior management skills; Low teacher motivation
4) Hypotheses: • **If the teacher were able to plan & prepare better, then she would implement the Lessons more consistently.** • **If teacher received more positive reinforcement/encouragement for her efforts, then her implementation would improve.** • **If teacher were more engaged with her students, the effectiveness of the Game, and her use of the Game would increase.**

FIGURE 4.4 Hypotheses.

was the right field for her, and was experiencing some signs of potential burnout. Therefore, Kelly believed it was critical that Ms. S. receive more positive reinforcement for her efforts. This would make it more likely that Ms. S. would use program components and that she would develop self-efficacy regarding her teaching and behavior management skills.

Based on her experiences as a teacher and coach, Kelly knew that it's generally easy to engage students in the program. Kelly reasoned that with a few simple changes, Ms. S. could increase student engagement, thereby making the Game more effective at reducing disruptive behavior. In addition, Kelly thought that strategies designed to improve Ms. S.'s relationship with her students might also increase Ms. S.'s enjoyment (i.e., reinforcement) of teaching.

From these hypotheses, Kelly identified three corresponding *goals* (Figure 4.5).

Next, Kelly identified a series of *action steps* for each goal (Figure 4.6).

For each hypothesis and corresponding goal, Kelly identified at least three coaching strategies intended to advance Ms. S. toward the goals, thereby improving implementation. As an example, to improve Ms. S.'s Lesson preparation, Kelly established a weekly meeting time during which she and Ms. S. planned the week's Lessons. During the first two planning sessions, Kelly modeled how to plan a Lesson, but also made efforts to shape Ms. S.'s planning skills. For example, early on, Kelly gave suggestions about how other teachers deliver particular Lessons and offered Ms. S. some options for Lesson-related activities. During the third planning session, the balance had shifted such that Ms. S. did the majority of the talking and made numerous suggestions about how she could carry out the Lesson. After that, Kelly and Ms. S. did not have formal planning sessions; rather, Kelly was able to check in with Ms. S. on her Lesson planning day to see if she had any questions.

Coach: Kelly School: Bayview Elementary Teacher: Ms. S. Date:	
2) Teacher Strengths: Good coach-teacher rapport; Teacher asks coach questions about modeled techniques and can demonstrate techniques; Students eagerly participate in Lessons and demonstrate good behavior during the Game when the coach leads each; Teacher demonstrates warmth and empathy towards students when working with them in small groups	
3) Influential Factors: Teacher stress (1st-year teacher, too much to do); Poor teacher engagement with students; Students do not appear motivated to behave well during Game; Poor general teaching skills (poor Lesson planning, poor organization); Poor behavior management skills; Low teacher motivation	
4) Hypotheses:	5) Goals:
• Plan & prepare • Positive reinforcement • Teacher engagement with students	• **Increase teacher's consistency with planning Lessons ahead of time** • **Increase positive reinforcement for teacher's implementation efforts** • **Increase teacher and student engagement in program components**

FIGURE 4.5 Goals.

Coach: Kelly	School: Bayview Elementary	Teacher: Ms. S.	Date:

2) Teacher Strengths: Good coach-teacher rapport; Teacher asks coach questions about modeled techniques and can demonstrate techniques; Students eagerly participate in Lessons and demonstrate good behavior during the Game when the coach leads each; Teacher demonstrates warmth and empathy towards students when working with them in small groups

3) Influential Factors: Teacher stress (1st-year teacher, too much to do); Poor teacher engagement with students; Poor general teaching skills (lack of meaningful assignments, poor organization); Poor behavior management skills; Low teacher motivation

4) Hypotheses:	5) Goals:	6) Action Steps:
1) Plan & prepare	1) Increase teacher's consistency with planning Lessons ahead of time	**1a) Schedule a convenient time in teacher's schedule to plan Lessons** **1b) Initially help teacher plan Lessons and then scale back assistance** **1c) Regularly 'pop in' during the scheduled Lesson times and maintain Lesson Log for teacher** **1d) Provide teacher with consistent praise and intermittent tangible reinforcers whenever any type of planned Lesson implementation is evident or observed**
2) Positive reinforcement	2) Increase positive reinforcement for teacher's implementation efforts	**2a) Provide praise (written and verbal) and tangible reinforcers** **2b) Acknowledge teacher's use of program on school-wide tootle board** **2c) Point out teacher's efforts to principal** **2d) Point out students' behavioral improvements following teacher's use of program skills**
3) Teacher engagement with students	3) Increase teacher and student engagement in program components	**3a) Initiate a dialogue with the teacher about her improvements and how to make Games and Lessons even more effective** **3b) Review and get feedback from students regarding the prize selection; add prizes identified by students as desirable** **3c) Encourage teacher to praise students during the Game** **3d) At the end of the Game, have a student select the prize** **3e) Encourage teacher sharing of examples and experiences during Lessons** **3f) Encourage teacher participation in Granny's Wacky Prizes** **3g) Model these strategies for teacher** **3h) Share ideas from other teachers that made the Lessons or Games more fun and engaging for students (e.g. books to read during Lessons, new prize ideas)**

FIGURE 4.6 Action Steps.

As Kelly phased out the planning sessions, she continued to stop by Ms. S.'s classroom at the scheduled Lesson time to monitor Ms. S.'s progress and provide positive reinforcement. This helped Kelly maintain a positive presence, rather than a punitive one, and Kelly provided Ms. S. with written and verbal praise when she saw evidence of a planned Lesson. She also, intermittently, provided tangible reinforcers (e.g., pencils, water bottle) for Ms. S.'s efforts. On the one day that Ms. S. failed to plan a scheduled Lesson because of competing priorities, Kelly assisted her in delivering the Lesson on the spot, thereby supporting Ms. S. and demonstrating ways the Lesson content could be modified to fit into the class schedule for the day.

Overall, the action steps were designed to provide an appropriate level of scaffolding to support Ms. S.'s skill development. Except for positive reinforcement, coaching strategies were phased out as Ms. S.'s skills and implementation improved, as indicated by the *short-term indicators of progress* (Figure 4.7).

Last, Kelly made notes of teacher progress through regular *assessment* informed by classroom observations, teacher reports, Lesson Logs, and Game Scoreboards (Figure 4.8).

Kelly also shared feedback (see Chapter 2 for tips on providing effective feedback) regarding Ms. S.'s progress according to the observational data she had collected as well as rubric data. For example, Kelly noted the increased use of teacher praise and student participation in the prize. She also praised Ms. S. for completing 9 of 10 of the Ten Easy Steps for Playing a Successful Game (Appendix I) while playing the Game in front of the rubric observers. This served to reinforce Ms. S. and to involve her more directly in setting goals for herself and monitoring her own implementation. Ms. S. set goals to become more consistent in her use of Scoreboards to keep track of Games and to enlist the students to remind her to play the Game more frequently. Ms. S. observed that her increased preparedness for the Lessons was related to increased student engagement in the Lessons and that she enjoyed when students participated in class. She began to identify new ways to increase student participation in all aspects of daily classroom activities (e.g., rotating classroom responsibilities, having students act out literary themes), not just PATHS to PAX GBG. Feedback from students to the coach indicated students enjoyed the increased opportunities for involvement in classroom activities. By the end of the year, Ms. S. and her students reported increased satisfaction about the classroom environment, and Game Scoreboard, Lesson Logs, and rubric data also demonstrated improved teacher implementation of the program (Figure 4.9).

Teacher implementation challenges are common when starting a new program. However, they can be addressed systematically through an iterative process of data collection, planning, and evaluation. When the evaluation and data suggest that progress is occurring, the plan can be expanded to include more ambitious goals. When the evaluation and data suggest progress is not occurring, it is helpful first to consider whether the plan is being implemented as intended. If not, then it is important to address barriers to plan implementation and to execute the plan with fidelity. If the plan is being implemented as intended, this may signal the need to consider whether something needs to be added to or changed in the plan. The use of a systematic process and a written plan provides the coach with a road map by which to navigate teacher implementation challenges, and provides the coach's supervisor with concrete information about the coach's conceptualization of how best to promote teacher implementation (see Chapter 6 for more on supervision).

Coach: Kelly	School: Bayview Elementary	Teacher: Ms. S.	Date:

2) Teacher Strengths: Good coach-teacher rapport; Teacher asks coach questions about modeled techniques and can demonstrate techniques; Students eagerly participate in Lessons and demonstrate good behavior during the Game when the coach leads each; Teacher demonstrates warmth and empathy towards students when working with them in small groups

3) Influential Factors: Teacher stress (1st-year teacher, too much to do); Poor teacher engagement with students; Poor general teaching skills (lack of meaningful assignments, poor organization); Poor behavior management skills; Low teacher motivation

5) Goals:	6) Action Steps:	7) Short-term indicators of progress:
1) Increase teacher's consistency with planning P2P Lessons ahead of time	1a) Schedule a convenient time in teacher's schedule to plan Lessons 1b) Initially help teacher plan Lessons and then scale back assistance 1c) Regularly 'pop in' during the scheduled Lesson times and maintain Lesson Log for teacher 1d) Provide teacher with consistent praise and intermittent tangible reinforcers whenever any type of planned Lesson implementation is evident or observed	**1a) Teacher has Lesson materials readily available during Lesson prep session with coach** **1b) Coach observes teacher deliver planned Lesson during scheduled Lesson time** **1c) Coach observes teacher deliver Lesson during scheduled time and the teacher demonstrates her preparedness (e.g., materials readily available, teacher knowledgeable about Lesson material)**
2) Increase positive reinforcement for teacher's implementation efforts	2a) Provide praise and tangible reinforcers 2b) Acknowledge teacher's use of program on school-wide tootle board 2c) Point out teacher's efforts to principal 2d) Point out students' behavioral improvements following teacher's use of program skills	**2a) Coach observes decrease in teacher's remarks regarding burden of program implementation** **2b) Coach observes teacher express appreciation for praise or reinforcer** **2c) Coach observes teacher working towards individual or school-wide incentives, as demonstrated through observation, Lesson Logs, and Game Scoreboards** **2d) Coach observes that program components specifically targeted by reinforcement increase (e.g., use of harmonica, # of Games played, etc.)**
3) Increase teacher and student engagement in program components	3a) Initiate a dialogue with the teacher about her improvements and how to make Games and Lessons even more effective 3b) Review and get feedback from students regarding the prize selection; add prizes identified by students as desirable 3c) Encourage teacher to praise students during the Game 3d) At the end of the Game, have a student select the prize 3e) Encourage teacher sharing of examples and experiences during Lessons 3f) Encourage teacher participation in Granny's Wacky Prizes 3g) Model these strategies for teacher	**3a) Students identify desirable prizes** **3b) Coach observes an increased use of teacher praise during the Game** **3c) Coach observes or Scoreboards indicate that students exhibit improved behavior during the Game** **3d) Coach observes teacher participate in wacky prizes with students** **3e) Coach observes that at least 90% of students who win the Game are enthusiastic about participating in prize**

FIGURE 4.7 Short-Term Indicators of Progress Toward Goals.

Coach: Kelly	School: Bayview Elementary	Teacher: Ms. S.	Date:

2) Teacher Strengths: Good coach-teacher rapport; Teacher asks coach questions about modeled techniques and can demonstrate techniques; Students eagerly participate in Lessons and demonstrate good behavior during the Game when the coach leads each; Teacher demonstrates warmth and empathy towards students when working with them in small groups.

3) Influential Factors: Teacher stress (1st-year teacher, too much to do); Poor teacher engagement with students; Poor general teaching skills (lack of meaningful assignments, poor organization); Poor behavior management skills; Poor teacher motivation.

7) Short-term indicators of progress:	8) Assessment:
1a) Teacher has Lesson materials readily available during Lesson prep session with coach 1b) Coach observes teacher deliver planned Lesson during scheduled Lesson time 1c) Coach observes teacher deliver Lesson during scheduled time and the teacher demonstrates her preparedness (e.g., materials readily available, teacher knowledgeable about Lesson material)	**Baseline (date):** When coach 'pops-in' during the identified Lesson time the teacher is often not planning on teaching a Lesson that day and makes excuses for why Lesson is not being taught. **One week later (date):** Teacher had materials readily available during Lesson prep session with coach. **Two weeks later (date):** During a scheduled observation, teacher taught Lesson that had obviously been planned for in advance (e.g., materials prepped, teacher knowledgeable about content, integration of classroom technology) .
2a) Coach observes decrease in teacher's remarks regarding burden of program implementation 2b) Coach observes teacher express appreciation for praise or reinforcer 2c) Coach observes teacher working towards individual or school-wide incentives, as demonstrated through observation, Lesson logs, and scoreboards 2d) Coach observes that program components specifically targeted by reinforcement increase (e.g., use of harmonica, # of Games, etc.)	**Baseline (date):** Teacher stated dissatisfaction regarding burden of program implementation. Coach did not observe use of even simplest program components (e.g., harmonica, Game) . **One week later (date):** Following contingency, teacher demonstrated use of harmonica and received praise and incentive (i.e., pack of pencils) . Teacher did not make any remarks about implementation burden and instead set goal to increase number of Games. **Two weeks later (date):** During a scheduled observation, teacher demonstrated Game to earn a second incentive and also provided current Game Scoreboard reflecting an increase from 0 to 1 Game per day.
3a) Students identify desirable prizes 3b) Coach observes an increased use of teacher praise during the Game 3c) Coach observes or scoreboards indicate that students exhibit improved behavior during the Game 3d) Coach observes teacher participate in wacky prizes with students 3e) Coach observes that at least 90% of students who win the Game are enthusiastic about participating in prize	**Baseline (date):** 90% of students who win Game do not participate in prize. Teacher does not deliver any praise for appropriate behavior during Game and sits down at her desk during prize. **One week later (date):** Students and teacher collaboratively identified desirable and undesirable prizes. Teacher delivered two praise statements during 5-minute Game when reminded by coach. Teacher used PAX sticks to choose a student to select the prize. **Two weeks later (date):** Teacher delivered two praise statements during Game unprompted by coach. The teacher, along with 90% of eligible students, participated in prize.

FIGURE 4.8 Assessment.

Coach Action Plan

Coach: Kelly	School: Bayview Elementary	Teacher: Ms. S.	Date:

2) *Teacher Strengths*: Good coach-teacher rapport; Teacher asks coach questions about modeled techniques and can demonstrate techniques; Students eagerly participate in Lessons and demonstrate good behavior during the Game when the coach leads each; Teacher demonstrates warmth and empathy towards students when working with them in small groups.

3) *Influential Factors*: Teacher stress (1st-year teacher, too much to do); Poor teacher engagement with students; Poor general teaching skills (lack of meaningful assignments, poor organization); Poor behavior management skills; Low teacher motivation.

4) *Hypotheses*:	5) *Goals*:	6) *Action Steps*:	7) *Short-term indicators of progress*:	8) *Assessment*
1) If the teacher were able to plan & prepare better, then she would implement the Lessons more consistently.	1) Increase teacher's consistency with planning Lessons ahead of time	1a) Schedule a convenient time in teacher's schedule to plan Lessons 1b) Initially help teacher plan Lessons and then scale back assistance 1c) Regularly 'pop in' during the scheduled Lesson times and maintain Lesson Log for teacher 1d) Provide teacher with consistent praise and intermittent tangible reinforcers whenever any type of planned Lesson implementation is evident or observed	1a) Teacher has Lesson materials readily available during Lesson prep session with coach 1b) Coach observes teacher deliver planned Lesson during scheduled Lesson time 1c) Coach observes teacher deliver Lesson during scheduled time and the teacher demonstrates her preparedness (e.g., materials readily available, teacher knowledgeable about Lesson material)	**Baseline (date):** When coach 'pops-in' during the identified Lesson time the teacher is often not planning on teaching a Lesson that day and makes excuses for why Lesson is not being taught. **One week later (date):** Teacher had materials readily available during Lesson prep session with coach. **Two weeks later (date):** During a scheduled observation, teacher taught Lesson that had obviously been planned for in advance (e.g., materials prepped, teacher knowledgeable about content, integration of classroom technology) .
2) If teacher received more positive reinforcement for her efforts, then her implementation would improve.	2) Increase positive reinforcement for teacher's implementation efforts	2a) Provide praise and tangible reinforcers 2b) Acknowledge teacher's use of program on school-wide tootle board 2c) Point out teacher's efforts to principal 2d) Point out students' behavioral improvements following teacher's use of program skills	2a) Coach observes decrease in teacher's remarks regarding burden of program implementation 2b) Coach observes teacher express appreciation for praise or reinforcer 2c) Coach observes teacher working towards individual or school-wide incentives, as demonstrated through observation, Lesson Logs, and scoreboards	**Baseline (date):** Teacher stated dissatisfaction regarding burden of program implementation. Coach did not observe use of even simplest program components (e.g., harmonica, Game). **One week later (date):** Following contingency, teacher demonstrated use of harmonica and received praise and incentive (i.e., pack of pencils) . Teacher did not make any remarks about implementation burden and instead set goal to increase set number of Games.

FIGURE 4.9 Completed Coach Action Plan.

3) If teacher were more engaged with her students, the effectiveness of the Game, and her use of the Game, would increase.	3) Increase teacher and student engagement in program components	3a) Initiate a dialogue with the teacher about her improvements and how to make Games and Lessons even more effective 3b) Review and get feedback from students regarding the prize selection; add prizes identified by students as desirable 3c) Encourage teacher to praise students during the Game 3d) At the end of the Game, have a student select the prize 3e) Encourage teacher sharing of examples and experiences during Lessons 3f) Encourage teacher participation in Granny's Wacky Prizes 3g) Model these strategies for teacher	2d) Coach observes that program components specifically targeted by reinforcement increase (e.g., use of harmonica, # of Games, etc.) 3a) Students identify desirable prizes 3b) Coach observes an increased use of teacher praise during the Game 3c) Coach observes or scoreboards indicate that students exhibit improved behavior during the Game 3d) Coach observes teacher participate in wacky prizes with students 3e) Coach observes that at least 90% of students who win the Game are enthusiastic about participating in prize	**Two weeks later (date):** During a scheduled observation, teacher demonstrated Game to earn a second incentive and also provided current scoreboard reflecting an increase from 0 to 1 Game per day. **Baseline (date):** 90% of students who win Game do not participate in prize. Teacher does not deliver any praise for appropriate behavior during Game and sits down at her desk during prize. **One week later (date):** Students and teacher collaboratively identified desirable and undesirable prizes. Teacher delivered two praise statements during 5-minute Game when reminded by coach. Teacher used Pax sticks to choose a student to select the prize. **Two weeks later (date):** Teacher delivered two praise statements during Game unprompted by coach. The teacher, along with 90% of eligible students, participated in prize.

FIGURE 4.9 Continued

Chapter 4 Reflection Questions

- What are the four steps of the Teacher Implementation Support Planning Checklist, or TISPC?

- Name the eight components of a Coach Action Plan, or CAP.

- Why are data important to the implementation support process?

- How are hypotheses beneficial to plan development?

- Think about your current strategies for working with teachers. How could the TISPC and CAP be helpful? What barriers might arise when using the TISPC and CAP? How will you overcome these barriers?

Lessons Learned

This chapter presents lessons learned throughout the years spent coaching classroom teachers. Despite a coach's best efforts with regard to engagement and training, implementation challenges are inevitable. Throughout the years spent coaching teachers, certain strategies have been used and adapted creatively to enhance teacher implementation. At the same time, despite best efforts to analyze data, develop plans, and use effective coaching strategies to support teachers, sometimes implementation of the program could not be improved substantially. This chapter is devoted to a review of common implementation challenges that may be encountered, along with strategies designed to address each challenge. Unlike skill challenges (Chapter 3) that are usually alleviated through additional coaching support (e.g., modeling, practice, feedback), the majority of the challenges described in this chapter occur when teachers have the necessary skills to implement the program, but some type of ambivalence or interference undermines the consistency or effectiveness of implementation. Case examples are provided of successes for each of the implementation challenges and, when applicable, examples in which the coaching strategies proved only minimally effective. These case examples are discussed with the wisdom provided by hindsight so that other coaches can learn from challenges already experienced by other coaches. The challenges presented in this chapter become increasingly difficult and tend to require increasing effort from the coach.

Objectives

- Familiarize yourself with the most common implementation challenges and how to be the most effective coach in handling these challenges.
- Learn key strategies designed to address common implementation challenges.

Introducing New Students to the Program

One situation coaches may encounter is helping teachers get new students familiar with the program. For example, teachers will need to create a PAX stick for each new student, add a stick with each new student's name to the Kid of the Day cup (a plastic cup that contains a popsicle stick with each student's name on it to select the Kid of the Day randomly, a second plastic cup can be used to store the sticks for students who have already had a turn being the Kid of the Day), review key elements of the program with the class, and teach the new students to play the Game.

In the following example, notice how the teacher repeatedly and seamlessly solicits student assistance as PATHS to PAX GBG "experts" to help teach a new student about the program.

 STELLAR!

In many urban schools there are constantly new students transferring in to and out of the classrooms. When this happens, one suggestion is to use the other students in the class to assist teachers in teaching new students about the program. In a lower elementary classroom, there was a new student who started after Winter Break, so the teacher and I met and discussed the best way to introduce the program to the new student. The following plan was developed collaboratively: The teacher started the day by going through the Kid of the Day process (as she normally would). As she chose a name from the Kid of the Day "need a turn cup" and put it in the Kid of the Day "had a turn cup," she explained this process to the new student and she added a stick with his name on it to the "need a turn cup." The class continued with the Kid of the Day process (e.g., giving the visor to the Kid of the Day to wear, posting his name on the Kid of the Day poster, and asking him to come to the front for Tootles). The teacher asked students to define a Tootle for the new student and then they proceeded with giving the Kid of the Day Tootles.

Next, she had the students define PAX and Spleem for the new student, then she taught and reviewed the PAX cues, offering praise as the students participated. In addition, the teacher explained the Game and I was able to sit by the new student as they played the Game in the classroom to prompt him quietly (e.g., whisper in his ear) and remind him of the rules/Spleems. Every team won the prize and the new student was able to see how much fun it was to win a Granny Wacky Prize! The teacher set up the rules for the prize as if this was the first time she had ever given a prize (e.g., reviewing level of voices, level of activity, what to do when the timer went off) and she "chose" a prize that was a quiet and lower activity prize. The prize was "air band," where students were to remain seated and pretend they were playing an instrument in a band. For the rest of the day the teacher had the new student "shadow" the Kid of the Day so that he could learn the routines of the class and more about the key concepts of the program. This was a big success because it helped the new student feel welcome in his new classroom and provided a review to the other students about key program components.

Later that day, the teacher and I met to plan for her next Lesson (which was the new student's first Lesson). The teacher started the Lesson with a mini review of all the key concepts learned so far (PAX cues, PAX language, Game). She was really creative and played a Game during which the students were put into their teams. She asked the teams questions and they received points for correct answers. After answering the question, the teacher and that team reviewed the key concept. For example, the teacher asked, "What do we use in the classroom to calm down?" The students answered by saying and pointing to the Calming Down poster on the wall. The team received a point and then the teacher reviewed the steps on the Calming Down poster. During the Game, the new student was the scorekeeper and the teacher had him repeat the answers to ensure understanding of the concepts. Later that week, the teacher taught the intended Lesson and reported it went really well; the students had a lot of fun "teaching" the concepts to the new student. She rewarded the class with a prize because they all did so well and had fun with the activity!

—Jenn Keperling, MA, LCPC

Introducing New Teachers to the Program

Another common challenge in schools is teacher turnover. This includes when teachers have long-term absences resulting from illness, family emergencies, or maternity leave, or when they leave their position before the school year ends (e.g., stress, burnout). High teacher turnover and long-term absences can cause significant disruptions to the classroom structure and routine. Sometimes schools have the resources and have time to plan for these changes in the routine, but often they do not. In these situations, there may not be a consistent substitute teacher to teach the class, and several different people may be sharing the responsibility (e.g., paraprofessionals, substitute teachers, student interns, other teachers combining classes).

If a school experiences a long-term teacher absence, the coach needs to develop a plan to help train the new substitute teacher and/or the new staff members who are helping in the classroom during this transition. It is important to note that, in these situations, schools may not have a permanent replacement for weeks or months; therefore, the coach should begin to train immediately any new staff identified to work in the classroom. One suggestion is to schedule a short training session for the new classroom teachers to review the training slides, materials, and curriculum binder, and to watch a video of high-implementing teachers. In addition, the coach needs to spend some time in this classroom modeling the Game and Lessons for the new teachers as well as provide feedback on their implementation. Students can also help in "teaching" the new staff various program components, such as Kid of the Day, the Game and PAX Stix. It is also important to connect the new teachers with other high-implementing teachers in the building who have been trained in the program, so they can answer questions and provide support when the coach is not in the building.

In this next example, note how the coach provided a lot of opportunities for the teacher to see PATHS to PAX GBG in action before training the teacher. Also notice how the coach helped prepare the teacher's classroom with the program elements, allowing him to jump into doing Kid of the Day and the other program components as soon as he was trained.

 STELLAR!

In one school, a new upper elementary school teacher started 3 months after the school year had started. His class was originally one large class with one teacher, but it was divided into two smaller classes when he was hired. The first step was to train him as quickly as possible so there was not a gap in program implementation; however, it was also important for him to have some time to transition to his new school and feel comfortable. He was trained his second week at the school during resource time and after school. The week before the training, he shadowed the original teacher before beginning with his new class, which allowed him to be able to observe the teacher implement many of the key elements of the PATHS to PAX GBG program. As the coach, I modeled the Game for the entire fourth-grade class while both he and the original teacher watched and took notes. The new teacher was also able to observe the original teacher doing Kid of the Day and teach a Lesson with the entire fourth-grade class.

After shadowing the original teacher for a week, the new teacher completed a brief training on both the Lessons and the Game, which included reviewing all the materials and watching exemplar videos of teachers playing the Game. Together, we created his PAX Stix (separating out the PAX Stix from the original class into two cups, one for him and one for the original teacher), his Kid of the Day Stix (separating his class from the original class), hung up program posters, and set up the PAX materials in his classroom. He received an incentive for hanging up his posters. I also visited his classroom with his administrator during a walkthrough, which encouraged the teacher to hang up the posters before the walkthrough.

We moved on to the Kid of the Day process and set the goal to do this each day. After a few weeks of checking in, he accomplished this goal and was given another incentive. In this situation, the original teacher had been implementing the program with the entire fourth-grade class, so the students were aware of the key elements of the program and had completed many of the Lessons before starting with their new teacher. We met with the original teacher and they came up with a plan that she would continue to teach the Lessons to the entire fourth grade (both classes) each week. The new teacher brought his students over to the classroom of the original teacher, who taught the Lesson with the assistance of the new teacher.

When the Lessons became routine, we focused on playing the Game in his classroom. This teacher was good with behavior management and believed he did not really "need" the Game to help with his classroom management; therefore, he was not entirely "sold" on playing the Game. However, he did agree to try it with his class and try to play at least one time per day. Overall, the teacher was successful at meeting his goal and played the Game about three to five times per week. As the coach, I provided incentives whenever I observed him playing the Game or using his harmonica. The key with this teacher was to take small steps to encourage him to implement the program because he was not only learning about it, but also he was making the transition to a new school and classroom.

—Jenn Keperling, MA, LCPC

Departmentalization

In some schools, grade levels are departmentalized based on subject area and teachers teach specific content areas to all the students. For example, one teacher may teach reading/language arts; another teacher, math; and the third teacher, social studies/science/health. In these situations, the coach needs to work with teachers to develop a strategic plan regarding when and who will be implementing the various components of the program with students each day. For example, one teacher could teach all the Lessons to students. Another option is to have all teachers give the Lessons to their homeroom class. It might also be decided that all the teachers will play the Game as well as use the cues and language throughout the day. Each teacher might complete the Kid of the Day process in the morning. In addition, the PAX Stix could travel with the students as they move from classroom to classroom, or all teachers might decide to have a set of PAX Stix for each of the various classes they teach.

In the following example, notice how the team tried out potential solutions before determining that assigning each teacher to deliver the Lessons to a particular group of students was the most effective solution for their situation.

 STELLAR!

In one lower elementary school, the team departmentalized and the students reported to one teacher for language arts and the other for math and science. They also rotated the times (morning/afternoon) they taught each section. It became apparent that each teacher played the Game with both sections, but it was sporadic with regard to which sections of students received the Lessons. One day I observed a group of students receive a Lesson on feeling sad. Later that day, they received the same Lesson from the other teacher. Meanwhile, the other group of students never heard the Lesson. We met as a team to think about this situation. One option was for only one teacher to implement the Lessons to both student sections to ensure all students received each Lesson. However, the teachers were hesitant about this because it would be unfair for one teacher to have to "do all the work," and it would be difficult for the other teacher to generalize the concepts throughout the day if she didn't also teach the Lessons. Another solution was to teach the Lessons at a specific day/time per week, regardless of which section of students they had. Although this worked initially, sometimes something (e.g., teacher absence) interfered with one of the two teachers being able to deliver the Lessons, thereby resulting in the same problem of certain students missing Lessons. In the end, the solution that worked best was to assign one of the two student sections to each teacher, who taught the Lessons at her convenience, but to only those students in the assigned section.

—Kelly Schaffer, MS

Performance Anxiety about Program Implementation

Some teachers may be nervous or anxious about implementing a new program in their classroom. Although some may be candid about their nervousness, most likely this will be something you discover as you explore the teacher's real barriers to implementation. Teachers who are anxious about program implementation may cancel appointments frequently with the coach, provide numerous reasons why they are unable to play the Game or teach the Lessons (e.g., not enough time in the schedule), or implement only a few components of the program in their classroom, such as Kid of the Day or using Tootles, but not teach the Lessons or play the Game. Some teachers may feel uncomfortable talking to students about social–emotional issues or they may feel they do not have the necessary skills to play the Game. For example, they may tell the coach, "I am scared to start talking with the kids about their feelings. Many of my students have trauma and I am afraid to 'open a can of worms' in my classroom."

In this situation, it is important for the coach to have discussions with the teacher about barriers to implementation and the true reasons they may feel uncomfortable implementing the program in their classroom. The coach should use lots of praise and positive reinforcement for the program components the teachers are implementing well. In addition, it is important to use lots of encouragement to let the teachers know they have the skill level to be successful in implementing the program. They may need repeated, frequent modeling and coteaching of the Lessons and Game with the coach. It may also be helpful to work with these teachers to set a realistic timeline and reasonable goals (e.g., chunking the program into smaller pieces), so teachers experience success.

In the following example, notice how the coach's initial visits to the classroom were low key in terms of the demands placed on the teacher. Rather than doing observations and feedback, the coach relied on modeling to help the teacher learn more about the program components. Also notice how the coach provided scaffolding to support the introduction of the Game while the teacher taught.

STELLAR!

I was working with a kindergarten teacher who canceled classroom observations repeatedly. In the beginning of the year, the teacher said it was because she did not have time to get the program started in her classroom. As a coach, I was very friendly and expressed understanding of her busy schedule, but was respectfully persistent in rescheduling another time for the observations. In addition, I started building rapport with this teacher in the hallways and teacher's lounge, making conversation that was not related to the program or her repeatedly missed appointments (she expressed a lot of guilt about always canceling appointments).

Eventually this teacher agreed to let me model a Lesson in her classroom. I was then able to start modeling Lessons on a regular basis, as well as stop by her classroom randomly to reinforce some of the program elements she had begun implementing (e.g., Tootle Notes, Kid of the Day). While spending time in the classroom (sometimes as brief as 10 minutes), I used it as an opportunity to model using the PAX language and praise with her students (e.g., "Tiara, I love how you are being a PAX leader by sharing your crayons"). Over time, the teacher became more comfortable having me in her classroom and shared she originally had not started the program because she felt the PATHS to PAX GBG program was for young teachers and she was too old to teach the program.

Although the teacher agreed to modeling in her classroom weekly, she still refused to let me observe her playing the Game or teaching a Lesson. She requested that we meet weekly on Wednesday mornings during her planning time to "discuss" the program. I continued to build a positive relationship with this teacher and was very supportive and encouraging of her progress. I would also comment on how much the students were enjoying getting Tootles and how proud they were when they were the Kid of the Day. During the weekly meetings, she said that, although she was now implementing the Lessons, Kid of the Day, and Tootles in her classroom consistently, she "[was] really intimidated and scared of playing the Game, it just seems so difficult to play the Game while teaching." Collaboratively, we developed a plan in which I started modeling very quick, brief Games for 3 minutes. She was amazed by how much the students enjoyed the Game and prizes. We also started by playing the Game while students were sitting at their tables (in their teams) doing seatwork, so it was easier to count Spleems.

Next, I suggested that I play the Game while she was teaching. She continued to be resistant to playing the Game by herself. I continued to emphasize how she simply needed to write on the whiteboard (next to the chair where she read stories on the carpet) "Team 1, Team 2, Team 3, Team 4" and then place tallies under the team names for Spleems. At this point in the relationship, I also used a lot of humor with her and modeled an attitude of not taking it too seriously but just trying it out!

Toward the middle of the school year, she agreed to try it but said she was really nervous. After she played the Game I used lots of praise (clapping excitedly and giving her a hug after the Game was over) and wrote her a Tootle. I also shared with her principal what a good job she was doing, and several weeks later he came to observe and praised her for the great work she was doing in her classroom.

After the principal observed her she told me, "I have no idea what I was so scared about or why it took me so long to just try playing the Game but I thought I would never be able to do it!" She also stated that, previously, she did not think she needed the program or help with students' behavior because they were kindergarten students and not as aggressive/disruptive as the older students in the building. However, after I modeled the Game and she started implementing other components of the program, she was impressed with how much more on task the students were, and the interactions among the students was much more positive in her classroom. At the end of the year, this teacher e-mailed me that she was so proud of herself for trying the program that she thought "she was too old for" and was really looking forward to starting the next year by implementing the program from the first day of school!

—Dana D. Marchese, PhD

Disruptive Classroom

As a coach, you may find some classrooms with high levels of disruptive student behavior. Students may be calling out, getting out of their seat without permission, talking with their peers, throwing things around the classroom, being disrespectful or yelling at the teacher, and possibly fighting with peers. A teacher in this type of classroom may have difficulty teaching the academic curriculum because the majority of their time and attention is focused on addressing students' disruptive behavior. These teachers may feel frustrated they are unable to teach the expected Lesson content each day because of the disruptive behavior in the classroom. The good news is that the program is intended to provide teachers with exactly those tools that can reduce disruptions and increase on-task behavior.

Create Structure

When there is a high rate of disruptions in a classroom, teachers may need additional support with classroom management strategies and routines. The coach can encourage these teachers to start from the beginning and create a list of classroom rules and routines with the students. The teachers need to teach, model, practice, and praise each rule with the students frequently. Teachers should be encouraged to use lots of positive reinforcement for appropriate student behavior, such as behavior-specific praise, writing Tootles, giving positive adult attention, and providing students with rewards or special jobs in the classroom. As coach, you could work with the teacher to ignore minor negative behavior and give all of your attention to those students who are following classroom rules appropriately. It may be helpful for the teacher to develop collaboratively with the coach a list of consequences for extreme negative behaviors. For example, they could identify which behaviors will be classroom managed and which behaviors need to be office managed, determine when parents will be called or asked to come to the school for a meeting, and so on. After this consequence list is created and shared with students, these teachers need to be very clear and consistent in their responses to disruptive behavior.

Introduce the Program in Small Steps

It may be helpful for the coach to work with these teachers to divide the program into smaller components. The coach could have the teacher revisit the PAX Vision and My Wonderful School (activities to introduce students to the PAX concepts of seeing, hearing, and doing more positive behavior to have a wonderful classroom and school) to engage students actively in creating a more positive classroom climate. The next steps would be to have the teacher implement consistently the Kid of the Day, create a Tootle Board, and provide students with multiple opportunities throughout the day to write Tootles. It can be difficult to play the Game unless teachers are able to obtain students' attention to signal the Game is starting (e.g., use PAX Quiet successfully). Encourage the teacher to use the harmonica consistently and praise students who give the teacher PAX Quiet in response to the harmonica. Over time, as these teachers gain control gradually of their classroom, begin implementing frequent yet very brief Games throughout the school day so that both the students and teachers experience success with the Game.

Establish Expectations

Expectations for students need to be explicit because teachers and students often have different ideas of standards for behavior. It may be helpful to identify specific times of the day that are difficult and then develop specific behavior expectations for that time. In one chaotic first-grade classroom, the students would sit on top of each other when they were called to the carpet, which led to lots of behavior issues. The coach assisted the teacher with creating "carpet expectations." They used balloons to illustrate the concept of personal space. The students then completed a worksheet the coach created that referred to PAX or Spleem on the carpet while they played a Game. The coach encouraged the teacher to continue using the language they had established (e.g., personal space) and praise students who met the expectations.

Practice Common Challenging Situations

Teachers who use discussion and who role-play can address disruptive behavior in a fun, collaborative way with students. One strategy is for the coach and teacher to solicit examples from the students of common situations that occur often in the classroom (e.g., neighbor kicking you while you are trying to work, you have no pencil, teacher talking to another adult, classmate making fun of you). When the teacher has a few minutes between activities (e.g., 3 minutes before lunch) or a significant chunk of time (e.g., resource class was canceled), the teacher can use the time to choose a situation at random, discuss it, have the students brainstorm various PAX/Spleem ways they could handle the situation, have students role-play their reactions and discuss, have students work in a group to create a T chart identifying both

PAX and Spleem ways to handle the situation, and/or have the students complete a writing about handling the situation.

For classrooms that have a daily class meeting, these scenarios can be incorporated as part of a "Situation of the Day" discussion about PAX and Spleem behavior. As an example, after school one day (early during the school year), one teacher discovered that someone had filled the bathroom sink with soap and turned on the water so that the bubbles were overflowing. The teacher took a picture and printed out an eight-by-ten-inch copy to use the next day during morning meeting. The teacher indicated she did not want to know who did it or why, but simply wanted to discuss it with the whole class. By removing the blame from the situation, the teacher was able to facilitate an effective discussion about why this was an unacceptable behavior for the classroom. The teacher and students also discussed why it might be tempting for someone to do, and what a person could get out of it. Together, they agreed on an appropriate consequence for this type of behavior. Nothing like this happened again that year.

Reward Appropriate Student Behavior

A teacher with a lot of disruptions in their classroom may tell the coach, "I am concerned that if I give my students the Game prizes, they will take advantage of me and (doing the prize)." Teachers who have difficulty with classroom management may be reluctant to give a prize to those teams that won the Game for fear the class will become disruptive during the prize and students will have difficulty settling down. These teachers may prefer to skip the prize and continue with academic instruction, or choose a prize that is not fun for students or that is used too often in the classroom as a filler activity (e.g., quiet reading, quiet art). For example, if the prize is wastebasket basketball, students may continue to throw paper balls after the timer has signaled the end of the prize, or they may throw the paper balls at each other. Assist these teachers in developing a list of appropriate prizes for their classroom that students will enjoy and want to work to earn, and that the teachers are able to administer quickly and return to instruction. Therefore, a prize such as wastebasket basketball is not an appropriate prize for a disruptive classroom; it may need to be a prize students can work to earn after the teacher is able to have more structure in the classroom.

Keep Students Busy

There are many reasons students engage in disruptive behavior, but a few of the more common reasons are unstructured time (e.g., downtime), boredom, and negative attention. One effective strategy for students who are frequently disruptive is to provide them with jobs throughout the day, such as Spleem counter, pencil collector, or paper collector, or have them hold the poster or book during a Lesson. By providing a role for students exhibiting disruptive behavior, the teachers provide structure for their time, combat boredom, and provide the opportunity for positive reinforcement and classroom recognition following a job well done.

Conduct a Teacher Self-Evaluation

Self-evaluation can be used to help teachers become more aware of their classroom behavior and to increase positive reinforcement toward students (Sutherland & Wehby, 2001). This may be particularly helpful in situations in which teachers indicate they have already tried something (e.g., praise), but with little or no positive results. The coach might observe these teachers and count the number of times the target behavior occurs. Then, in a discussion with the teachers, ask them to estimate the number of times the behavior occurred during the observation phase. Provide the observed count, noting this observation was simply a snapshot of behavior and it is likely the desired behavior is more frequent at other times. If the teachers overestimate their use of praise, the coach can assist them in developing a plan to increase praise. If the teachers estimate accurately or underestimate their use of praise, the coach can also provide examples of praise and a brief discussion of the potential effectiveness of praise.

In the following example, notice how the coach validated the teacher's frustration and developed strategies collaboratively for introducing program components gradually, thereby leading to a slower, but more successful rollout of the program in the classroom. Note also how the development of routines and teacher modeling of program components helped support effective program implementation over time.

 STELLAR!

I was working with an upper elementary teacher who experienced a highly disruptive classroom during the school year. During informal classroom visits, he remarked frequently how "kids today don't respect adults and they don't care about their education." His rubric scores were satisfactory, suggesting he had the skills to play the Game and deliver Lessons; however, he rarely turned in Scoreboards and, although his Lesson Log was on pace, the quality of the Lessons needed improvement. When he confided his anger about his students to me, I expressed empathy and acknowledged that, as a teacher, he has one of the most challenging jobs. I let him know I was impressed with his resilience. We talked about how PATHS to PAX GBG offers strategies to help with classroom management and to improve the overall environment. We first worked on playing the Game for a shorter amount of time more frequently and consistently. We came up with routine times to play (transitions and independent work at first, then during instruction) and also decided to play the Game whenever the behavior problems started to increase. In addition, we tackled the environment issue slowly by just doing Tootles during his most difficult time: when the students returned from lunch. We made this a daily routine (allowing each student to write two Tootles to whomever they wanted when they came back from lunch). This helped calm the students and get them ready for the afternoon's instruction. We then moved on to the Lessons and how they can help with the environment. We found the Control Signals Poster and the Problem-Solving Box to be very effective at peaceful conflict resolution. I also guided him to use the Control Signals Poster whenever he felt angry or stressed. Using these opportunities to use the control signals might serve the dual purpose of reducing his immediate stress as well as modeling appropriate emotion regulation behavior for the students. Validating the teacher's frustration and helping him use PATHS to PAX GBG to reduce disruptive behavior and conflict, and manage his own stress helped this teacher get back on track and be successful with consistent implementation and improved classroom management and environment.

—Michael Muempfer, MA

In the next example, consider the coach's perspective that the high rates of disruptive behavior were a result of the absence of routines and expectations in the classroom. Consider the potential similarities and differences between this teacher and classroom and the one in the previous example. What other strategies do you think you might try in this situation?

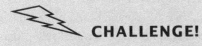

CHALLENGE!

Early during my coaching career, I was faced with working with a lower elementary (K– 2) teacher who lacked general classroom management skills. There was very little structure or routine in place. She often allowed the students to move freely around the room with little or no consequences. Something as simple as a student needing to get a crayon often would result in a big classroom disruption. Expectations were not made clear to the students, which led to many misunderstandings (e.g., "he stole my pencil," when really the teacher told him to borrow it), which naturally led to outbursts and fights. Behaviors spiraled out of control so quickly it often appeared the classroom was out of control.

My approach with this teacher was to model, multiple times, the steps for playing the Game. Each time I modeled the Game, I would have the teacher complete the Good Behavior Game Modeling Checklist (Appendix A) as I went through each of the steps. After each modeling session we would debrief and review the GBG Modeling Checklist, either immediately or later in the day. Eventually, she began to play the Game as well. When she first started, I would stand near her and prompt each step as she played. It got to the point where the teacher was willing and able to play the Game successfully, which led to some small pockets of peace throughout the day, but overall the environment was still chaotic and out of control.

As powerful and successful as the Game can be, it can be doomed to fail if the teacher does not have basic control of the classroom to begin with. Without established routines, clearly posted rules, procedures, and consequences, it is difficult to implement any type of intervention program successfully. As a new coach, I stayed narrowly focused on specific program elements (e.g., steps of the Game). In hindsight, if I had focused on helping the teacher establish basic routines and expectations for the classroom, I probably would have yielded greater results.

In general, this classroom, or any classroom, needs to be ready to play the Game for it to truly be successful. If a classroom is not ready and you simply trudge ahead (like a teacher who trudges through a Lesson for which students are not prepared), you cannot expect positive results.

—Kelly Schaffer, MS

Teacher Stress and Burnout

Many teachers report that teaching is stressful. Teaching is challenging work, and teaching in urban schools is a particularly challenging job. Children growing up in the inner city often experience stressors related to poverty, violence, trauma, and familial distress that interfere with their academic achievement. As a result, these children exhibit significant behavioral or emotional problems that disrupt the learning environment. Resources are tight, and there are often not enough support staff (e.g., social workers, other mental health professionals) to help children develop appropriate social-emotional, coping and behavioral skills. Many teachers identify successful strategies for dealing with these challenges so they can teach their students effectively. However, in some cases, teachers experience significant distress related to the challenges of teaching, and this stress interferes significantly with their ability to engage fully with coaching staff and to be onboard with implementing the program. The following strategies may be useful in helping teachers manage stress: empathize, offer the program as a stress reducer, identify stress reduction strategies, lighten the load, reframe, and choose your battles.

Empathize

Validate teachers' feelings by making empathic statements (e.g., "It sounds like things in the classroom have been tough lately. I can see why you feel stressed.") and normalizing the stress ("Teaching is one of the most challenging professions. Many teachers feel stressed or burned out from time to time. That's a totally natural response to the pressure of the school environment."). Praise the teacher for continuing efforts in the classroom to help children despite the stress and identify specific things that are genuinely going well in the classroom. Often teachers feel validated and supported when coach's use these strategies, as opposed to the coach pointing out what the teacher is not doing well or needs to do differently, and adding more things to the teacher's already full plate!

Offer the Program as a Stress Reducer

When teachers feel stressed, it can be a great opportunity to remind them that one of the major benefits and outcomes of the coaching and the PATHS to PAX GBG program is that it helps to reduce teacher stress. Use of the calming down strategies such as the Turtle Technique or Control Signals Poster can help teachers manage stress in the moment and serves a dual purpose of modeling the technique for students (Jennings & Greenberg, 2009). In addition, other Lessons on topics such as problem solving and goal setting may assist teachers in channeling stress in a more productive way. For example, stressful classroom situations provide an opportunity for teachers to model Lesson strategies for calming down and thinking through the consequences of various solutions, and determining what to do if the chosen solution doesn't work the first time. Finally, consistent use of the Game and PAX cues during times of stress can help maintain order and a positive classroom environment during times of stress.

Identify Stress Reduction Strategies

It may be helpful for you to assist the teacher in identifying other strategies that can be used in the classroom to reduce stress. Examples of strategies that teachers and coaches have identified include deep breathing, pleasant imagery, closing the shades, listening to relaxing music during their lunch break, walking outside during lunch, and calling a friend during lunchtime. In one classroom, a brief morning yoga routine for the teacher and students was an effective stress-reducing strategy. It can also be helpful to encourage teachers to take their lunch break every day, instead of working through lunch, so they can feel a bit more refreshed during the second part of the day. The coach may also talk with the teacher about self-care strategies they can use in their everyday routine to help reduce stress (e.g., schedule a time to meet a friend for coffee or dinner, exercise, meditate, go to sleep earlier than usual, take a relaxing bath). It may be helpful to set a small goal and encourage teachers to try one new self-care strategy, then check in later to see how they feel after trying the strategy.

Lighten the Load

Stressed teachers may be particularly appreciative of offers to help in the classroom. For example, you might offer to teach a Lesson or Game. The coach might also use "load lightening" as a reward for teacher implementation of the program, such as by offering to teach a Lesson contingent on the teacher maintaining a Tootle Board. Similarly, the coach may be able to help teachers "lighten the load" in other ways, such as demonstrating how to be more effective with their time management and organizational skills, and how to delegate tasks and identify things they can say no to on their to-do list.

Reframe

If the coach cannot offer direct strategies for improving teacher stress, it may be useful to help teachers think about problems in their classroom in a different way through *reframing*. Reframing provides teachers with alternative explanations that help reshape their beliefs about their students and their problems. This is done by placing the teachers' experience in another "frame." An example, is included in the following box.

COMMUNICATE!

Teacher: My student has these incredibly long angry outbursts when I tell him to do something. He's really out to make it difficult for me.

Coach: Do you suppose he might be really testing the strength of your limit setting to see if he can get you to lose your cool or back down?

or

Teacher: My student has gotten incredibly worse this week. He is impossible to handle and I've sent him to the office twice already. He's wearing me down.

Coach: You know, I often see kids in school who regress to test the security of the limits in their environment before they take a major new step forward in their development.

Choose Your Battles

It is important for teachers to understand that it is better to pick one specific classroom problem or problematic behavior to target at a time, rather than try to address all the problems at once (which is more overwhelming and likely to contribute to stress). The coach might say, "As a teacher your resources are not unlimited. Think about choosing those battles that are really important to you and save your energy for those. For example, no hitting, using an indoor voice, and doing assignments may be more important to you than sitting with bottoms completely on the chair or keeping pencils in the box. In that case, it's not worth expending your resources in battle for those causes." This helps teachers prioritize which classroom rules they are prepared to enforce and which ones they can ignore for the time being. There is a greater likelihood problems will be resolved with this approach, although it may seem that it will take longer than addressing multiple problems or behaviors at the same time. If teachers experience significant distress regarding classroom problems, it may be difficult for them to select just one issue on which to focus first. In these instances, it may be helpful for the coach as a neutral observer to offer suggestions about how to select which problem to tackle first that would give the teachers the "biggest bang for their buck."

In the following real-life example, notice how the coach provides validation to create a safe environment for the teacher to verbalize her stress and vulnerabilities. Also notice how the coach used reinforcement and small steps toward implementation success to enhance the teacher's self-efficacy.

 STELLAR

I worked with a teacher who moved to Baltimore City from a rural area in the Midwest immediately after completing her undergraduate degree. This teacher canceled many of my initial visits to her classroom but eventually agreed to meet during her planning period. In the beginning, she spent the majority of the coaching sessions crying uncontrollably with her head down on the table and would not speak. The first few times I sat with her and did not say much (I did not mention the canceled observations or program implementation). She continued to cry in future sessions but eventually talked about how she was so stressed and overwhelmed, and that teaching in Baltimore was not what she expected. She admitted feeling scared of most of her fourth-grade students (a few of the boys were literally more than twice her size), especially when they got in her face, yelled, swore at her, or threw chairs and desks. She knew she had lost complete control over the class and was concerned about the safety of the students in her class (as well as her own safety) because of the dangerous fights.

As a result of the unsafe behavior in the classroom, the principal had other school staff coming in and out of the classroom all day to "help" this teacher. This teacher expressed that she felt frustrated because each person had a different idea about what should be her priority to fix her classroom and would express disappointment with the lack of instruction and extent of behavior problems in her classroom. In addition, she felt she had lost the respect of her students completely because they knew she could not do her job (e.g., gain control of the classroom).

Throughout the course of the year, I worked to build rapport with this teacher and gain her trust in talking about the stress/challenges she was having with her job. I normalized her experiences as a first-year teacher new to Baltimore and used a lot of praise and encouragement to help build her self-efficacy as a teacher. When we began meeting, she said she could not even *think* about PATHS to PAX GBG because it was too overwhelming with everything else she needed to do to improve in her classroom (e.g., safety, behavior, instruction). Therefore, I realized that it was unrealistic to expect her to follow the pacing guide other teachers in the building were using. Instead, I focused on rapport building and small steps toward implementation. First, we discussed how the Game could be used to help improve students' on-task behavior and we developed a list of prizes she thought her students would enjoy. I took on the role of playing Games with her students in the classroom and hallway, which spurred her motivation for playing the Game when she saw its effect on student behavior. Her enthusiasm for the Game and fun prizes helped improve her relationship with the students. Next, we talked about how the Lessons, Tootles, and Kid of the Day would help her students have more positive interactions and relationships with each other as well as help make her classroom a more positive environment. Over time, we were able to develop a feasible plan to chunk the program into smaller components. As she experienced small successes (e.g., improved relationships between her and the students and with each other, decreased behavior problems, a more positive classroom environment) with different components, she was more willing to try other elements of the program.

—Dana D. Marchese, PhD

Developmentally Appropriate Expectations for Students

Sometimes teachers may have expectations for their students that are not developmentally appropriate. Examples include expecting that younger students can sit still and quiet for more than 5 minutes without anything to do, that students can complete challenging assignments independently without assistance, or that students should know how to behave when rules and behavioral expectations have not been explained to them. Developmentally inappropriate expectations may arise as a result of a number of factors, including the teacher coming from a higher grade to teach a lower level or the teacher generalizing from a few exceptional students who meet the behavioral expectation to all of the students. When teachers have developmentally inappropriate expectations for students, they may become frustrated because the program does not appear to be effective at improving behavior. This can result in decreased use of program components. Therefore, it can be useful to remind teachers the class is comprised of students with different behavioral abilities, just like a range of academic abilities, and to discuss appropriate expectations for students of that grade level. Empathize with their frustration and explain that, although it is extremely frustrating, some students need more frequent reminders, and so on.

One concept to use is shaping. Explain that sometimes learning can be a process. The coach may say something such as, "Remember when you talked about how hard it is to get your student to sit in his seat for an entire Lesson? Well, some kids get overwhelmed with a big job and do better when tasks are broken down into smaller parts that they can learn one at a time. You can teach kids this way by using a technique called *shaping*." Then, explain the principles of shaping using other examples from the teacher's classroom. Shaping is similar to scaffolding assignments. This approach can help generate discussion and provide opportunities for you to reinforce and expand on important points teachers raise as they react to the idea of shaping.

Analogies and metaphors can be particularly helpful in explaining strategies and theories of behavior change to teachers. Here are a few that can be used:

- *Flossing analogy*: "Teaching children is like flossing your teeth; you have to keep doing it over and over to get long-term results." This analogy conveys that daily repetition and constant monitoring can achieve long-term results, although it doesn't seem to be accomplishing much day by day.
- *Children wearing L plates*: "In England, when one is learning to drive, an L plate for 'Learner' is put on the car. Imagine your students also have an L plate on their back. This will remind you to be patient and tolerant when students make a mistake. Children are, after all, learners in life." This analogy helps remind teachers of children's developmental processes. They are still learning and, like the child who is learning to ride a bike, will wobble and make mistakes.

In the following case example, notice how the coach used reframing to help the teacher recognize developmentally appropriate expectations for her students. Also notice how the coach and teacher developed strategies collaboratively to facilitate student learning. See how this, paired with coach assistance in lightening the teacher's teaching load, brought about improved teacher implementation.

 **STELLAR!**

I was working with a lower elementary teacher who had developmentally inappropriate expectations for her students. During informal classroom visits, she often yelled at her students and became increasingly frustrated with their confusion. In addition, she often snapped at her students over minor misbehaviors, and disruptions in the classroom were becoming more frequent. When she asked me why the students couldn't handle the workload, I reminded her these students are very young and full of energy, and that it is normal for students to become restless when sitting for long periods of time or when they are learning something new. We reframed how she thought about her students. Rather than expect they should know how to do everything as soon as instructions are given, the teacher realized she should expect they will need instruction, demonstration, and perhaps even some one-to-one feedback. We came up with a few ideas, such as having the teacher demonstrate more frequently the tasks she wants her students to do and shortening her Lessons into mini Lessons and then providing an activity to assess her students for understanding before moving on. We also talked about how the Game could help her students to focus on the tasks at hand. These initial strategies were moderately successful in terms of reducing her frustration level toward students, but it wasn't until I offered to lighten her load by playing the Game in her classroom and teaching some academic lessons as well as PATHS to PAX GBG Lessons that her implementation improved. By first observing me and then by identifying time to play the Games during Lessons, the teacher had the support she needed to get back on track and be moderately successful with consistent implementation.

—Michael Muempfer, MA

Unpredictable Circumstances

As a result of decreased funding, a lack of resources, high teacher turnover, and increased student disruptive behavior, some schools are operating in a crisis mode and therefore may not be able to implement the program because of a more reactive focus of "putting out fires" as opposed to a proactive, preventive approach. At times, the coach might encounter situations in which schools are closed for extended periods of time as a result of weather-related issues (e.g., snow, extreme heat, power outages from storms). As a coach, you might also be in a school that experiences grief or tragedy (e.g., loss of students, family members, or staff to illness, community violence). It is important for the coach to remain flexible and remember that these closings may cause changes in teachers' schedules that may affect their implementation of the program. Be empathetic in these situations and make revisions to the pacing guide if necessary, but also be sure to develop a plan to help teachers maintain implementation or get back on track because the structure of PATHS to PAX GBG allows teachers and students to continue to move toward their academic goals even in the face of unpredictability.

In the following example, try to put yourself in the shoes of the coach, whose school experienced a significant loss. Notice how the coach followed the lead of the school staff but also looked for cues that teachers were ready to get back to teaching. Also think about how the coach's modified pacing guide and her willingness to teach the Lessons eased the burden for one particular teacher and also provided consistent program delivery for students.

 STELLAR!

Working as a coach this year, I encountered an unexpected event that not only impacted implementation of the program, but also the overall school climate. Over Winter Break, a young second-grade teacher at the school passed away unexpectedly. Quite understandably, this was devastating to the students and staff of the building. On returning from break, the administration basically told the teachers to forget about instruction for the first few weeks back from break and to focus on helping students cope with the loss. The funeral was held during the second week back from break and the teachers were expected to return to "business as usual" the following Monday. Missing two solid weeks of instruction led to teachers falling behind rapidly on all curriculum and systematic deadlines related to the teaching of core content standards (e.g., reading and math benchmark assessments). As a coach, I felt it was important to give teachers time to get back into instruction and get caught up with the core content before addressing the needs of the program. I was careful to respect their wishes, and give them time as they readjusted to instruction. However, within a few weeks, most teachers were eager to get back on track and responded well to a modified Lesson pacing guide that I designed for each teacher based on his or her individual needs.

This was a relatively small school with only two teachers per grade level, and second through fifth grades were departmentalized (one teacher on the team was responsible for teaching language arts and reading; the other teacher was responsible for teaching math and science). Understandably, the teammate of the teacher who passed away had an extremely hard time returning to "business as usual." She was dealing with a variety of emotional challenges: extreme grief coupled with constant reminders that stemmed from the students they shared (who were also grieving and displaying their emotions in a variety of ways). In addition, she was also struggling with the logistical implications of her students no longer having a stable teacher for language arts and reading (there were three long-term substitutes brought in for the remainder of the year). In an effort to ease the workload for this teacher, I offered simply to teach the program curriculum to all second graders. This served several purposes; it not only eased the burden for the teacher how was having difficulty coping but also it ensured all students (in both classes) were receiving the same exposure to the Lesson content. In addition, the PATHS to PAX GBG instruction was provided by the same person every time, thus providing some needed stability in the daily routines of these still recovering students. This process of me teaching the Lessons continued through late spring, when the teacher slowly began teaching the Lessons again herself (to both classes).

To deal successfully with a tragedy like this, or with any other sort of unexpected change in school personnel, the key is to remain flexible but determined. Respect the staff and the students and their need to grieve. The coach needs to understand things may not go right back to normal quickly, and every principal will probably handle the return to rigorous study a bit differently. I tried to be there in any way that I could to support those with whom I had worked so closely and to let them know I was ready whenever they were to get back to our Lessons. I didn't push them or try to force anything, but made my presence known and did my best to ensure that, within a reasonable timeframe, all students were once again receiving the intervention Lesson content.

—Kelly Schaffer, MS

In the following example, consider how the teacher's frequent absences interfered with her ability to set up classroom routines and to implement the program consistently. Notice how the coach focused on increasing implementation of the major components of the program, rather than all the components. Also notice what the coach said she might have done differently in hindsight.

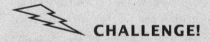 **CHALLENGE!**

I worked with a lower elementary teacher who was having some medical issues and was often absent from school. She did not have classroom routines in place and she seemed to have a loose teaching style in which she allowed her students to get up as they pleased (e.g., to sharpen pencils) and to call out answers. The teacher often sat at the back of the class instead of walking around the classroom (mostly because of medical issues). She was very nice and friendly, but made many excuses for why she didn't do parts of the program or why she couldn't meet with me. Often, she explained that, because of her absences, she had many other things on which to catch up that interfered with her implementation.

The first step was to develop rapport with this teacher, which was fairly easy to do because she was friendly and welcoming. She also was a fairly skilled teacher; however, she had a loose style of behavior management for a large class, which allowed for a lot of misbehavior. She wasn't always strict on counting Spleems, so I frequently reviewed the importance of tracking Spleems accurately.

It was difficult for this teacher to be consistent because of her frequent absences. We created collaboratively a revised pacing guide for the Lessons. Some weeks the teacher followed our updated pacing guide and other weeks she did not teach any Lessons. One thing that seemed to work was hanging her Scoreboard on the chalkboard if it wasn't up when I visited. This helped remind her to play Games during the week. Looking back, it may have been helpful to prompt the teacher to do this as the year went on as opposed to doing it for her. However, because I was visiting her classroom on a weekly basis, this system worked well.

Setting goals and providing incentives were effective at getting the teacher to accomplish smaller tasks; however, it was often not successful at sustaining her implementation. This teacher did not get into a routine of writing Tootles or having a Tootle Board, but I did not focus on this because there were other larger concerns (e.g., Games, Lessons, Kid of the Day). Usually she had a Kid of the Day (students reminded her if she forgot), although she would not always remember to do the Kid of the Day Tootle. Looking back now, I could have spent more time modeling this procedure and having the teacher identify a specific time (e.g., immediately in the morning) each day to do Kid of the Day. As the coach, I could have checked in during the identified time to be sure she was following through. Again, because of her frequent absences, it was difficult to get her to be consistent with daily activities. Overall, she did her best with implementation when she was at school.

In our discussions, I would make a connection to how well her students behave during the Game and what she is expecting of them during those times (e.g., setting expectations, following through with rules). Although she agreed with this, she was not consistent in using this style in her daily teaching. Looking back, one thing I could have done differently is to work with this teacher and her class to review classroom rules and observe her more during her daily teaching practices to give her specific feedback on ways to keep a structured environment and stick to a daily schedule. After a lot of hard work, this teacher improved in playing the Game consistently and correctly, teaching all the Lessons in our updated pacing guide by the end of the school year, having a Kid of the Day every day, using her harmonica and PAX language, and offering more praise to those students who were behaving in a positive manner! She also improved her classroom structure as a result of playing the Game.

—Jenn Keperling, MA, LCPC

Competing Demands

One of the most common barriers coaches experience is that schools do not have sufficient time in their schedules for teachers to participate in coaching. There are several options to address this barrier. First and foremost, be understanding, empathetic, and respectful of the multiple demands principals and teachers "have on their plate." Next, be flexible and offer multiple options for days and times to schedule coaching and/or training sessions, including before or after school, during faculty or team meetings, planning periods, or weekends; or as part of a luncheon in which the program provides a catered lunch for the school staff. Issues related to time commitment can also be prevented by providing principals and teachers with information about coaching sessions (e.g., frequency, duration) so they can figure out ways to incorporate these sessions into their schedules. Finally, be sure to listen carefully to the principal and understand clearly the true barrier in a given situation. It is possible the principal may have other concerns regarding the program and is using "not having enough time" as an excuse for not permitting the time teachers need for professional development and coaching. *We have found that when teachers and principals participate consistently in the coaching and find it beneficial (e.g., see the coach as a resource) they are more willing to make time in their schedule for coaching requirements.*

Even in schools that consistently implement the program there may be specific times during the year that implementation decreases throughout the school. For example, it is common for teachers to deviate from their routines and schedules before or after a holiday or school break (e.g., Winter Break, Spring Break) as well as toward the end of the school year. During these times, it is also likely for teachers to reduce their implementation of the program. In addition, program implementation often decreases during statewide testing and preparation. Sometimes schools revise their schedules to make more time for test preparations, which often leaves teachers with little time to implement the program in their classroom.

The benefit of knowing this information is that the coach can plan in advance how to structure coaching during these times of the year. For example, the coach might offer assistance in other areas, such as making copies for teachers so they have more time to implement program components in their classroom. This also helps to build rapport and a positive working relationship with teachers. As a coach, you may also offer to plan with teachers and make suggestions for how to integrate the program into the revised testing schedule. Emphasize that the program is not meant to be an extra thing for the teacher to do, but is actually intended to help teachers and students meet academic objectives for other subject areas.

Similarly, suggest teachers play the Game during test preparations, and share the rationale that if students are more focused during test preparation (e.g., there are fewer disruptions during instruction), students will have higher test scores. The coach could also meet with teachers before testing to create a plan for testing that best fits their individual needs. For instance, some teachers prefer to use the week before testing to prepare for testing, and they teach the Lessons during the week the test is being administered (e.g., in the afternoons after testing is completed); others prefer to continue teaching the Lessons consistently before the test days and take a break from teaching the Lessons during the actual testing week (this option reflects the pacing guide, which suggests teachers skip teaching Lessons during the testing period).

In the following example, notice how the coach validates the teacher's concerns regarding her time demands and works with the teacher to set small goals collaboratively for increasing implementation. Also notice how the coach shares some of the load in terms of implementation, thereby enhancing the coach–teacher relationship and achieving goals through teamwork.

STELLAR!

I was working with a lower elementary teacher who expressed frustration about having to fit the program into her already packed schedule. She also shared her perception that the program took a significant amount of time each day. When observed, she scored high on implementation and positive affect. This teacher was able not only to teach the key points in the Lessons and play the Game with her students, but also she was able to do both very well. However, she turned in Game Scoreboards that showed infrequent Game playing (e.g., only one to four Games per week) and she was also inconsistent with the Lessons (e.g., some weeks she taught two Lessons but other weeks she did not teach any Lessons).

As a coach, I expressed empathy, acknowledged the time constraints on all teachers, and let her know this was a common concern (normalized her experience). We agreed to meet to find ways to fit the program into her busy schedule and to identify ways to shorten the amount of time it takes to deliver the required program components. During this meeting, I began by highlighting her strengths and remarked how impressed I was with her level of implementation when she was able to fit it into the schedule. I asked her open-ended questions such as: How do you find time some weeks to fit in two Lessons? She replied that she often used the time on Fridays, when her class didn't have a resource, to teach one to two Lessons. She also said she played the Game when she remembered and that her students reminded her to play. We discussed various times to play the Game during the school day. She identified after lunch as the most important time to play the Game because her students were usually off task and disruptive after lunch because of the lack of structure in the cafeteria and the transition back to learning. We set the goal to play a Game every day after lunch and to start with just focusing on playing that one Game each day.

My plan was to get her to play one Game every day and make this a regular part of her routine, then increase the amount of times she played the Game each day (e.g., two times per day), and take small steps to achieve our final goal of playing the Game three times per day. We talked about the Lessons using the same philosophy of taking small steps to work up to teaching two Lessons per week. I offered to teach one Lesson per week while she got caught up on other things and/or just took some time for herself because she was feeling stressed. The teacher committed to teaching one Lesson per week and I agreed to teach one Lesson per week to get back on track with the pacing guide. We also made a few modifications to the pacing guide (e.g., combining a few Lessons, removing review Lessons) to make it more attainable. Overall, both the teacher and I were successful with this plan. By working together, we built a positive relationship and it helped motivate the teacher. During most Lessons I taught, the teacher remained in the classroom and caught up on work at her desk, which helped reduce her stress. Last, when I taught Lessons I also played the Game or PAX timer surprise (which is a generalization strategy in which the teacher chooses a student's PAX stick randomly from the cup and does *not* announce the student's name, but when the timer goes off if the identified student is on task, that student earns a prize for the entire class. If he or she is not on task, the teacher does not announce the student name and continues with instruction) to model additional strategies for the teacher and show how easily it could be fit into her daily routine.

—Jenn Keperling, MA, LCPC

In this next example, notice how the coach identified the primary barrier to implementation (e.g., emphasis on test scores) and attempted to relate PATHS to PAX GBG to academic achievement as a way to increase teacher implementation. What other strategies might you use in this situation?

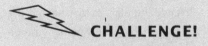

CHALLENGE!

With so much emphasis on standardized testing in schools today, it's not uncommon to find teachers who are stressed about how well their students will do on the tests. I worked with an upper elementary grade teacher whose primary concern was the upcoming tests in the spring; therefore, he focused most of his time and energy on test preparation. This teacher was not aware of the positive impact the program has been shown to have on student performance.

The rubric data on this teacher showed he had remarkable skills when he did implement the Lessons. He was well prepared and had a talent for keeping the students engaged. However, his Lesson Logs and Game Scoreboard data showed he did not implement the Lessons regularly and was not playing the Game consistently. He shared his concern that the Lessons and Game took too much time away from preparing for the spring tests.

Because he was focused on test results, I thought that showing this teacher student performance data might persuade him to implement the program. Unfortunately, after sharing relevant results (e.g., playing the Game consistently with students increases on-task behavior) from several studies he still did not change his mind about the program/implementation. He was adamant he did not have enough time to implement the Lessons or Game because he had to reach certain academic gains by testing time. As a coach, I hypothesized that one of the major barriers was he was a new teacher and he was worried about making a good impression on administration, as well as his students achieving good test scores. He did not have enough teaching experience to realize that for students to achieve high test scores, teachers do not have to dedicate all class time to drilling math and reading concepts, and that by incorporating other types of learning, such as social–emotional learning, test scores can also be raised.

Because other efforts were not successful, I tried to praise this teacher for his efforts whenever he did teach a Lesson, play the Game, or use any of the other program components. This was easy to do because he was a fantastic teacher and his innate ability to reach his students was truly impressive. I also praised his efforts to administration and let them know how phenomenal he was at teaching the Lessons. This teacher had a great way of making the Lessons his own and relating to his students in a way that was natural. I was able to get him to try the Kid of the Day routine and, when I observed him doing Kid of the Day, I used a lot of praise. Unfortunately, he implemented Kid of the Day for a few weeks but then stopped, because he wanted to spend the time focusing on content on which the students would be tested.

I also invited several other coaches to watch him teach a Lesson and they praised his ability to teach the Lessons. This strategy was also unsuccessful in getting him to implement the program consistently. Because he was a new teacher, I am not sure if there was anything I could have done differently as a coach to change his outlook or focus in his classroom. I was very careful not to do anything that could have hurt the relationship I had worked on building with him. It is possible that if administration would have been more supportive of the program and focused less on test scores, this teacher also would have invested more time into implementing the program.

—Sandy Hardee, MS

Disorganization

Some teachers exhibit levels of disorganization that affect program implementation. The teacher may have difficulty finding the various materials to play a Game or teach a Lesson (e.g., timer, harmonica, curriculum binder). This can be frustrating for teachers and interferes with the success of the Game and Lessons (e.g., downtime for students, low student engagement). As a result of not being able to access necessary materials quickly, teachers' implementation of the program may be low or inconsistent. In a disorganized classroom there may be a lot of unnecessary clutter (e.g., large stacks of papers scattered around the room and on the teacher's desk).

The goal in working with teachers with a disorganized classroom is to help them organize their classroom and be more efficient with their time, and develop routines and systems so they can locate their materials quickly each day. This helps alleviate downtime while the teacher searches for materials during the Lesson or Game and helps to maintain the pace of the Lesson. This strategy also reduces the possible perception of teachers that the program is overwhelming or "one more thing they have to do." As a result of being more organized, they will have increased student engagement, more time for academic instruction and the program, and increased on-task student behavior. The following organizational strategies are suggested to help teachers in a disorganized classroom organize their classroom:

1. **PATHS to PAX GBG area.** The simplest strategy is for teachers to designate an area for all program materials so they are easily accessible. Some teachers have used a table or countertop to place all the copies and materials they need for the day, in order, according to what they need first, second, and so on. Similarly, an extra desk or supply table by the teaching area can help organize the materials needed for a Lesson before starting. This not only applies to PATHS to PAX GBG materials, but also it is important to have a designated area for all items needed for that school day (e.g., copies of all handouts, pens, pencils, highlighter).

2. **Cart on wheels or large colorful bin.** Suggest the teachers have a cart on wheels or a large colorful bin (a neon bin will help them locate it easily when they are busy) in their classroom that has all their PATHS to PAX GBG materials (e.g., curriculum binder, timer, clipboard with the Game Scoreboard, PAX Stix, Lesson plans). The cart could also have any other materials teachers need frequently during a school day, such as extra sharpened pencils, blank paper, whiteboard markers, and so on.

3. **Apron or tool belt.** Wearing an apron or tool belt that contains the timer, harmonica, PAX Stix, pens, and so on, can make things easier for teachers to find them. Strategies such as hanging the harmonica on a magnetic clip on the chalkboard/whiteboard can help with organization, but also with prompting a teacher to use specific materials when they are stored in a convenient location and viewed often. Another suggestion is to clip the timer to the lanyard that holds the harmonica so these tools are around the teacher's neck for easy access.

4. **Planning.** As a coach, it is important to encourage teachers to take a few minutes at the end of each day to prepare for the next day and to arrive at school a *few minutes early* in the morning to prepare and organize their classroom for the day, make copies, and so forth.

5. **Systems.** Organized teachers often have multiple systems in place in their classrooms. For example, materials and manipulatives are clearly labeled in colorful bins or on shelves and there are routines for procedures such as a morning routine, end-of-the-day routine, and so on. In organized classrooms, there is an identified space for all materials (e.g., homework bin, jar with extra sharpened pencils).

6. **Student assistance.** It can be very helpful to involve students in the organization process. One strategy is to have teachers verbalize their actions as something is being set down (e.g., "I am putting the prize box on this table. Remind me where I put it when I'm looking for it in a little bit."). Students enjoy the challenge of demonstrating a better memory than

the teacher and they soon get in the habit of watching and remembering where objects are placed, which can serve as a source of amusement as well as a significant time saver. Instead of spending several minutes searching for the timer before starting a Game, teachers can simply say, "Does anyone remember where I put the timer?" Inevitably, within seconds, several students will point to where it is.

In the following example, note how simple strategies are effective at improving implementation. Also notice how the initial strategy was tweaked to improve its effectiveness and to capitalize on student responsibility.

STELLAR!

I was working with an upper elementary teacher who had extreme difficulty keeping her Game materials organized. As a result, when a good opportunity arose to play the Game, she often could not find the timer, Scoreboard, or prize box and thus would get frustrated and not play the Game because it was taking too much time. I observed this several times when I was in her classroom informally, and the data she turned in each week reflected this. Often, Scoreboards would have one to three Games for the entire week. However, when I had a formal observation scheduled, she was able to implement the Game with high fidelity. Her students responded well to the Game and the teacher acknowledged that her students liked the Game. She expressed a desire to play the Game more often, but couldn't seem to develop a plan to be able to do this on her own.

First, we agreed to put the Scoreboards on a clipboard (I provided one with a pen attached) so that it would be easier to find. Then, the teacher designated a place where she would keep her timer, prize box, Scoreboard, and pen. The teacher chose her teaching station (cart with the projector on it) located in the middle of the room as her designated place. Although this change helped initially, it did not solve the problem completely because, throughout the day, the materials were not always put back in the designated place. The teacher admitted she often set down the timer (or prize box, Scoreboard, and so on) wherever she was in the room when she was done with it. When another opportunity arose to play the Game, she was back to square one—not knowing where her materials were. I suggested wearing an apron, but the teacher did not think she would be able to follow through with this strategy. Together, we came up with the strategy that ultimately helped her locate Game materials easily at a moment's notice. It became the Kid of the Day's job to ensure materials were put back on the teaching station. The teacher began to get in the habit of handing the Game materials to the Kid of the Day as she finished with them, rather than setting them down in a random location. She explained this to her students and they agreed to be responsible for the materials. If she "forgot" and set the timer (or another material) down in a random location, the Kid of the Day had permission to get up and bring it back to the PATHS to PAX GBG materials area. It is important for coaches to have lots of ideas for organizational strategies that have worked well for other teachers; however, the coach needs to work collaboratively with the teacher to determine what will work best for that individual teacher in his or her classroom. For example, many teachers love the apron or tool belt idea, but others may not like wearing something around their waist.

—Kelly Schaffer, MS

In the following example, notice how the coach uses collaborative planning to increase the teacher's preparation for the Lessons. Also notice that, in this case, coaching sessions were frequent and did not result in significantly improved implementation, as sometimes happens. What other strategies do you think might have increased teacher implementation in this example?

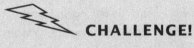

CHALLENGE!

I worked with a lower elementary grade-level teacher whose implementation suffered because of disorganization and a lack of classroom routines. It was evident from informal observations that one of the biggest barriers to this teacher teaching Lessons during the scheduled time was that her morning "routine" lacked structure and often took 30 to 60 minutes when it could take about 10 minutes. This teacher would get flustered when she got behind with time and then often skipped her PATHS to PAX GBG Lesson to move on to the next subject.

As a coach, the first thing I tried was to identify a time convenient with her schedule to meet and discuss how I could be helpful. Often "something came up" for the teacher and we had to reschedule. After a few cancellations, I confirmed our appointment with her that morning and also checked with administration to ensure that it did not interfere with any other school meetings. During our meeting, I worked with the teacher to adjust the pacing guide based on where she currently was with the Lessons and to help her achieve success in being able to get through the curriculum in a timely manner so she did not "feel behind." In addition, I offered to teach some Lessons for her. When I taught the first Lesson, I asked her to fill out the PATHS to PAX Lesson Modeling Checklist (Appendix DD) and comment on specific things she observed me doing during the Lesson that she liked or maybe she would do differently. At the end of the Lesson, I also played the Game with the class so the teacher could observe me implementing each step of the Game with fidelity. Then, the teacher and I met to discuss what she observed. She did not take many notes on the Modeling Notes Sheet and did not appear to be paying attention during the modeling.

During the next scheduled observation, I noticed the teacher was running behind with her morning routine. Throughout the Lesson I helped the teacher by adding key points. As the Lesson came to an end, I guided the teacher to play the Game with her class during the activity portion of the Lesson. I praised the teacher for all the components she demonstrated well and, regarding feedback, I only chose to have her focus on one thing: pacing of the Lessons. The next week we worked together to plan four Lessons collaboratively. I sat with her as we completed the Lesson planning sheet and went over each Lesson explicitly so she was prepared for each Lesson. I was very hopeful that the next 2 weeks would go well with the Lessons. Both the teacher and I were assigned a few tasks to complete before the Lessons were implemented. Unfortunately, the teacher did not complete her tasks and we had to postpone the Lessons once again.

Next, I offered to prepare all the materials for the upcoming Lessons so the teacher would have everything she needed to teach the Lessons. In addition, I asked a colleague to visit the classroom with me and sit with the teacher while I modeled a Lesson and Game. During the modeling, my colleague engaged in discussions with the teacher about concerning issues such as pacing and ignoring minor disruptive behaviors. Over time, this teacher began teaching the Lessons consistently on a regular basis. I provided a lot of positive reinforcement for implementing the Lessons. Next, we focused on the quality of implementation in our coaching. My colleague and I visited the classroom often to offer support. We also used incentives as she continued to play the Game more often, which increased her Game playing.

Looking back on this situation, one thing I could have done differently was to offer incentives for implementation earlier during the school year, because the incentives seemed to be effective at improving her implementation of the program. It may have been helpful to have the teacher teach two Lessons and then I could teach one Lesson. This may have motivated her to keep up with the Lessons knowing I would be providing her with a "break" every third Lesson. If we had more time in the school year, having her observe high-implementing teachers in their classroom and/or watching a videotape of her Lessons might have helped improve her Lesson delivery.

—Sandy Hardee, MS

Negative Classroom Climate

Some classrooms have a very low rate of praise or positive statements and a high rate of reprimands, harsh comments, and removal of students from the classroom. Teachers who rely heavily on punitive strategies may seldom use precorrects or preventative strategies to prepare students for activities. Teachers may use more of a *reactive model* (e.g., "putting fires out") in their interactions with students as opposed to a *proactive model*. For example, teachers might focus more attention on what students are doing incorrectly as opposed to noting the positive behavior of students or those students who are following the classroom rules. The teacher may say, "My students will eat me alive if I show any vulnerability. If I am more positive and use praise, I will lose control of my classroom." It is possible teachers are unaware of their own unmanaged stress and how it is interfering with their ability to regulate their own emotions successfully, which is resulting in a negative classroom climate.

Being punitive can be harmful to both students and teachers. Research suggests that negative teacher affect directed toward kindergarten students had detrimental effects on students' academic and social achievement in fourth grade (Hamre & Painta, 2001). Teachers who display negative emotions and behaviors frequently are at risk for burnout (Kavanagh & Bower, 1985). Therefore, the goal is to increase teachers' use of positive teaching strategies (e.g., praise, positive reinforcement, ignoring minor negative behaviors) and create a positive learning environment for students by increasing program implementation. Listed here are a few coaching strategies that may be helpful in this situation:

1. **Acknowledge the behavioral challenges in the classroom and check in with teachers' feelings** "Wow, this was a tough day in your classroom. You had to spend a lot of time dealing with misbehavior. How are you doing right now?"
2. **Validate teachers' experiences**. Reflect on teachers' emotions and normalize. "Yes, I think it makes sense that you feel stressed. I think that's completely reasonable given the situation. I feel tense and I'm not even their teacher."
3. **Ask what teachers would like for the classroom environment to be like** "I notice you often have to spend a lot of time correcting student misbehavior, which then this interferes with your teaching. What do you think about that? Would you rather you didn't have to yell so much to get students to behave? When you envision your ideal classroom, what does it look like in terms of how students behave, how you interact with them, and how you feel?" By asking these questions, the coach can elicit a classroom vision that is likely more positive. The coach can then use this information to set shared goals.
4. **Offer assistance and hope toward the shared vision**. "It sounds like you would like for your classroom to be calmer and more productive. I would love to help you. There are a few strategies that other teachers in similar situations have found helpful. For example, right now you have to yell to get students to stop misbehaving, but sometimes certain strategies can be put in place to encourage students to behave and to stop misbehavior before it escalates." Using collaborative, nonblaming language can increase the likelihood the teacher will discuss positive behavior management strategies. For example: "Do you think we could work together to develop a plan to try a few simple things to see how they work in your classroom? Great! Maybe we could start by reviewing some of the strategies we've already talked about to determine which ones might have the best chance at helping your classroom be a calmer and more productive classroom."
5. **Review rationale for praise and other positive strategies**. First, normalize the teacher's frustration and use of a raised voice. Next, point out the limits of its effectiveness. Explain that in a crowded room with lots of noise and raised voices, it's more likely that someone would stop and turn toward a novel noise such as a harmonica, than toward another loud

voice. Emphasize that attention is a powerful reinforcer and that by giving negative attention to those students who are disruptive, the teacher may be encouraging and reinforcing their disruptive behavior inadvertently. Instead, it is more effective to increase praise and attention for those students who are following classroom rules.

6. **Model positive behavior management strategies**. Make a special effort to provide frequent praise comments and positive reinforcement to students, particularly those who exhibit frequent disruptive behavior. Promote the use of Tootles (e.g., peer Tootles, adult-to-student Tootles, student-to-teacher Tootles, a Tootle Board) and consistent implementation of Kid of the Day components (e.g., special roles for the Kid of the Day, Kid of the Day Tootles/compliments). Create immediate opportunities for teachers to use these strategies (e.g., harmonica) before you leave the classroom. Teachers who frequently move students away from the main group of students as a punishment for misbehavior sometimes have difficulty deciding when to reintegrate the student into the group. Assist the teacher with developing behavioral goals for misbehaving students to be moved back into the group when the behavioral goal has been demonstrated or accomplished.

7. **Post classroom cues**. It can be helpful to post visual cues in the classroom to serve as reminders about the use of positive classroom management and self-calming strategies. Smaller desk signs can be posted in key locations, such as on a dry erase board on which the teacher writes frequently, on the overhead projector, and by the light switch. Another opportunity for reminders is to make notes on GBG Scoreboards to remind teachers to use praise statements during the Game.

8. **Provide reinforcement to teachers**. Praise and attention are powerful reinforcers and often teachers who display negative affect toward students do not receive a lot of positive reinforcement from administration and their mentors. They may receive reprimands from administrators and frequent frustration because of their students' behavior. Therefore, lots of genuine praise from the coach may be particularly effective for these teachers. Similar to how praise is applied to shaping student behavior, the coach should provide heavy reinforcement (e.g., praise, tangible rewards) initially for even small changes in teacher behavior toward students. Observe the teacher's use of positive classroom management strategies to then provide the basis for positive feedback for the teacher. Examples of such opportunities include making notes during the Game or Lesson of specific praise statements the teacher delivers, followed by a discussion about the effectiveness of the praise in increasing positive student behavior and positive reinforcement for the teacher. The coach may also want to discuss how it feels to receive the praise and incentives as an adult, then link it to how effective it is for students to receive similar types of positive reinforcement, encouragement, and acknowledgment for what they are doing well.

In the next example, notice how the coach's use of active ignoring and praise with a student who consistently demonstrated disruptive behavior served to motivate the teacher to try the same approach. Also notice how the coach modeled positive reinforcement with the students and also provided lots of positive reinforcement to the teacher as well!

STELLAR!

I worked with a lower elementary grade-level teacher who was often punitive toward her students. She focused frequently on the negative behaviors her students were exhibiting in the classroom, thereby causing a lot of important instruction time to be lost on disciplining students. The negative comments the teacher made toward students as well as the energy she spent on arguing with students contributed to a negative classroom environment. Informal observations of the teacher and rubric data all showed the teacher was losing lots of instruction time disciplining students and giving negative attention to their behavior.

First, I modeled the concept of active ignoring while I played the Game for the teacher and the school mental health professional. The mental health professional was able to use concepts modeled during the Game to guide discussions with the teacher about specific students in the classroom. The three of us discussed how I used active ignoring for a student who was trying very hard to get my attention during the Lesson. As soon as the student who was trying to gain my attention changed his behavior and followed the behavior expectations, I praised him verbally in front of the entire class. In addition, I also suggested the teacher praise the student so that I could ensure she was aware of what had actually just happened. We also discussed how that student made significant efforts to remain on task and stay focused after receiving praise. This meeting was very effective in taking the time to discuss with the teacher how active ignoring was successful with this student. I encouraged the teacher to try this approach as well and she seemed particularly motivated to do so after she observed the change in her student's behavior.

After this meeting, I continued to visit this teacher several times a day to "pop in" and see how things were going. Sometimes merely my presence served as a reminder to try techniques we had discussed. I also used a lot of praise whenever I observed the teacher being positive toward students, especially when I observed her using praise to reinforce desired student behaviors. As a result of these consistent visits and modeling lots of praise in the coaching relationship, the teacher increased her use of praise with students significantly. In addition, I provided tangible incentives to the teacher for playing the Game more often. Because she appeared to enjoy being recognized for her efforts, I also provided her with written Tootles and also gave her public recognition for being positive in the classroom. The regular classroom visits also provided me with frequent opportunities to model for the teacher as well as to intervene whenever necessary to diffuse situations in which the teacher might have normally focused on negative behaviors. It wasn't always a perfect situation and there were times it seemed like the teacher may have forgotten what we had worked on, but those times were less frequent as the school year went on. *As a coach it is important to be flexible and remember everyone has bad days!* On these more difficult days I tried to offer extra help in the classroom to give the teacher a break. This helped to build our relationship and to show the teacher I was there as a resource when she needed me.

—Sandy Hardee, MS

In this next example, notice how the coach's use of modeling and positive reinforcement did little to improve the teacher's interactions with students and her implementation of the program. What might you do to address these issues if you experience a similar situation?

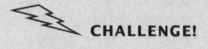

CHALLENGE!

I worked with a lower elementary grade teacher who had low student engagement and was very punitive with students. The teacher was often exhausted by the end of the day and reported she did not like her job. Unfortunately, the students in her class had learned to get the teacher's attention by being disruptive as opposed to being on task. This teacher had a slow start with the implementation of the Lessons and playing the Game.

First, I modeled a Lesson to show how quick and easy it is to follow the manual. I asked the teacher to complete the PATHS to PAX Lesson Modeling Checklist (Appendix DD) while I modeled, hoping she would notice the amount of praise I was giving to all students, especially the students she considered to be overly disruptive. However, the teacher was very distracted and did not appear to be paying attention when I modeled. After multiple discussions with this teacher, it seemed she was going to have difficulty using praise regularly. Therefore, I tried to encourage the teacher to focus only on Kid of the Day at first. I praised her and rewarded her efforts for being consistent with this process. The praise was successful at getting her to complete the Kid of the Day routine every morning. She did a great job completing the full-page Tootle and I was always quick to acknowledge the Kid of the Day whenever I came into the classroom. Unfortunately, this appeared to be one of the few times this teacher used praise consistently.

Next, I encouraged her to implement the use of the general Tootles and to model it for her own students. She created her own Tootle writing corner and had a great way of making it easy for students of all levels in her classroom to be able to write Tootles to each other. I also encouraged students to write Tootles to the teacher so she could understand how it feels to receive them. The teacher responded positively to my Tootles as well as to Tootles from her students; however, this did not seem to increase her level of positive interactions with her students.

Because I noticed a lot of negative interactions happening in the hallway, I prompted the teacher to play the Game on the way to the cafeteria and on the way to resource classes. I also modeled the recognition of desired behaviors in the hallway and ignored negative behaviors. I shared with the teacher that overall positive behavior increased when I recognized one student's appropriate behavior (e.g., standing quietly with PAX hands at their sides). The teacher acknowledged this connection but continued to focus on the negative behaviors of a few individual students.

Although we had great discussions about the strategies modeled in her classroom, overall this teacher was inconsistent with following through on using the strategies. Often she would express how much she disliked her job. She appeared to give little effort to teaching and her students. As the school year went on, it was more difficult to connect with her because she took little responsibility for the negative classroom climate and often blamed the students.

This teacher eventually got in a routine of implementing the Lessons consistently, but continued to be punitive and expressed little interest in changing her behavior.

—Sandy Hardee, MS

Low Teacher Engagement

Despite a coach's best efforts there are some teachers who are not engaged in the program. Although there are many potential reasons for low engagement, we have found two major reasons in our work with teachers. One potential contributing factor to low teacher engagement involves problems with the coach–teacher relationship. Although often it is difficult to identify with certainty the true reason for a mediocre relationship, a coach is usually quite perceptive when a teacher does not behave in a positive way toward the coach. This may reflect personality differences unique to the coach–teacher dyad, or the coach may notice the teacher does not appear to have positive interactions with other school staff as well. Also, it may be possible the coach irritated or offended the teacher inadvertently without realizing it (e.g., teachers may feel they do not need help in managing their own class and the coach is suggesting they do, just by being there) or the teacher develops a negative association with the coach because of the extra demands they feel that implementing the program has put on them.

Another potential contributing factor to low engagement involves the program itself. When a new program is introduced into the school setting, teachers may have mixed feelings about learning the new skills and participating in the program. They may be interested in seeing what the program has to offer, but they may have concerns about the time needed to effect it or other program requirements. Often, teachers may already feel overwhelmed or have "too much on their plate" or see this as "one more thing to do." In some cases, teachers may have already established a successful learning environment and feel they don't need additional assistance. In other cases, teachers may believe the program won't work with the students they teach (e.g., urban youth) or the principles of the program don't match their beliefs about how adults should manage behavior problems (e.g., children should not be rewarded for positive behavior but should just do what is expected of them). Problems with teacher engagement may be manifested in a variety of ways (e.g., cancellation of coaching sessions, low implementation of program components, hostility toward coach). Fortunately, there exist some strategies that may enhance teacher engagement with the coach and program.

Strategies to Enhance Teacher Engagement

Establish an Alliance

The coaching relationship has been identified as one of the primary mechanisms of change (DeHaan, 2008; Kemp, 2009). In the first meeting as well as during subsequent meetings, convey to teachers you are not there to judge or evaluate the teachers or to be a spy for school administrators. Assuage any anxieties teachers might have regarding your perceptions of them as ignorant and in need of help, or that you represent outside experts who don't really understand the school environment. Instead, present yourself as being on the same team as the teachers and therefore are working toward the dual goals of student social–emotional development and enhanced learning (O'Broin & Palmer, 2009). Indicators of positive alliance include the teacher having an "open-door" policy for you to enter the classroom without an appointment, the teacher being willing to meet with you during free time (e.g., lunch, planning period), and the teacher seeking you out for feedback.

Emphasize Program Benefits

It is also important to demonstrate to teachers the *benefit* of the program for them and their students, and how the program connects to their goals/values for their students and classroom. When possible, use the language the teacher has used explicitly (e.g., "You mentioned it was important to you that your students have a positive experience with community and learn how to be good citizens. One way that some teachers have created this in their classroom is by . . . ."). Strive to make the connection quickly and clearly for teachers between program strategies and promotion of their students' social–emotional and behavioral development, as well as a more positive classroom and school environment. This can be done by sharing anecdotes of your own use of the program in the classroom or of the impact of the program on other students and teachers with whom you have worked. In addition, in some cases you might find it helpful to discuss results from research studies that demonstrate program effectiveness.

Address Questions about Relevance

Concerns about the *relevance* of the program may come up in a number of scenarios. For example, in the case of teachers with solid classroom management skills, teachers may perceive that what they are already doing works well for them, so there is no need to learn or implement the program skills. To address relevance, it is important to find ways to explain the connection between the program and the teacher's situation. In the case of teachers with solid skills, acknowledge and reinforce their effective strategies (e.g., praise) while explaining the importance of consistency across classrooms and within the school environment. In other words, point out that their use of program components promotes consistent expectations within the school and provides additional opportunities for students to practice good behaviors, thereby increasing the likelihood students will demonstrate appropriate behavior not just in that teacher's classroom, but also throughout the school, ultimately making behavior management easier for everyone. Moreover, consistent use of program components by all teachers and other school staff provides a universal schoolwide system and common/

consistent language throughout the building. Seek out effective teachers for feedback routinely with regard to program techniques or as a peer consultant who can serve as an invaluable resource to other teachers in the program. If teachers do not feel they need additional support at this time and everything is going well in their classroom, communicate to them that they are learning a set of "tools" they might not need now, but perhaps could use at some later time. There are very few students who don't go through some difficult time in their life when these tools could prove helpful. Even teachers with solid positive behavior management skills may have something they would like to see improved in their classroom. Through observation, you might obtain a more accurate idea of the teacher's behavior management skills and might develop some ideas about any program components that may be helpful in this classroom. After praising the teacher for all the wonderful things going on in the classroom, it might be helpful to ask if there is anything at all the teacher would like to improve—even something small (you have this coaching time scheduled anyway). If so, try to connect it to program components or suggest that, although they may not have classroom management issues, they may like to try Kid of the Day, Tootles, and so on, to make their classroom environment even more positive.

In other cases, teachers may express that the children in their classroom are particularly challenging or that there is little they can do because the children need outside help (e.g., therapy) or because it is the responsibility of parents to teach their children how to behave. In other situations, teachers may view their teaching position as temporary (e.g., a teacher nearing retirement, a long-term substitute who is filling in while another teacher is on maternity leave) and may not believe there is any point in starting something new before another transition occurs. In this situation, explicate the relevance of the program by empathizing with the teacher's situation and pointing out that the teacher actually has a lot of influence with regard to how the children behave when they are at school. Teachers typically spend approximately 40 hours a week with their students—more than most parents spend with their children and certainly more than most therapists spend with their clients. Just as teachers have the opportunity to teach their students about math or reading, so, too do teachers have an opportunity to influence the social, emotional, and behavioral skills of the students.

Give to Get

To increase engagement, sometimes it is helpful to "give" a little extra to challenging teachers. What you "give" depends on the teacher, but you might consider providing classroom materials and other resources teachers find helpful, as well as treats such as hot chocolate on a brisk winter morning or snacks/candy during a team meeting. In addition, you could lend an extra hand during classroom time to assist teachers with academic activities unrelated to the program. These thoughtful gestures may enhance teacher engagement in two ways. The first is that they help to improve the coach–teacher relationship by demonstrating thoughtfulness that is unrelated to and completely noncontingent on program implementation. So, the coach provides the treats or assistance simply as a gesture of kindness and teachers' positive perception of the coach and their willingness to work with the coach may increase. The second way this approach might improve engagement has to do with reciprocity. Specifically, when the coach provides a treat or assistance, teachers may feel a slight sense of obligation to reciprocate in some way, either by engaging more with the coach or implementing the program to a greater extent. This strategy is not intended to manipulate teachers, but rather to capitalize on naturally occurring social forces that operate on interpersonal interactions so that improvement in teacher engagement, program implementation, and, ultimately, child outcomes can occur.

Identify Key Opinion Leaders

It can be very effective to identify teachers who are respected by their peers to use as exemplars for the program. Having these "key opinion leaders" voice support for the program serves as encouragement to others who are struggling with the program and may influence those positively who are not yet committed to the program (Atkins et al., 2008). Moreover, key opinion leaders are often more influential than mental health providers on issues of student behavior management (Atkins et al., 2008). Key opinion leaders can be helpful to support the program, but they can also sabotage the program if they do not have buy-in (e.g., encourage teachers not to implement the program, say it does not work). It is important to spend time at the school and identify the key opinion leaders as well as to develop a strong positive relationship with these individuals.

Make Concessions

Although it would be ideal for teachers to work hard to catch up on the implementation of all the program components they are not using, this is unlikely to happen given a teacher's historical lack of engagement. Although you might be inclined to ask this teacher to implement one small component, another strategy that may be successful is to ask the teacher to make a large commitment (e.g., playing the Game three times per day). Teachers who are not engaged will likely turn down the request, thereby providing the coach the opportunity to make a smaller, more reasonable request (e.g., playing the Game once a day). By making these concessions, the coach then increases the likelihood the teacher will also make a concession and agree to the smaller request.

Initiate Gentle Discussion

It can be uncomfortable for a coach to have direct discussions with teachers regarding low engagement; however, sometimes direct discussion can be very effective at identifying the barrier to teacher implementation. Such discussions can be initiated in a respectful, nonconfrontational manner. You might begin by asking open-ended questions about how the program is going in the classroom to elicit the teacher's perspective. If nothing is forthcoming, you might try a more direct approach. For example, you might say, "I noticed you often cancel our meetings. I know you are very busy, but I also wanted to check in to see if there was something I did" or "I was wondering how excited you feel about doing the program right now. I noticed a couple of times you said you plan on do the Lessons and Games regularly, but that it's hard to get consistency going. That's completely normal; it can be really challenging to do the Lessons and play the Game on a regular basis. I was wondering if we could talk about what might be getting in the way so perhaps we could figure out how to make it more manageable or more relevant to your classroom." In addition, data can be used to facilitate discussion. For example, you could point out data trends from Game Scoreboards and Lesson Logs (e.g., "I noticed your Scoreboards this week contain fewer Games than Scoreboards from previous weeks").

Emphasize the Positives of Being Part of a Team

It can be helpful to reframe the use of program strategies for this particular teacher as contributing to the team through ensuring consistency across classrooms. Reinforce teachers who demonstrate solid teaching and behavior management skills by indicating the teacher has "shining star" potential, can serve as a model for other teachers, and that there is the possibility of videotaping the teacher for training purposes (if the teacher would find that reinforcing).

Reinforce Progress

In conjunction with the strategies just described, consistent use of praise for even the smallest evidence of program implementation (e.g., hanging the Control Signals Poster, writing a Tootle) might foster increased use of program components. Providing teachers intermittently with tangible reinforcers (e.g., classroom supplies, teacher reward) may also enhance teacher implementation.

In the next example, notice how the engagement issue appeared to be with the coach–teacher relationship. Look for ways the coach persisted with trying to develop a positive relationship with this teacher, despite the poor rapport they had initially. Also notice how praise and rewards served to improve the coach–teacher relationship as well as reinforce teacher implementation of the program.

 STELLAR!

When I first started working with one lower elementary grade-level teacher she would interrupt me mid sentence, and tell me she did not have time to speak with me at that moment, and would walk away quickly before I could ask about a more convenient time to meet with her. After some reflection, based on her behavior, it was clear she did not wish to be bothered during her lunch time. Taking this into consideration, I started visiting her classroom during times when I saw students working in small groups and noticed she seemed a little more open to talk to me during these times.

One day after modeling the Game in her classroom, she appeared to be upset with something I had done. Because I was having difficulty building a relationship with this teacher, I wrote her a Tootle for a great activity she did with her students. She responded to the Tootle by smiling and thanking me. Next, this teacher did a great job using the PAX language throughout the school day, but was not playing the Game with her students. I started to praise her for specific PAX elements she was using in her classroom. As I increased the use of Tootle Notes for her fantastic work, she increased her use of PAX elements in her classroom and began to generalize throughout the day.

In addition, I asked a colleague who had a lot of experience with this grade level to help me engage the teacher more with PATHS to PAX GBG. There were a few times the teacher canceled a meeting with us, and as frustrating as that may have been, we never showed that frustration to the teacher. Instead, we "rolled with it" and acted like it was no big deal to change the meeting to a different day and time. When we met with the teacher, we brought her some chocolate, which was helpful in getting the teacher to warm up to the coach and engage in meaningful conversation. Both my colleague and I praised the teacher verbally and with written Tootles at every opportunity. It was obvious by her reaction when she received praise that she appreciated our efforts. After a short time, the teacher began implementing some of the techniques we had discussed with her. Again, we followed that with praise. After the teacher witnessed other teachers receiving a nice tangible incentive for playing the PAX Game in their classrooms, she began playing the Game more. Offering a grade-level incentive for her and her teammate to win a substantial incentive and schoolwide recognition also got her to play the Game more often. She definitely responded well to praise and recognition from her peers and other colleagues. Overall, it appeared that scheduling meetings at a convenient time for the teacher and providing verbal, written, and tangible reinforcement on a consistent basis were most effective in improving this teacher's implementation of PATHS to PAX GBG.

—Sandy Hardee, MS

In the following example, notice how the coach used a broader, schoolwide approach to involve everyone in the program, thereby creating a sense of PAX community and perhaps reducing the instances of low engagement. Also notice how the coach enlisted successfully the assistance of key opinion leaders and implemented simple rapport-building strategies to engage a disengaged teacher.

 STELLAR!

I was working in a school in which the principal was excited initially about PATHS to PAX GBG, but when the program started, the principal did not prioritize it. This is understandable because principals have numerous priorities as building administrators; however, we know it is critical to have support from administration for a program to be successful. First, I gave each school staff member, even the custodial staff, a harmonica to use in the building. The harmonica is a unique PATHS to PAX GBG tool. Over time, more and more staff members wore the harmonica and used it, thereby promoting the program and enhancing staff engagement throughout the building.

However, the harmonica was just the first step. I started using positive reinforcement, specifically by recognizing every teacher in the school by using the Staff Tootle Board and highlighting a special Teacher of the Week. I found that including other staff, such as the administrators, in addition to the classroom teachers really helped to build relationships at the school. There was one administrator that could not remember my name and barely acknowledged me when I entered the school building. I used Tootle Notes with this administrator to acknowledge her support for the program and let her know I appreciated her efforts. As a result, this administrator started to talk about the program on the morning announcements and started using her harmonica in the building. I continued to praise her efforts and support for the program.

I began to make "friends" and allies with the most influential teachers and staff members (e.g., key opinion leaders) in the building. This approach took effort with regard to identifying the key figures in the building, letting them know about the program, and earning their support. For instance, I discovered that one teacher I was trying to get to support the program always ate her lunch in the staff lounge, so I started eating my lunch in the lounge during her lunchtime. We started talking and making connections to things we had in common, which built a foundation for a positive working relationship. I would often refer to those topics and tried to find other ways to connect with her. Eventually, I talked with her about the program and she started playing the Game more and implementing Lessons. I played Games in her classroom and taught a few Lessons for her. It took some time to build a relationship with this teacher, but it was definitely worthwhile. She also encouraged her grade-level teammates to play the Game more often. This strategy was successful because this teacher was well respected among staff for being a genuinely good teacher who obviously cared for her students. By gaining the support of this teacher, she was influential in encouraging other teachers to implement the program.

—Sandy Hardee, MS

In the next example, observe how the teacher's perspective that she was being forced by her administrator to use the program interfered with her engagement and implementation. Notice how the coach tried to address the teacher's concerns repeatedly, but to no avail. Consider what other strategies you might try if faced with a similar situation.

CHALLENGE!

Sometimes teachers do not engage with a new program because they feel as if they are being forced by administration to participate in it. I worked with one upper grade elementary teacher who felt this way. The initial modeling was very success-ful in her class, but seeing the effect of the Game on her students' behavior did not engage her as it does with most teachers. This teacher did not want to play the Game with her students immediately after I modeled. She appeared nervous so I did not "push" her to try. A few days later, we met to discuss her impressions of the Game and modeling. She told me how upset she was that she was being forced to participate in this program without her consent. I tried to explain that, although her principal agreed to participate in the program, I would not be reporting spe-cific information to her principal. I also explained to her I was a former teacher (in the same school district) and my students really enjoyed it—and so did I, as their teacher. She thought that was fine, but still did not want to participate. I decided to let it go. I offered to model the Game again in her class, which she declined. I gave her the rest of the week to calm down.

The next week I met with her team (she was present) and I reintroduced myself. I told them about how I was a teacher and the same thing that was happening to them happened to me. I told them how well my students responded to the program and how beneficial I found the program as a teacher. Next, we discussed the plan for coaching. I reiterated to the group that I was going to be there often and I hoped we could work together. I also emphasized that my job was not an evaluator and that anything shared between us would be confidential and not shared with administra-tion. This information seemed to be helpful and my "challenging" teacher said she would do the program but she was not enthusiastic about it.

Her first rubric score was good; however, she only played the Game about four times a week. We discussed convenient opportunities to play the Game and I tried to stop in to watch her play it. She allowed me into her classroom to watch; however, she did not play the Game while I was in the room. Sometimes I would sit there for an hour with her teaching but not playing the Game. When I prompted her to play the Game she would give a reason why she could not play it (e.g., "Not now. It's not the right time. I don't want to interrupt the Lesson"). I continued to have conversations with her about how the Game is an overlay to instruction and not an interruption. She would listen to my suggestions but disagreed. As a coach, I offered to model using her Lesson plans (or I could create a Lesson based on the topic they were studying) but she refused.

Overall, this teacher was very angry about being "forced" to do a program she had no prior knowledge of before the school year began. In my experience, when teachers see PATHS to PAX GBG in action, they love it! However, this teacher had some issues with her principal and was not interested in trying the program. It took a tremendous amount of time and effort to gain this teacher's trust and get her to "try out" the program. In the beginning, it seemed she wanted to sabotage the program to spite her principal, but when she realized I was only trying to help her and her students, she began to implement the program gradually.

—Michael Muempfer, MA

In the following example, notice how the teacher's low engagement with the coach as well as what might be considered lack of reinforcement from her job interfered with her implementation of the program. Note the creative strategies the coach used to increase rapport and to support the teacher in taking small steps toward increased implementation. Also observe how, in this instance, administrative pressure increased, rather than interfered with, teacher implementation.

 **CHALLENGE!**

A challenging coaching experience I had was working with a lower elementary teacher who struggled with general classroom management, mostly because she had poor engagement with her students. Her students appeared not to be engaged as a result of the teacher's lack of planning (e.g., lack of planning meaningful assignments, which led to challenges with behavior management). At times, it seemed the teacher was completely overwhelmed by the day-to-day expectations of the teaching profession. On multiple occasions she commented on not having enough time to "get it all done." It was difficult to determine whether the teacher was not successful because she was overwhelmed by teaching in general or because she lacked the knowledge to be able to engage her students, which led to disruptive behaviors spiraling quickly out of control, leaving little energy for teaching tasks. Either way, on most days she appeared to be disengaged and was not motivated to make any changes. She was frequently absent, arrived late, or left early. Quite often, when I arrived for a scheduled appointment, she would tell me she had somewhere else to be (e.g., special education meeting, resource) and rush out of the room.

Typically, when I have encountered teachers who struggle with management, simply modeling the GBG with their class tends to promote buy-in and gives me an opportunity as a coach to begin to work in the room. Unfortunately, this was not the case in this situation. This teacher was not eager to have me model in the first place, and she was absent on the first two occasions I was supposed to model for her. I was politely persistent with rescheduling and, eventually, was able to demonstrate the Game for her. As I do with all teachers, I gave her the Good Behavior Game Modeling Checklist (Appendix A) and asked her to follow along as I played the Game with her students. She sat in the back of the room, on her computer, while I modeled the Game. Looking back, I should have told her I would collect the checklist as soon as

I was done to ensure she paid attention. After I model the Game it is standard practice to ask the teacher to play a Game immediately. Much to my surprise, this teacher agreed. With prompting from me—and with checklist in hand—she was able to play the Game successfully with her class. Her students were engaged in their work and responded really well to the challenge of showing PAX! I used this as a talking point with her on subsequent occasions, pointing out how "on task" her class was when she played the Game. However, the teacher still avoided playing the Game on her own. Unfortunately, she rarely had any Games on her GBG Scoreboards, and when I would visit her classroom I did not see any evidence of the program components.

I needed more than the "standard" coaching strategies with this teacher. I started simply by spending a lot of time in her classroom (at least 45 minutes each time I was in the building one to two times per week). My initial goal was to observe her and pinpoint the best way to reach her. However, after the first two observation sessions, it was clear to me this teacher did not like when I observed her teach. She tended to yell at the students to sit and be quiet, rather than try to engage them in any type of learning activity, and she seemed reluctant to start anything while I was in the room. She would say she was about to initiate some sort of learning activity, but rarely followed through. The students spent an exorbitant amount of time in transition with nothing to do. To elevate any pressure the teacher might have felt when I simply sat and observed, I began to develop reasons to sit down while I stopped in her room for a normal check-in visit. For example, on one occasion I had a bunch of papers scattered on my clipboard and in my bag when I went to hand her a standard coaching flier. I asked, "Do you mind if I sit back here and organize my papers for a few minutes before I go visit the next teacher?" She eagerly agreed. It may sound like an interesting approach, but I felt like it helped put her at ease and even allowed this teacher to see that I also struggled with work-related duties from time to time. I also began to use this "observation" time to help the teacher get classroom duties done (e.g., hang Tootles, replace bulletin boards). Although this did not increase her implementation, it helped build a positive relationship with her. She did not run out of the room immediately or make excuses as soon as she saw me.

When I felt like we had a good relationship, I started to model and prompt elements of the program. For example, when the teacher attempted to get the students' attention I would use PAX Quiet and praise the students for responding, then I would remind the teacher to use this strategy. Often she would acknowledge my suggestions, but there was no follow-through from her. At times, I varied my approach and addressed the students rather than the teacher directly (e.g., "Boys and girls, remember to respond using PAX Quiet when you hear your teacher use the harmonica."). Looking back, it seemed more effective when I addressed the students, and it may have been helpful to shift my focus from the teacher to the students. If I initiated the Game, the teacher was very willing to allow me to play with the class; however, she would not participate when I asked her (e.g., "Can you tell me if you see any Spleems?"). Again, I would point out the difference in student behavior when the

Game was being played and the teacher would agree, but she would not play the Game on her own. She would often say, "They do like the Game, but I don't have time for it" or "I lost my prize box."

I began to feel frustrated by the lack of change and effort put forth by this teacher. It seemed that she recognized the difference the program elements made with her students, yet she made no effort to implement them on her own. It was difficult for me to spend time in the room without feeling discouraged. However, as a professional, I continued to put forth the effort and try to think of new ways to engage this teacher. Along with the standard coaching practices, I continued helping out in the room as well as prompted and modeled program elements. As the year progressed, the teacher began to feel more comfortable with using the different program components and even began to wear (and sometimes use) her harmonica!

A major shift happened with this teacher after she had a meeting with her administrator. Although I don't know the specifics of the meeting, it appeared she was reprimanded by the administrator in some way because she asked me to write a letter stating she was working with me. Of course, I wrote the letter and used this as an opportunity to continue to build a relationship with this teacher. From that point forward, she began to play the Game and use PAX Quiet. I praised and rewarded her frequently with incentives while continuing to work on her skill level with program elements. Similar to my experience working with this teacher to implement the program, progress with her skill level was a slow process. For example, after the PAX Quiet cue, she would yell at the students who did not respond, rather than praise those who responded appropriately. During the Game she was inconsistent with the behaviors she counted as Spleems. She would often have a harsh tone of voice and/or skip imperative steps (e.g., setting the timer, picking the prize). I varied my approach with providing feedback to this teacher—at times giving written feedback and other times modeling explicitly. On multiple occasions I would make suggestions in the moment by whispering in her ear (e.g., "Rather than pointing out that it was Billy that Spleemed, simply state the team and behavior, then praise the others for staying on task"). Although I made numerous attempts to help her improve her implementation, her skill level did not improve significantly. Although this teacher increased her implementation throughout the year, I am not sure it was a result of the coaching. The meeting with her administrator seemed most effective at prompting her behavior change.

—Kelly Schaffer, MS

In this next example, notice how the teacher's students exhibited appropriate behavior despite the teacher's low implementation of the program. How do you think this might be related to the teacher's willingness to play the Game? Notice how the coach tried a number of different strategies to develop rapport, provide reinforcement, and help enhance the "fun" of PATHS to PAX GBG. What other strategies might you consider in this situation?

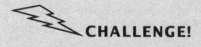

CHALLENGE!

I worked with an upper elementary teacher whose class was very well behaved because she had a "militant style" and the kids appeared afraid of her. The teacher reported she did not agree with many elements of the program (e.g., Granny's Wacky Prizes, made-up words like Tootles); however, she did buy in to some aspects of the program (e.g., Kid of the Day, teaching the Lessons). When teaching the Lessons, she agreed with the main points and thought they were important to teach to her class; however, this was only when she had time to do so, and she often came up with excuses for why she couldn't find the time (e.g., testing, report cards).

With this teacher, my first step was to attempt to develop rapport. At times I felt uncomfortable entering her class or even saying hello to her. She often walked by me in the halls without looking at me, so I did my best to be friendly and understanding with her, especially in the beginning. I tried to find ways to give her incentives for implementing key elements (e.g., Kid of the Day). She immediately started Kid of the Day and chose to type her Tootles (which she called *compliments* because she refused to call them *Tootles*) on her computer and display them on the overhead projector as she typed. She was consistent with this process and did it every day, although the process was rigid and did not seem like a lot of fun. It was good she used the Tootles, because it helped create a positive relationship between her and her students, and it allowed her to compliment a student which she might not have done previously without doing the Kid of the Day Tootle. Looking back, I could have tried to observe this process more often and give her some feedback about having fun with the process. However, I am not sure she would have been receptive to this type of feedback.

The teacher did a good job with the Lesson, hitting all the main points, but her Lessons were too long (45 minutes) and not much fun. The students were learning and she allowed them to participate and have discussions, but it was all very structured. Because the teacher was behind in teaching the Lessons and reported not having enough time as a result of state testing and other school-related commitments, I observed her Lessons throughout the school year and offered suggestions to the teacher, such as keeping the Lessons brief (e.g. 20 minutes). I tried continuously to free up some of her time by having her stick to the time frame, but she was pretty rigid in sticking to the Lesson script. We revised her pacing guide to combine some Lessons, skip some along the way, and teach three Lessons during some weeks so she could catch up. She did end up catching up by the end of the school year, but took off from teaching Lessons and playing the Game during testing and during the few weeks leading up to the testing.

The teacher rarely played the Game because she did not like many parts of the Game (e.g., Granny's Wacky Prizes) and did not like using the made-up terms, such as *Spleem*. She said that she viewed her students as adults and had a difficult time allowing them to be kids and have fun. She allowed me to come in to model the Game and her students would ask me constantly if we could play it when I visited the classroom. Looking back, I could have tried to use the students more in getting her to buy in to playing the Game, possibly showing her the times they did an excellent job with the Game and showing her how easy it is to play and integrate it into daily teaching.

Sometimes the teacher would use PAX language (e.g., PAX hands in the hall), but mostly she would yell *procedure* and all her students would sit or stand in the ready position. She would not use her harmonica and preferred using a dog clicker. When she clicked the dog clicker, her students would all sit up straight and in the ready position. There were a few times she would joke with her students and I would try to recognize these times and praise her to promote having fun with her students, but this did not seem effective in changing her behavior.

Many strategies that I used typically with other teachers were not successful with this teacher because she did not buy in to the entire program. She had her style of structured teaching and a rigid personality, and it was apparent I was not going to change that. I did my best to work with her and offer her incentives for trying key parts of the program. In the school, she was viewed as a good teacher who produced great test scores and had a well-behaved class, so I don't think she thought she needed any help. It made it very difficult to work with her, but I continued to check in with her, was friendly and positive, and I tried to offer suggestions and help along the way.

Overall, she did improve and was consistent with a few aspects of the program. She consistently did the Kid of the Day process every day, gave out Tootles (although she still would only called them *compliments*) and put them on her Tootle Board, and she taught all the Lessons. However, she did not improve on playing the Game consistently. When she did play it, she did a good job with all the key steps and her students enjoyed playing.

—Jenn Keperling, MA, LCPC

In the next example, notice how these students also demonstrated high levels of appropriate behavior despite low implementation of the program. What similarities and differences do you see between this teacher and classroom and the one in the previous example? What else would you have tried to improve teacher implementation?

CHALLENGE!

I experienced a coaching challenge with an upper grade-level teacher with playing the Game. She felt she had good classroom management and her students didn't need to play the Game. This teacher did have good classroom management. The students were generally on task, and when they became off task, the teacher quickly prompted them to get back on task. The students almost always complied. Although this teacher was skilled in playing the Game, she averaged less than one Game per week throughout the course of the school year.

After my initial observation of her playing a Game, I had high hopes. This teacher did a fantastic job with her first try with it. Her students responded well when I modeled the Game, but, more important, they responded positively when she played. During the next 2 weeks, she played just a few Games. I asked her why and she said she simply forgot. She also reported she felt compelled to play the Game when I was in the room, but did not when I was not present. I met with her several more times during lunch and/or resource to discuss the situation. She said the Game was too intrusive to her instruction and that whenever her students got off task she would bring them back quickly. I then offered her suggestions for when it would be easy to play (e.g., independent reading, independent work, group work, transitions, playing in hallway during transitions to lunch/resource). She said she would try. During the next few weeks, Game frequency went up slightly, but soon thereafter she regressed back to playing less than one Game a day.

I then asked her to identify the time of day when her students were most disruptive. She informed me the transition back from lunch was the most challenging time of the day. I modeled a Game for her during this time and the students were very on task. The teacher commented she had never seen them do so well. She played it just one other time coming back from lunch because she said she always forgot to play. I also explained to her that although she is a high-quality teacher, her students would benefit learning the Game and self-control for future teachers. We also discussed the benefits of having students practice going from highly excited states to calm focused states (experienced during the PAX Game). She agreed, however her frequency never improved. She continued to score high on the rubrics. My final attempt was to get her to submit some feedback for why she felt the Game wasn't necessary in her class, and what advice I could give other teachers who might want to implement the program and/or best teaching practices. Although she agreed to do this, I never received her feedback.

Unfortunately, this teacher did not play the Game consistently because she felt it was easier to prompt attention quickly when her students became off task. Fortunately for her, the class complied. Although she agreed with all my suggestions, she didn't use them because she was never in "need" of them. Even in situations when it would have made life a bit easier (the transition back from lunch), she felt it wasn't worth it. I would have liked to go back and visit her the following year. She may have had an exceptional class the prior year and may have needed PATHS to PAX GBG the next year.

—Michael Muempfer, MA

Throughout this chapter, common implementation challenges were presented, along with a variety of strategies that have been developed to reduce the interference of these factors for program implementation. Although there are bound to be obstacles to implementation that arise, anticipating these challenges can help pave the way for collaborative problem solving and successful resolution of these barriers.

Chapter 5 Reflection Questions

- How can teachers introduce new students to a program?

- What are some strategies you can use for a teacher who is anxious about implementing a new program?

- As a coach, name three things with which you can help a teacher in a classroom with lots of disruptive behavior?

- What are three organizational strategies you can suggest to teachers to help them organize their classroom?

- Thinking about the many challenges presented in this chapter, what might you have done differently than what the other coaches attempted? How can you prepare for these types of the challenges in your own coaching?

Selection, Training, Supervision, and Observation of Coaches

The purpose of this chapter is to discuss the importance of selecting effective coaches as well as providing training, supervision, and ongoing observation of coach activities.

Objectives

- Learn how to select effective coaches and engage them in successful coaching relationships.
- Understand the importance of providing training, collaborative supervision, and ongoing observation of coach activities.
- Develop skills to become a supportive and positive supervisor.

Coach Selection

All the coaches on the PATHS to PAX GBG project in Baltimore City were employees of the project. For long-term sustainability of the program in the schools, it might be ideal for coaches to be employees of the school district, which is often the case for coaches involved in literacy and other academic programs. Coaches can be mentors, lead teachers, school psychologists, school-based mental health clinicians, or peer teachers. The strategies and techniques discussed in this book are intended for anyone working with a classroom teacher. It is important for the coach–teacher relationship to be collaborative and that, regardless of coaches' position, they remain nonjudgmental, positive, and supportive!

Because of their central role in facilitating teacher implementation, it is necessary to select effective coaches. Important considerations include prior coaching or teaching experience, familiarity and fit with program rationale and components, and personality characteristics. All our coaches had considerable experience working in public schools either as former teachers or school mental health clinicians. Experience working with the student population is an important selection criterion. For example, in Baltimore City, all the coaches had experience working in an urban school setting. Our coaches understood concepts essential to teaching: classroom organization, academic pacing and instruction, developmental levels of students, and behavior management. Moreover, because some of them had been former teachers who had been trained in the GBG, they demonstrated clear understanding and skill with the program components, which allowed them to share their own teaching experiences with the teachers they coached and to develop empathy for teachers facing classroom challenges. Those who had not received previous training in the program still demonstrated knowledge of and positive attitudes toward program principles and components.

Desirable personality characteristics included credibility, affability, empathy, confidence, ability to lead, professionalism, and flexibility. Coaches need to be credible to the teachers and administrators with whom they will work (Neufeld & Roper, 2003). Their professional expertise (i.e., knowledge and skills) and deportment (e.g., professionalism and trustworthiness) reflect their credibility (Neufeld & Roper, 2003). Coach likeability is critical to the development of relationships with teachers and reinforcement of teachers through the use of praise. Moreover, coaches who are skilled socially are better able to create their own social networks in the schools. Empathy is particularly important for coaches because they work with teachers who encounter challenges in the classroom on a daily basis. Confidence and the ability to lead enable coaches to train, to deliver constructive feedback, and to engage in effective collaborative problem solving around implementation. Often, it is beneficial for coaches to be independent—not dependent on a lot of support. Furthermore, dealing with dynamic school schedules, teacher and administrator personalities, and a variety of classroom situations requires flexibility. Similar characteristics of effective coaches have been noted by other programs as well, including the America's Choice literacy program (e.g., Poglinco et al., 2003).

Training

Coaches also require training and ongoing support (e.g., supervision) to improve their knowledge and skills (Neufeld & Roper, 2003). Training for coaches consists of a 5-day workshop involving didactics, video review, demonstration, skill rehearsal/role play, and feedback. Before the workshop, coaches are given program materials, videos, and manuals to review. Training consists of two main parts: (a) program components (2 days) and (b) coaching (3 days).

The first 2 days of the training are focused on the components of PATHS to PAX GBG. At the beginning of the training, the rationale and evidence for the program are reviewed, followed by instruction about each of the program components. Coaches watch videotape demonstrations of teachers implementing program components. Videotape demonstrations are discussed in terms of the relative strengths and weaknesses of teacher implementation. Trainers, who may be expert coaches, also demonstrate modifications to program components when applicable to help coaches visualize the flexible application of the program to various classroom situations. Coaches participate in skill rehearsal and receive positive and constructive feedback from the trainers regarding their demonstration of program components.

The latter 3 days of the training are focused on effective coaching strategies and follow a structure similar to that of the initial 2 days. First, the rationale and evidence for coaching as a supportive implementation intervention are reviewed. Then, there didactics regarding coaching procedures and tools are discussed (e.g., how to conduct a team meeting, how to use incentives). Then, trainers demonstrate specific coaching strategies and discussion centers on the application of these strategies to different teacher situations. Survey data from other coaching programs (e.g., Poglinco et al., 2003) suggest coaches often feel uncomfortable providing constructive feedback to teachers and many avoid working with resistant teachers. Thus, coach training involves direct discussion about challenging coaching situations. Case examples are provided to facilitate brainstorming and the development of action plans for resolving implementation issues. Coaches also participate in skill rehearsal of coaching strategies and receive positive and constructive feedback from the trainers regarding their skill demonstration. Accurate completion of the coaching forms (e.g., Game Scoreboard Log [Appendix Q], Lesson Log [Appendix O], Good Behavior Game Modeling Checklist [Appendix A]) is also reviewed during training. In addition, trainers accompany the new coach into the field to the first few coaching sessions to provide support and feedback related directly to "real" coaching sessions. This helps new coaches acquire the confidence needed to work effectively with teachers.

Supervision

Sustainability

Coaches participate in weekly supervision meetings with supervisors (e.g., expert coaches, faculty researchers, supervisors) and participate biweekly in individual supervision. Additional supervision via e-mail, phone, or in person is provided on an as-needed basis, particularly when coaches have identified crises or coaching challenges with low-implementing teachers.

Group Supervision

Supervision meetings are structured and data driven, typically lasting 2 to 3 hours. An agenda is created for each meeting, but the structure of each meeting follows the same basic outline:

- Review spreadsheet of individual teacher implementation (e.g., Games played per day, number of Lessons taught each week)
- Review teachers with moderate implementation challenges
  - Indicators/evidence of implementation challenges (e.g., behind on Lessons, not playing Games regularly?)
  - Hypotheses regarding implementation challenges
  - Action Plans: prioritize targets for change, interventions, assessment
- Review teachers with significant implementation challenges
  - Indicators/evidence of implementation challenges
  - Hypotheses regarding implementation challenges
  - Action Plans: prioritize targets for change, interventions, assessment

- Discuss check-ins and successes with high-implementing teachers
- Conduct logistics and planning

Before the supervision meeting, coaches provide their supervisor with information for each teacher regarding the Lessons delivered and number of Games played during the previous week, as well as copies of their Lesson Log (Appendix O) and Game Scoreboard Log (Appendix Q). This helps the team assess the extent to which the teacher is on target with regard to the guidelines of the program. In addition, the coaches provide completed Coaching Logs (Appendix R) that detail the frequency and type of coaching contacts during the previous week.

A portion of these meetings is spent noting briefly which teachers are on target with their Lessons and Games, and discussing strategies to reinforce, praise, and acknowledge these teachers. A much larger proportion of time is spent discussing teachers who are behind in their Lessons and/or Games or who are demonstrating significant implementation challenges, such as missed Lessons, hostility toward students, and so forth. For these teachers, the team reviews the Coach Action Plan (Appendix CC), or CAP, systematically using the structure in Table 6.1.

In general, these discussions reflect a collaborative problem-solving approach to teacher implementation and parallel the process in which coaches engage with teachers. The goal is not only for the group to identify collaboratively effective strategies for the coach to implement, but also to provide an opportunity for coaches to reflect on their coaching and that of others. Similar to teacher implementation, improved coaching results from the observation of others' coaching strategies, reflection on teacher responses to their coaching, and receipt of feedback about their coaching performance (Neufeld & Roper, 2003).

In the interest of feasibility, a general guideline is for coaches to rely on the simplest and most time-efficient strategies with proven effectiveness with regard to enhancing implementation for that particular teacher. In other words, start with the strategies that provide the "biggest bang for the buck." Therefore, it is important for supervisors to ask detailed questions regarding implementation of the Action Steps in the CAP (Appendix CC) to get a true understanding of the teacher's skill level, coaching relationship, strategies, and so on. The questions provided in Table 6.1 provide information about the use and effectiveness of specific Action Steps. However, sometimes an Action Step is unsuccessful because it was not implemented fully by the coach as a result of barriers that interfered with the coaching session (e.g., not enough time) or because of a skills deficit on the part of the coach with regard to implementing that particular strategy. A fruitful discussion should result in the identification of two to three strategies the coach will implement to support the teacher in making progress toward implementation goals.

Individual Supervision

Individual supervision sessions often occur to review the coaching sessions involving challenging teachers or classroom situations. These sessions may occur in the office, but it is very helpful for the supervisor to travel into the field with the coach to observe the teacher and classroom targeted for discussion. Supervisory principles mirror the core coaching principles

TABLE 6.1 Supervision Guidelines for Discussing Teacher Implementation Challenges

Step	Example	Individual
Provide status of teacher implementation relative to previous weeks.	"The teacher had not been using the harmonica, but I heard her use it even before I went into the classroom this week." "The teacher is still behind with his Lessons, although he said he would be able to make them up this week."	Coach
Elicit information about Action Steps implemented by coach.	"Which Action Steps did you use with the teacher?"	Supervisor
Elicit information about teachers; response to Action Steps.	"How did the teacher respond when you [Action Step]?"	Supervisor
Elicit coach's appraisal of Action Steps.	"Do you think [Action Step] was successful? If not, what got in the way of [Action Step] not being successful?"	Supervisor
Consider next steps.	"Will the teacher continue to improve using these Action Steps or are additional steps necessary?"Brainstorm: "What additional strategies could we use with this teacher?"	Supervisor + Coaches
Plan next coaching session with teacher.	"What can be done to make the Action Steps more successful? What Action Steps can be added to enhance teacher implementation?"	Supervisor + Coaches

(i.e., collaboration, supported skill development, constructive feedback, and positive reinforcement), and the structure of supervision sessions parallels the structure of coaching sessions:

1. **Identify the positives.** First, the supervisor and coach discuss what went well during the coaching sessions. This sets the tone for a positive coaching interaction by providing coaches the opportunity to reflect on their specific strengths and for the supervisor to provide positive reinforcement.

2. **Identify areas for improvement.** Areas for improvement may include issues such as teacher resistance to coach's suggestions, difficulty with identifying an appropriate solution for a challenging classroom situation, or coaching style. Often, coaches are able to reflect on the challenges of the coaching session and identify areas for improvement. In some circumstances, the supervisor also may have noticed something of which the coach is not aware, so the supervisor may suggest an area of improvement for collaborative discussion (e.g., "Did you notice the teacher did not seem to join in the discussion about how to improve her use of the PAX cues? I get the sense that if she were more involved in the discussion and generated some ideas of her own, she might be more motivated to use the cues. What do you think?"). In general, it is best to identify just one or two concerns so coaches can address each successfully before moving on to other concerns.

3. **Express empathy and align with the coach.** Keeping in mind the collaborative approach and the large responsibilities of the coach, it is important for supervisors to express genuine empathy and validate the coach's perspective when addressing areas for improvement. This may be done through reflective listening to express understanding (e.g., "It sounds like you get really frustrated when the teacher does not do the Lesson even though she says she will. I can see why you would feel that way."). Normalizing the situation based on the experiences of other coaches (e.g., "I think this is a really common challenge for coaches."), putting the situation into perspective (e.g., "Fortunately, most of your teachers do follow through when they say they will do something."), and instilling hope (e.g., "I think if we work together we might be able to improve her delivery of the Lessons.") can also go a long way in validating a coach's concerns.

4. **Elicit coaches' perspective.** Engaging in dialogue that promotes coach reflection about the situation and their own coaching strategies will promote coach skill development and problem-solving ability. This can be done by asking the coach a series of questions to clarify the problem (e.g., "What do you think needs to be changed so teacher implementation improves?"), identify what has been tried (e.g., "What have you tried that you thought might work in this situation?"), and propose additional solutions (e.g., "In addition to the great strategies you've already tried, do you have any other thoughts about anything else that might work?"). In some cases, this dialogue might identify a way to tweak the strategy to make it more effective. In other cases, this discussion may lead to the brainstorming of other possible strategies on which the coach and supervisor can expand.

5. **Reinforce, reflect, and expand on coaches' suggestions.** Praise is one of the most powerful techniques to influence behavior change and is a core coaching principle. The role of a coach is a demanding one, particularly when coaches are dealing with challenging teachers or classroom situations. Praise from a supervisor can increase coach efficacy and motivation by reinforcing their positive ideas and efforts with teachers. After reinforcing coaches' positive ideas or behaviors, supervisors can validate the coaches' perspective (e.g., "So your thought is if the teacher prepared the Lessons ahead of time, the students would be better behaved during the Lessons. I think you're right about that."). The expansion component brings in a complementary or compatible solution (e.g., "I do think if the teacher prepared the Lessons ahead of time, classroom disruptions would be reduced. Right now it seems that preparing the Lessons on his own is challenging for him. Are there ways we could support him with Lesson preparation until he masters this skill on his own?"). Reinforcement and reflection are also great strategies to use when coaches implement a new skill. Praise for the coach's willingness to practice a new skill paired with asking open-ended questions (e.g., "What do you think was different about talking to the teacher in this way?" or "How did the teacher respond differently when you asked directly but gently about barriers to her playing the Game regularly than when you asked her if she played the Game this week?") reinforce behaviors and also help coaches develop insight about the connection between program components and student behavior.

6. **Provide constructive feedback and explain rationale**. Coaches recognize the value of the coaching and are receptive to supervisor support to improve the effectiveness of their coaching skills. Constructive feedback is best conveyed by identifying strengths, providing a rationale, and then identifying means for improvement. For example, "I really like the way you have a lot of ideas about how to use program components in the classroom. You are very flexible and really willing to give suggestions to teachers in a way that is constructive. It seems you could take your coaching to the next level, and therefore improve teacher skill development, by using strategies that help teachers reflect on their own teaching. For example, this might include asking them to draw conclusions about how their students responded to certain program components, or asking for their opinion about how to modify a particular component so they can generalize it to other school situations outside the classroom."

7. **Generalize**. Another way to make explanations and suggestions meaningful and applicable is to help coaches adapt and generalize strategies they have used with one teacher or classroom situation to another. Generalization of skills across teachers and situations serves as an indication of skill development and an understanding of the program rationale and the principles of behavior change. After discussing a particular problem area or coaching strategy, a supervisor might ask, "How would this work in a different setting? Are there situations in which this wouldn't work?" Discussions about these questions help coaches learn how to apply strategies to a variety of situations.

8. **Summarize and set goals**. Another aspect of the collaborative supervisory role is to review and summarize. Setting goals fits well into the collaborative supervisory model because it is through practice and feedback that coaches become more effective and empowered, and less dependent. It is also important that coaches share with their supervisor real-life experiences of trying out their new skills so any discussions, feedback, and problem solving are meaningful and practical. Ideally, after discussion with the supervisor, coaches identify an area on which they would like to work before the next meeting, and they establish concrete goals for practice (e.g., "We've spent some time talking about offering opportunities for teachers to reflect on student responses to program components. What do you think would be a reasonable and manageable goal for incorporating this into your coaching sessions? Okay, so the next time we meet, I'll ask you how it's been going with regard to increasing teacher reflection."). When checking in about these goals, supervisors should provide lots of positive reinforcement for progress and address any obstacles that appear to have gotten in the way of a coach achieving stated goals. It is particularly important for supervisors to express confidence in coaches' abilities to use skills effectively.

9. **Request feedback**. To demonstrate a collaborative approach further, it may be helpful for supervisors to ask for coach feedback to identify any potential concerns or resistance coaches may experience. For example, "We've been discussing how to improve teacher engagement with the program, and my goal was to work with you to identify one or two strategies that we think might have the best chance at achieving this. Was I helpful in that regard or do we need to discuss this more?"

10. **End on a positive note.** In addition to improving coaching effectiveness, the goal of the supervision meeting is to maintain the collaborative relationship; thus, it is helpful for supervisors to end the session on a positive note. This can be accomplished by providing verbal praise (e.g., "You're doing a great job increasing the number of Games your teachers play. Keep up the good work!"), thanking coaches for their efforts (e.g., "I'm really impressed with how frequently you meet with your teachers. Thank you for all the effort you are putting into your coaching."), providing encouragement (e.g., "I think you came up with some great strategies today and I am hopeful that we'll see improvement with your teachers soon."), and using humor.

Enhanced Supervision

Effective supervision often parallels the developmental process of effective coaching. The relationship between supervisors and coaches is of primary importance. Effective supervisors express interest in coaches as individuals and professionals, empathize with and validate the difficulties of being a coach, use praise and rewards to shape and reinforce high-quality coaching, demonstrate their willingness to get out in the field, and use a collaborative approach to solve teacher implementation challenges.

Occasionally, supervisors may find the supervision process with coaches also parallels the coaching process in terms of challenges. Supervisors can enhance the supervision process by supporting coach implementation of coaching strategies directly, increasing engagement in the supervision process, assisting in improving time management and organizational skills, promoting problem solving as a way to reduce coach stress, and helping coaches optimize their use of behavior change principles and scientific methods. Each of these strategies is discussed here briefly in turn.

Supporting Coach Implementation of Strategies

Coaches are very busy; sometimes, low implementation occurs because of their large caseload. In these instances, it can be helpful for supervisors or other coaches to provide support, such as checking in with teachers who need extensive support. Low implementation of coaching strategies may also occur because teachers demonstrate many areas for improvement and coaches are not sure where to begin. To address this situation, it is helpful for supervisors to review teachers' Action Plan with the coach to prioritize coaching strategies. Simply identifying a starting point can help bring clarity to the next steps coaches should take to support teacher implementation. Sometimes a coach does not understand or does not have the skill to implement a strategy, and this contributes to low implementation. In these situations, it can be helpful to work one-on-one with the coach to discuss the strategy and its rationale, as well as to rehearse the strategy within the context of a role-playing scenario in which the supervisor first models the strategy by playing the role of the coach and then observes the coach play the role of him- or herself, followed by feedback and discussion. To take this one step further, a supervisor may even accompany the coach to the classroom to observe or even demonstrate the coaching strategy when appropriate. In general, extra support coupled with clear expectations, goals, and timelines can help improve low implementation.

Increasing Engagement in the Supervision Process

Coaches who experience low engagement in supervision may not participate during group supervision sessions, may display verbal or nonverbal signs of defensiveness during supervision, or may appear to be ambivalent to suggestions when discussing cases. In these situations, it is important for supervisors first to think about their own contribution to the situation with regard to their relationship with the coach. Supervision involving case discussion may hit a sensitive spot for even those coaches who are most engaged and responsive to constructive feedback, and may be harmful to an already fragile supervisor–coach relationship. Conversation surrounding nonwork topics (e.g., coach's interests, sports) and involvement in fun activities (e.g., holiday parties, sporting events) can enhance the supervisor–coach relationship.

In addition to relationship-building activities, a supervisor can enhance engagement by building an alliance with the coach. Accompanying the coach to classrooms provides a prime opportunity for the supervisor to see firsthand the challenges that coach faces on a daily basis, and can then be incorporated into a discussion about the teamwork necessary to improve the classroom (e.g., "Wow, even with three adults in the classroom, many of those students were not following directions. Would it be helpful if I accompany you to that classroom a few more times so that together we can try out the strategies we think have the best chance for success?"). An emphasis on collaboration can also build the supervisor–coach alliance. In contrast, an expert model of supervision is likely to undermine the self-efficacy of the coach and increase defensiveness and resistance to supervision.

Another factor that deserves attention is whether the dynamics of the group supervision meeting increase the likelihood that a coach views the process as evaluative, aversive, or inefficient. Seating arrangements may help or hinder engagement in the supervision process. For example, sitting interspersed among the coaches may foster coaches' perceptions of a collegial atmosphere, as opposed to supervisors sitting on one side of the table with coaches on the other. Although coach accountability is important, a heavy emphasis on outcomes (e.g., number of Games and Lessons, implementation level of teacher) may have the unintended consequence of increasing coach defensiveness as well as the quantity of coaching rather than the quality of coaching. In contrast, an emphasis on the collaborative and developmental process of designing and testing effective coaching strategies will elicit rich information about the strategies coaches have tried, how they've implemented them, and what works or needs improvement. By conceptualizing every interaction with a teacher as a learning opportunity rather than a pass/fail, coaches may become more engaged in supervision and related activities, such as role-playing challenging situations.

Assisting in Improving Time Management and Organizational Skills

Some coaches may need support and supervision in being more organized and efficient with their time. Working with teachers in schools can be very challenging for coaches as a result of competing demands. It is important for coaches to be organized so they can find things quickly when needed. Time management and organization are key components for coaches to complete their work successfully.

Supervisors can support coaches by using supervision time to discuss time management and organization strategies. In this next section, we share some very specific strategies our coaches have used and have found to be helpful. First, it is important to prioritize tasks. Often, coaches are asked to help with a multitude of tasks (e.g., covering classrooms, being on hand for lunch duty, making copies, dealing with crises). Have coaches make a list of what needs to get completed each day and try not to get pulled into other activities. It also may be helpful to take a few minutes at the beginning and end of each day to plan what was accomplished that day, then make a list for the next day. Second, identify one calendar system or planner that works best for the coach and be consistent. Some people prefer planners to write each appointment/meeting whereas others prefer to use their phone or electronic calendar on e-mail. It can be helpful to write or type everything "to do" in one place, and record it immediately so it is not forgotten. When making a schedule, be sure to estimate as accurately as possible how long each task will take, then block off enough time in the schedule to complete each task. Next, if coaches are working in multiple locations or schools, it may be beneficial to plan meetings back-to-back that are in the same location/school to reduce travel time. In the event that a meeting is canceled or teachers are unavailable, it is helpful to be have work on hand to take advantage of time that has been freed up. Last, we recommend coaches keep folders with them of the teachers with whom they are currently working in case there is unexpected downtime. To stay organized, coaches may prefer to have individual file folders with different colors for each teacher or each school, a larger accordion/expanding file folder, or one large binder with dividers to organize each teacher's information. Similarly, if coaches are working in several different roles, it is critical that they keep their electronic files organized as well. They can create separate folders for each project and have folders within larger folders for each teacher to access documents quickly when needed.

Promoting Problem Solving as a Way to Reduce Coach Stress

Coaching is a challenging job. Coaches deserve a lot of credit for going into classrooms day after day, adapting to the inevitable schedule changes or crises that arise on a weekly basis, and supporting teachers who may not want their support. Conscientious coaches who do not experience job stress likely do not exist. Coach stress can manifest in different ways. For example, a coach may adopt avoidance tactics, such as through procrastination (e.g., "I'll see that challenging teacher tomorrow") or inefficient time management (e.g., scheduling too many appointments in one day so coach–teacher meetings are too short to allow the coach to tackle challenging situations). Another reaction to coach stress might involve devoting an inordinate amount of time to "crisis" situations. This is done with the good intention of helping out those involved in the crisis, but sometimes the stress makes it difficult for a coach to rally additional support from the school administration whose involvement is critical to resolving the crisis. Much time and energy may also be spent worrying or venting about cases, which has the downside of taking away time from productive problem-solving and solution-oriented approaches. In the worst case, coaches question their self-efficacy as a coach or develop a sense of learned helplessness and believe nothing they can do will improve the situation. This can lead to coach burnout. In extremely challenging teacher or classroom situations, it may be true there is little the coach can do, but it is usually not the fault of the coach; rather, there is likely something awry with the fit of the teacher with the specific school, or the teacher may need to consider a career change.

Supervisors can help reduce the interference of coaching stress by recognizing, normalizing, and validating stress for coaches, particularly stress related directly to dealing with challenging coaching situations. Checking in about a coach's self-care and stress reduction strategies can help supervisors assess stress levels and facilitate discussion about how to manage stress. Allowing some time for emotional venting about challenging professional situations may be helpful in terms of understanding and validating the scope of the problem, but it is important for supervisors to keep sight of the ultimate goal of applying a systematic problem-solving method to reduce stress by enhancing coach self-efficacy in resolving challenging coaching situations. The process of problem solving within the context of an Action Plan for the teacher includes identifying the problem, brainstorming possible solutions, evaluating the costs and benefits of each potential solution, and selecting one or more strategies to try. During this process, it can be helpful for the supervisor to model identification of a variety of solutions without evaluating them. Just getting a number of solutions down on paper can help coaches see there is hope in these situations. In addition, systematic problem solving allows supervisors to use insight-building approaches to help coaches evaluate the effectiveness of the strategies they are currently using or those that supervisors notice the coach gravitates (e.g., procrastination, trying to help everyone on everyone else's schedule).

Helping Coaches Optimize Their Use of Behavior Change Principles and Scientific Methods

Many clinical psychologists receive direct training in principles of behavior change and scientific methods, but this is not necessarily the case for other professionals who may serve as coaches, such as social workers, counselors, or teachers. As discussed throughout this manual, coaching can be enhanced through the regular application and generalization of these principles as well the use of data and hypothesis testing. Therefore, it is important for supervisors to expose coaches to information regarding these principles and methods, and there are a number of ways to do so.

One strategy is to provide didactics about major principles of behavior change (e.g., positive and negative reinforcement, differential reinforcement, antecedent management, goal setting), many of which are core features of the program. Reading or discussing scientific research on the effectiveness of behavior change principles may also be helpful in increasing coach confidence in each strategy's effectiveness and may help coaches develop the expectation that behavior can change, and they have the tools to facilitate teacher and student behavior change.

Although coaches focus much of their efforts on helping teachers apply behavior change principles to students, it is important to have discussions regarding the specific application of these principles to teachers to identify how these principles are related to implementation. For example, with a teacher who often misplaces supplies, what stimulus or antecedent control strategies could be used to increase the likelihood she will play the Game when the coach is not present? How might repeated pleasant chats with a low-implementing teacher reinforce low implementation inadvertently? Can the reinforcement contingencies be changed to shape greater implementation? What is the rationale for having a teacher participate actively in setting implementation goals? Discussions such as these can improve the efficiency of supervision because, rather than having case discussions that are focused on individual teachers (e.g., "What can be done to improve Ms. McDonald's use of the Game?"), supervision might entail discussion focused on the principles of behavior change (e.g., "How is reinforcement operating for Ms. McDonald?").

It can be disheartening for coaches to implement what should be an effective coaching strategy with teachers and not see any improvement the following week. Adopting language reflecting scientific values (e.g., hypothesis testing) may help coaches think about how to use the data they collect to develop and test hypotheses within the context of an iterative process and the teacher's Action Plan. Emphasizing a data-driven hypothesis testing approach to coaching may help reduce the stress coaches sometimes feel about selecting the "right" strategy and having it "work" immediately, and, more important, may improve the effectiveness of coaching.

Weaving in the language of other psychological principles can help alert coaches to other factors or biases operating in a given situation. For example, with low-implementing teachers, coaches might have a tendency to make the "fundamental attribution error" by assuming these teachers have some innate characteristics (e.g., laziness, meanness) that prevent them from implementing the program. These personality assumptions are confirmed inadvertently when the "Hawthorne effect" occurs in the context of rubric observations during which teachers demonstrate their skills (e.g., the teacher is lazy because he played the Game during the rubric but won't play otherwise). By highlighting the normal tendency of all humans to make the fundamental attribution error and the nature of the Hawthorne effect, supervisors can expand the discussion beyond presumed personality characteristics to include consideration of the environmental contingencies that operate for these teachers. This approach encourages a productive hypothesis testing approach to improving teacher implementation.

Taken together, these strategies can promote effective supervision that can support effective coaching. Observation and feedback, other key elements related to the sustainability of effective coaching, are discussed next.

Observation and Feedback

Logistics sometimes preclude videotaping the coaching sessions with teachers, although this would be ideal so these videos could be reviewed during weekly meetings. Videotapes may provide the opportunity for others to offer their interpretations of the nuances of the coach–teacher interactions, thereby lending insight to how to address a challenging situation. As mentioned, in many cases, it is helpful for supervisors to conduct field visits to observe teacher implementation and provide a better understanding of teacher strengths, challenges, classroom context, coach–teacher interactions, and coach implementation of Action Steps.

To provide a structure for the observation, supervisors use the Coach Observation Form (Appendix EE). The goal of this form is not only to capture a snapshot of the coaching session, but also to provide coaches with feedback about their professional strengths and areas for continued development (Neufeld & Roper, 2003).

In the Coaching Strategies section at the top of the form, supervisors check off which strategies the coach used. For strategies that were used by the coach, the supervisor also provides a qualitative rating from 1 point (Needs Improvement) to 4 points (Advanced). Using a coding manual (Quality Coaching Code Descriptions [Appendix FF]), the supervisor can indicate which components of each strategy the coach implemented. For example:

1. Modeled techniques.
   - Provided rationale and brief highlights of skill before modeling.
   - Demonstrated skill.
   - Discussed skill components after modeling.
   - Discussed student response to modeled technique.
2. Engaged teacher in modeled element.
   - Asked teacher to share an example.
   - Requested teacher to practice skills students are learning (e.g., Turtle Technique).
   - Encouraged teacher participation in prize.
   - Praised teacher.

In the General Coaching Style and Behavior section at the bottom of the form, supervisors again indicate coaching behaviors observed (e.g., warm tone of voice, reflected/praised teacher's feedback and suggestions) and provide qualitative ratings ranging from 1 point (Needs Improvement) to 4 points (Advanced). Following observations, feedback can be provided to the coach (as discussed earlier in the "Supervision" section in this chapter), and additional skill rehearsal and feedback may occur. Note that expectations about a coach's use of certain coaching strategies may need to be adjusted depending on the situation, whereas coaching style and behaviors are generally applicable across coaching sessions. For example, when immediacy of feedback to teachers requires prioritization, it may be that the coach will only be able to catch the teacher for a few minutes. Given time constraints, it might be difficult for coaches to model or set goals with teachers; therefore, coaches might rely on a more direct and instructive approach than they might if given more time. However, although strategies and style might be modified, one would still expect that those implemented by the coaches be delivered with a high level of quality.

After observation, it is helpful for supervisors to provide constructive feedback to coaches in a timely manner. Effective supervisors elicit the coach's perspective during the feedback session and typically follow a structure similar to that used during individual supervision (i.e., identifying positives, noting areas for improvement, expressing empathy, reinforcing and expanding on coach suggestions, providing feedback and rationale, generalizing, setting goals, requesting feedback, and ending on a positive note; see the "Individual Supervision" section earlier in this chapter).

Because the coach is an integral part of the coaching process, successful implementation of coaching depends on the selection of coaches who have high-quality interpersonal skills as well as the ability to develop technical expertise in the program. Training, ongoing supervision, and observation/feedback of coaches provide a parallel process to the support role coaches provide for teachers, thereby increasing the likelihood of successful implementation of the program.

Chapter 6 Reflection Questions

- What are some desirable personality characteristics of coaches?

- Why is it important for coaches to have supervision?

- What are three things on the agenda for group supervision of coaches?

- Why do you think the supervisory principles mirror the core coaching principles (collaboration, supported skill development, constructive feedback, and positive reinforcement)? How would this be beneficial?

- How can videotaping be helpful in supervision?

Conclusion
Moving Forward

Coaching teachers is a challenging yet invigorating task. Being an effective coach requires persistence, commitment, and flexibility. As you prepare for your role as a coach, you have already taken the important step of reading this book to learn more from the rich experiences of the coaches in Baltimore City who have led the way with developing strategies to support teacher proficiency effectively with PATHS to PAX GBG. You are aware that if we are to bring important change that improves the outcomes of the students in our school buildings, prevention and evidence-based interventions are needed. As a coach you will encounter barriers to the effective implementation of evidence-based interventions in the schools.

This book provides some suggestions and ideas for how to overcome many of the barriers to implementing these interventions effectively through ongoing coaching. In addition to paying close attention to establishing positive coach–teacher relationships, our coaches use many strategies that reflect core principles of behavior change, such as modeling, reinforcement, and performance feedback (Chapter 2). These coaching strategies have been shown to impact the implementation of interventions in classrooms. Using modeling, reinforcement, and performance feedback with the teachers you hope to support will increase positive outcomes for their students. Our model is a flexible approach that promotes coach expertise; indeed, the Baltimore coaches used their talent, creativity, and experience to enhance the strategic application of these principles across a variety of teachers, classrooms, administrators, and school settings. As described in our Universal Coaching Model (Chapter 3), these strategies are intended to have high impact and are focused on immediate success and reinforcement of teacher skill proficiency. Systematic data collection (Chapter 3) allows coaches to monitor and assess teacher skill and performance challenges (Chapter 3). The challenges encountered while coaching teachers have required and inspired a "never give up" approach to coaching that has informed our data-driven Indicated Coaching Model (Chapter 4) and that continues to motivate our entire team to develop collaboratively novel solutions to barriers that arise and interfere with program delivery (Chapter 5). We have shared many lessons learned. We hope that you find our candid reveal of the challenges we faced and methods for overcoming these difficulties useful and perhaps inspiring. As the lessons learned that we share (Chapter 5) illustrate, there is still room for refinement and innovation of the coaching model, yet it is our hope the strategies in this book as well as the case formulation approach that guides our coaching approach will be beneficial to other coaches in their support of teacher implementation of school-based interventions.

We learned a great deal from our teachers, schools, and students as we coached evidence-based interventions in the Baltimore City schools. If possible, consult and process your experiences with others who offer coaching to teachers. Having conversations can stimulate innovation and important ideas. Our team has taught us that innovation and problem solving are very important toward helping teachers become proficient in new skills. As you move forward with your work as a coach, we suggest you, too, learn and grow from the opportunities you face in the classroom.

Appendix: Forms

Forms included here are also available on the website of *Oxford Clinical Psychology*, where you can print, save, and complete them electronically. You may access them at www.oxfordclinicalpsych.com/coachingteachers. The following forms are contained in this Appendix:

Good Behavior Game Modeling Checklist

Name: _____   School: _____

Coach: _____   Date: _____

Instructions: Use this checklist to take notes as you watch a PAX Good Behavior Game.

Before the Game

____ Used PAX Quiet (harmonica and signal) to get the students' attention *before* to starting the Game.

____ Told students how long the Game would be played. Length of Game: _____

____ Reviewed the directions for the activity to be completed during the Game.

____ Reviewed for which Spleems and/or PAX behaviors the teacher would be looking during the Game.

____ Set the timer in front of the students and announced the start of the Game.

During the Game

____ Referred to the time remaining (or lapsed) at some point during the Game.

____ Made students aware that Spleems were being counted.

____ Responded to Spleems unemotionally.

____ Was able to observe and track all Spleems during the Game.

____ Announced the Game was over as soon as the timer went off.

After the Game

____ Reviewed the number of Spleems each team received.

____ Made students aware of which teams won the Game.

____ Reviewed which behaviors caused the Spleems to be counted, then guided the teams on what to work on for the next time the Game is played.

Granny's Wacky Prize

____ Chose a random prize from the prize box.

____ Showed enthusiasm for the winning teams.

____ Explained the expectations for the prize clearly.

____ Used the timer to time the prize. Length of prize: _____

____ Used PAX Quiet to get students' attention when the prize was complete.

Tootle Note

[1]**PAX *Tootle* Note**

Dear

_____

_____

_____

_____

_____

_____

TOOTLE WRITER   DATE

What a PAX Leader!

Thanks for making Spleems go down.

[1]This Tootle Note entitles you to recognition, praise, and honor for helping *make* our school a wonderful place today.

Coach–Teacher Collaborative Planning Sheet

Teacher _____ School _____ Grade _____ Date _____

Lesson Title _____ Lesson # _____

Lesson Date _____ Start Time _____ Length of Lesson* _____

*Consider time allotted when thinking of how to pace the Lesson.

During the Lesson

Classroom Teacher's Role: _____

PATHS to PAX Coach's Role: _____

Major Lesson Concept(s)

_____
_____
_____
_____

Tasks to Complete before the Lesson

_____
_____
_____
_____
_____
_____

Materials Needed

_____
_____
_____
_____
_____

After the Lesson: Self-Checks

☐ I stated the objective clearly.

☐ I related the Lesson to other learning.

☐ I was able to stay on topic; the Lesson content was appropriate and related throughout the entire Lesson.

☐ I assessed students' understanding throughout the Lesson.

☐ My pacing was good throughout the Lesson; I was able to stick to the time allotted.

☐ My affect and energy were genuine and appropriate throughout the Lesson.

You have been Tootled!

Tootles & Tootle Boards!

*Tootles help to create a positive classroom environment!

Please Remember to:

- *Write Tootles to your students* and hang a few on your Tootle Board
- *Prompt students* to write Tootles to other students (e.g., during "Tootle time" as students finish their work, as students enter the classroom in the morning or after lunch) and hang a few on your Tootle Board
- *Update your Tootle Board.* At the end of the week or biweekly, students can take Tootles home. New Tootles can be written and hung at the start of each week.
- *Review all Tootles* before they are hung on the Tootle Board. Return to sender if Tootles are inappropriate.

Other Things to Remember:

- *Younger children* can draw pictures on their Tootles or dictate to the teacher what they want written on the Tootle. Sentence starters and finishers can also be used (e.g., "You are [nice/helpful/a good friend]").
- *Prompt older children* to write Tootles that focus on other students' traits and characteristics (e.g., respectful, intelligent). This also helps build their vocabulary.

Tootle Board Checklist

Teacher:_____ School:_____ Grade:_____

Coach:_____ Date:_____

During a brief classroom visit today, the following elements of the Tootle Board were observed:

☐ Tootle Board is hung in the classroom.

_____

☐ Current (less than 2 weeks old) Tootles written *to students from students* are posted on the Tootle Board.

_____

☐ Current (less than 2 weeks old) Tootles written *to students from adults* are posted on the Tootle Board.

_____

☐ Current full-page Kid of the Day Tootle is posted in the classroom.
Remember to send a copy of the full-page Tootle home with the Kid of the Day!

_____

Please contact your coach if you have any questions about Tootle boards ☺.

Coach Information (Name, email, phone)

APPENDIX F

Lesson Pacing Guide

Week	Pre-Kindergarten and Kindergarten	First Grade	Second Grade	Third and Fourth Grade	Fifth Grade
Oct 18–22	Prep 1: Prize Box Prep 2: PAX Stix L1: Classroom Vision L2: PAX Quiet and Hands	Prep 1: Prize Box Prep 2: PAX Stix L1: Classroom Vision L2: PAX Cues	Prep 1: Prize Box Prep 2: PAX Stix L1: Classroom Vision L2: PAX Cues	Prep 1: Prize Box Prep 2: PAX Stix L1: Classroom Vision L2: PAX Cues	Prep 1: Prize Box Prep 2: PAX Stix L1: Classroom Vision L2: PAX Cues
Oct 25–29	L3: Introducing the Path to PAX (P2P) Animals L4: PAX Leader and PAX Promise	L3: Beat the Timer L4: P2P Readiness	L3: Beat the Timer Prep 3: Baseline L4: Kid of the Day (Tooling)	L3: Beat the Timer Prep 3: Baseline L4: Kid of the Day (Tooling)	L3: Beat the Timer Prep 3: Baseline L4: Kid of the Day (Tooling)
Nov 1–5	L5: P2P Kid of the Day L6: PAX Voices Prep 3: Baseline	L5: Are You a PAX Leader? Prep 3: Baseline L6: Kid of the Day (Tooling)	L5: Are You a PAX Leader? Prep 4: Teams L6: Intro to the Game	L5: Are You a PAX Leader? L6: The Golden Rule Prep 4: Teams	L5: Are You a PAX Leader? L6: The Golden Rule Prep 4: Teams
Nov 8–12	L7: Tootles I L8: Beat the Timer Prep 4: Teams	L7: Activities on Tooling Prep 4: Teams L8: Intro to the Game	Prep 5: Review of P2P Concepts Prep 6: Go PAX, Stop Spleems Cues L7: Intro to Feelings L8: Feeling Happy, Sad, and Private	L7: Intro to the Game Prep 5: Go PAX, Stop Spleems Cues L8: Cooperative Learning Skills	L7: Intro to the Game Prep 5: Go PAX, Stop Spleems Cues L8: Cooperative Learning Skills

Week	Pre-Kindergarten and Kindergarten	First Grade	Second Grade	Third and Fourth Grade	Fifth Grade
Nov 15–19	L9: We All Have Feelings L10: Intro to the Game Prep 5: Go PAX, Stop Spleems Cues	Prep 5: Go PAX, Stop Spleems Cues L9: Intro to Feelings L10: Feeling Happy, Sad, and Private	L9: Home Tootles L10: Self-Control I (Steps for Calming Down)	L9: Listening to Others L10: Home Tootles	L9: Feelings Review L10: Home Tootles
Nov 22–24	L11: Home Tootles	L11: Home Tootles	L11: Self-Control II (Learning Self-Control) L12: Peer Tootles	L11: Self-Control 1 (Control Signals Poster) L12: Peer Tootles	L11: Peer Tootles
Nov 29–Dec 3	L12: Feeling Happy L13: Twiggle Makes Friends Prep 6: Secret Game	L12: Feeling Fine, Excited, and Tired L13: Peer Tootles	L13: Control Signals I (Anger Management) Prep 7: Secret Game L14: Control Signals II (Using the Control Signals Poster)	L13: Self-Control 2 (Solving Problems in Groups) L14: Self-Control 3 (Thinking Ahead) Prep 6: Secret Game	L12: Control Signals Poster, Part 1 L13: Control Signals Poster, Part 2
Dec 6–10	L14: Feeling Sad L15: Tootles II	L14: Feeling Scared or Afraid, and Safe Prep 6: Secret Game	L15: Feeling Fine, Excited, and Tired L16: Feeling Scared or Afraid, and Safe	Prep 7: Creating a Problem Box L15: Problem-Solving Meeting 1 L16: PAX Roles	L14: Recognizing and Controlling Anger, Part 1 L15: Recognizing and Controlling Anger, Part 2 Prep 6: Secret Game
Dec 13–17	L16: Mad or Angry I L17: Peer Tootles	L15: Feeling Mad I L16: Feeling Mad II	L17: PAX Roles L18: Feeling Mad or Angry I	L17: Intro to Feelings L18: Recognizing and Controlling Anger	L16: P2P Feelings Dictionary *L17: My Own Feelings Story
Dec 20–23	L18: Feeling Scared or Afraid	L17: P2P Review Lesson	L19: Feeling Mad or Angry II (Baxter and His Temper)	L19: Feeling Calm or Relaxed and Tense	L18: PAX Roles
Dec 24–Jan 2	NO LESSONS ~ Winter Break ☺				

Week	Pre-Kindergarten and Kindergarten	First Grade	Second Grade	Third and Fourth Grade	Fifth Grade
Jan 3–7	L19: My Feelings L20: Mad or Angry II	L18: PAX Roles L19: Self-Control I (Anger Management)	L20: P2P Review Lesson Prep 8: Creating a Problem Box L21: Problem-Solving Meeting I	L20: Feeling Guilty L21: Feeling Jealous	L19: Treasure Hunt: Problem-Solving Review, Part 1 L20: Treasure Hunt: Problem-Solving Review, Part 2
Jan 10–14	L21: Turtle Story Part I L22: Turtle Story, Part II	L20: Self-Control II (Anger Management) L21: Self-Control III (Baxter and His Temper)	L22: Problem-Solving Meeting II (School Transitions) L23: Feeling Shy and Lonely	L22: P2P Feelings Dictionary *L23: My Own Feelings Story	L21: Identifying Problems and Feelings L22: Identifying Solutions
Jan 18–21	*23: Turtle Story Review L24: Turtle Technique Review	L22: Feeling Calm or Relaxed L23: Control Signals I	L24: Making Friends (Baxter Makes a New Friend) L25: Listening to Others	L24: Feelings Intensity	L23: Consequences: What Might Happen Next?
Jan 26–28	L25: Appropriate Turtles I	L24: Problem Discussion, Angry Arthur Prep 7: Creating a Problem Box	L26: Fair-Play Rules L27: Decision Wheel	L25: Best Friends, Part 1 L26: Best Friends, Part 2	L24: Trying Out Your Plan (Refusal Skills), Part 1 L25: Trying Out Your Plan (Refusal Skills), Part 2
Jan 31–Feb 4	L26: Appropriate Turtles II *L27: Appropriate Turtles Extension Activity	L25: Problem-Solving Meeting I L26: Problem-Solving Meeting II	L28: Problem-Solving Meeting III (Friendship/Recess Problems) L29: Feeling Jealous and Content or Satisfied	L27: Best Friends, Part 3 L28: Best Friends, Part 4	L26: Making a Good Plan L27: Trying Your Plan and Evaluating What Happens Next
Feb 7–11	L28: Calm and Relaxed L29: Sharing and Caring I	L27: Feeling Surprised L28: Problem Solving, Privacy, and Telling Your Feelings	L30: Different Points of View L31: Surprised, Expect; Anticipating Consequences	L29: Best Friends, Part 5 (Making Up) L30: Intro to Manners	L28: Trying Again: Obstacles, Part 1 L29: Trying Again: Obstacles, Part 2
Feb 14–18	L30: Sharing and Caring II L31: Twiggle's Special Day	L29: We Are Best Friends L30: What Is a Friend?	L32: Accident, On Purpose L33: Feeling Proud	L31: Playing by the Rules L32: Avoiding Gossip	L30: Solving Problems (Dear Problem Solvers) L31: Making New Friends

Week	Pre-Kindergarten and Kindergarten	First Grade	Second Grade	Third and Fourth Grade	Fifth Grade
Feb 22–25	L32: Advanced Tootles / *L33: "Turtle" Review Activity I	L31: Feeling Lonely / L32: Making Friends	L34: Feeling Guilty / L35: Feeling Embarrassed or Humiliated	L33: We Are All Unique / L34: Respecting Others	L32: Joining Other Kids, Part 1 / L33: Joining Other Kids, Part 2
Feb 28–March 4	L34: Feelings Review / L35: Making Choices	L33: Feeling Shy / L34: Feeling Embarrassed	L36: P2P Review Lesson / L37: Baxter's Challenge	L35: Problem Solving, Test Taking	L34: Problem Solving, Test Taking
March 7–11	L36: Solving Problems / L37: Solving Problems with Friends, Part 1	L35: P2P Review Lesson / L36: Accident, On Purpose	L38: Making Up with Friends / L39: Feeling Frustrated	NO LESSONS ~ Maryland School Assessment Testing	
March 14–18	L38: Solving Problems with Friends, Part 2 / *L39: "Turtle" Review Activity II	L37: Manners I / *L38: Manners II	L40: Being a Good Winner / L41: Being a Good Loser		
March 21–25	L40: Comfortable/Uncomfortable / L41: Different Types of Feelings	*L39: Manners III / L40: Fair-Play Rules	L42: Feeling Disappointed and Hopeful	L36: Problem ID 1 / L37: Problem ID 2 (Confident vs. Confused)	L35: The Eagles and The Playoffs, Part 1 / L36: The Eagles and The Playoffs, Part 2
March 28–April 1	L42: Frustrated / L43: Excited	L41: Problem Solving, Test Taking	L43: Problem Solving, Test Taking	L38: Problem ID 3 (Why Things Happen) / L39: Goals	NO LESSONS ~ MSA Science Testing
April 4–8	*L44: "Turtle" Review Activity III / L45: Proud	NO LESSONS ~ Stanford 10 Testing		40: Setting Positive Goals / L41: Reaching Our Goals	L37: The Eagles and The Playoffs, Part 3 / L38: The Eagles and The Playoffs ("I" Messages)

Week	Pre-Kindergarten and Kindergarten	First Grade	Second Grade	Third and Fourth Grade	Fifth Grade
April 11–15	L46: Tired	L42: Listening to Others L43: Sharing	L44: Feeling Greedy or Selfish and Generous L45: Fair/Not Fair I	L42: Generating Solutions 1	L39: Dealing with Teasing, Part 1 L40: Dealing with Teasing, Part 2
April 18–25	NO LESSONS ~ Spring Break ☺				
April 27–29	Choose two lessons to revisit and complete supplemental or extension activities.	L44: Decision Wheel L45: Feeling Curious or Interested, Bored	L46: Fair/Not Fair II L47: Feeling Generous and Giving	L43: Generating Solutions 2	L41: Managing Our Feelings, Part 1 L42: Managing Our Feelings, Part 2
May 2–6	Choose two lessons to revisit and complete supplemental or extension activities.	L46: Feeling Proud and Ashamed L47: Feeling Frustrated	L48: Feeling Worried L49: Feeling Malicious and Kind	L44: Generating Solutions 3 (Thinking Takes Time) L45: Coping with Difficult Problems	L43: Forgiving or Resentful L44: Feeling Rejected or Excluded
May 9–13	Choose two lessons to revisit and complete supplemental or extension activities.	L48: Feeling Disappointed and Hopeful L49: Problem Discussion on Frustrated or Disappointed	L50: Teasing I L51: Teasing II	L46: Being Responsible *L47: Being Responsible and Creating Change (Biography of Aung San Suu Kyi)	L45: Stereotypes and Discrimination, Part 1 L46: Stereotypes and Discrimination, Part 2
May 16–20	L47: P2P Review L48: Saying Goodbye	L50: P2P Review Lesson	L52: P2P Review Lesson	L48: Social Responsibility (A Class Project to Improve the School)	L47: Being Responsible: A Class Project of Commemoration

Kid of the Day

*The Kid of the Day procedure helps to create a positive classroom environment!

Tips for Kid of the Day

- Have a Kid of the Day *every day*.
- Write the *Kid of the Day Tootle* (give one copy to the Kid of the Day and hang the other copy in the classroom for the day).
- Have the Kid of the Day wear a *Kid of the Day identifier* (e.g., hat, beads, button).
- Write the name or hang a picture of the Kid of the Day on the *Kid of the Day poster (as pictured here)*.

Other Things to Remember

- Choose the Kid of the Day *randomly* by using the **"had a turn/have not had a turn" cups** (these should be separate cups with a set of sticks other than the PAX Stix).
- Every child in the class should have a turn as the Kid of the Day before any child is Kid of the Day for the second time.
- *Don't take the Kid of the Day honor away* from a child (if a child is misbehaving, you may remove identifier until the child can act like a PAX leader again).
- *Prompt the Kid of the Day* to act as a PAX leader (e.g., "Is that what a PAX leader would do? As the Kid of the Day, I need you to be my number one PAX leader!").

Kid of the Day Guidelines

Six Questions to Ask Yourself ...

1. Do I have a Kid of the Day *every day*?

2. Do I have a *system* in place for choosing the Kid of the Day *randomly* (*not based on behavior*)?
   - Kid of the Day status is not taken away from a student as a result of behavior (i.e., used as a punishment).

3. Does my Kid of the Day wear an *identifier* (e.g., hat, sash, sticker)?

4. Is my Kid of the Day *identified* somewhere in the classroom (e.g., poster, picture display)?

5. Is my Kid of the Day given *special roles* throughout the day (e.g., line leader, messenger, helper for the PATHS to PAX Lesson)?

6. Do I complete the full-page written Tootle for my Kid of the Day?
   - Is the full-page Tootle *posted* in the classroom?
   - Is a copy of the full-page Tootle *sent home*?

A teacher who is fully implementing the Kid of the Day would answer YES to all of the above questions. Please contact your coach if you have any questions.

Coach Information (Name, email, phone)

Ten Easy Steps for Playing a Successful Game

1. Use PAX Quiet (harmonica and signal) to get students' attention. (*Tip*: Do not continue until all students have responded to the signal.)

2. Tell the students that all of you will be playing the Game for ___ minutes.

3. Review the activity directions and specific Spleems to which they might be prone during that time. (*Tip*: Also review common Spleems you have noticed lately in your classroom.)

4. Set the timer and announce the Game has begun.

5. Mark Spleems accurately. Your focus should be on their behaviors. *Do not* ignore any Spleem! Respond to each Spleem unemotionally, such as "Red team, that was a Spleem." (*Tip*: Do not call out any individual. Address the team as a whole.)

6. Announce the Game has ended as soon as the timer rings. (*Tip*: Use PAX Quiet to get students' attention.)

7. Review the team wins. At this time, also review the Spleems you marked during the game. (For example, you might say, "Most of the Spleems were for calling out without raising your hand. A few were for not starting the assignment right away." These types of statements help students realize exactly which Spleems you are marking so they can fix that negative behavior.)

8. Choose a random prize from the prize box. Show enthusiasm for the winning teams! (*Tip*: Prizes should be short and something the students perceive as fun.)

9. Set the timer for the prize. (*Tip*: Prizes usually last no more than 1 minute.)

10. Use PAX Quiet to get students' attention when the prize is completed. (*Tip*: If all students do not respond to the signal, discuss removing that particular prize from the prize box until they show they can follow signals.)

Remember: Keep it positive!! Everyone (**teacher & students**) should be having fun !!

APPENDIX J

My Most Wonderful School

My Most Wonderful School

Name: _____

Date: _____

The Greatest Classroom

Name: _____   Date: _____

The Greatest Classroom

_____

_____

_____

_____

_____

 Guidelines for Conducting
a High-Quality Lesson

1. Start the Lesson by stating the objective so students are ready for the content that will be covered.

2. Make a connection between the current Lesson and previous Lessons of a similar theme.

3. Read your audience. Children's affect and behavior reflect their level of engagement. If you maintain an appropriate pace, your students will stay engaged throughout the Lessons.
   - Lessons should not take longer than 20 minutes.
   - You can always cut down the number of examples you provide or responses you take from students to save time.

4. Use your emotional expressions and the tone of your voice to your advantage during the Lesson. Remaining positive and animated even on difficult days will help your students to remain engaged and to have a positive experience during the Lesson.
   - Remember that you are a model for the students.
   - The Lessons provide an opportunity for classroom behavior to shift.

5. Make connections between the Lesson topic and the experiences of you and your students (both within and outside the classroom).
   - You can always change the examples provided in the Lesson to ones you think are most relevant to your students.
   - Use the techniques presented through the Lessons to work out classroom problems (e.g., peer conflicts, challenges during the Game).

6. Don't forget to extend the Lesson to other parts of the day by integrating it with literature or making connections during other subjects such as social studies.

Good Behavior Game Implementation Rubric

Program Component Being Rated	Rating				
	4	3	2	1	0
Preparing Students for the Game	*All* of the following: • Teacher gets the children's attention before starting the Game by using PAX Quiet with harmonica. • Teacher gives clear and concise directions for the activity, including specific behaviors (e.g., please stop working on your writing project, put your essay in your folder and put your folder in your desk) the children will be completing during the Game. • Teacher identifies or references the Spleems that will be counted during the Game. • Teacher sets the timer in full view of children and announces they will be playing the Game for ____ minutes. • Teacher announces, "The Game starts now," or in some other way makes it clear to students the Game has started (e.g., the sound of the harmonica signals the start of the Game).	*Four* of the following: • Teacher gets the children's attention before starting the Game by using PAX Quiet with harmonica. • Teacher gives clear and concise directions for the activity, including specific behaviors (e.g., please stop working on your writing project, put your essay in your folder and put your folder in your desk) the children will be completing during the Game. • Teacher identifies or references the Spleems that will be counted during the Game. • Teacher sets the timer in full view of children and announces they will be playing the Game for ____ minutes. • Teacher announces, "The Game starts now," or in some other way makes it clear to students the Game has started (e.g., the sound of the harmonica signals the start of the Game).	*Three* of the following: • Teacher gets the children's attention before starting the Game by using PAX Quiet with harmonica. • Teacher gives clear and concise directions for the activity, including specific behaviors (e.g., please stop working on your writing project, put your essay in your folder and put your folder in your desk) the children will be completing during the Game. • Teacher identifies or references the Spleems that will be counted during the Game. • Teacher sets the timer in full view of children and announces they will be playing the Game for ____ minutes. • Teacher announces, "The Game starts now," or in some other way makes it clear to students the Game has started (e.g., the sound of the harmonica signals the start of the Game).	*Less than three* of the following: • Teacher gets the children's attention before starting the Game by using PAX Quiet with harmonica. • Teacher gives clear and concise directions for the activity, including specific behaviors (e.g., please stop working on your writing project, put your essay in your folder and put your folder in your desk) the children will be completing during the Game. • Teacher identifies or references the Spleems that will be counted during the Game. • Teacher sets the timer in full view of children and announces they will be playing the Game for ____ minutes. • Teacher announces, "The Game starts now," or in some other way makes it clear to students the Game has started (e.g., the sound of the harmonica signals the start of the Game).	Teacher does not attempt to prepare the students for the Game. or Teacher does not play the Game during the scheduled observation.

Program Component Being Rated	Rating				
	4	3	2	1	0
Choice of Activity	Teacher has chosen an appropriate activity for the students to complete while playing the Game **All of the following:** • Teacher is able to be an observer (does not need to interact with students) • Teacher displays appropriate skill level—one that is not too easy or to difficult for students. • Teacher ties the educational purpose to the curriculum (the Game is not just busywork).	Teacher has chosen an appropriate activity for the students to complete while playing the Game **Two of the following:** • Teacher is able to be an observer (does not need to interact with students) • Teacher displays appropriate skill level—one that is not too easy or to difficult for students. • Teacher ties the educational purpose to the curriculum (the Game is not just busywork).	Teacher has chosen an appropriate activity for the students to complete while playing the Game **One of the following:** • Teacher is able to be an observer (does not need to interact with students) • Teacher displays appropriate skill level—one that is not too easy or to difficult for students. • Teacher ties the educational purpose to the curriculum (the Game is not just busywork).	Teacher has chosen an appropriate activity for the students to complete while playing the Game **None of the following:** • Teacher is able to be an observer (does not need to interact with students) • Teacher displays appropriate skill level—one that is not too easy or to difficult for students. • Teacher ties the educational purpose to the curriculum (the Game is not just busywork).	Teacher choose an inappropriate activity. or Teacher does not choose an activity chosen; students are not given a task to complete while playing the Game. or Teacher does not play the Game during the scheduled observation.
Timing the Game A phone timer or stopwatch is appropriate to use. A watch or clock on the wall needs to have a countdown mechanism. With phone timers it is usually clear teachers are setting the timer at the beginning of the Game, or you may hear the timer buzz at the end of the Game, letting you know teachers set the timer on their phone.	Timer is used to time the Game. **And both of the following:** • Timer is placed in a visible/ auditory location and teacher acknowledges when Game time has ended (e.g., "The timer went off and that is the end of our Game."). • Time is referred to (e.g., "There are 3 minutes left in the Game.") at least one time for a 5-minute (or less) Game and at least two times for Games lasting longer than 5 minutes.	Timer is used to time the Game. **And one of the following:** • Timer is placed in a visible/ auditory location and teacher acknowledges when Game time has ended (e.g., "The timer went off and that is the end of our Game."). • Time is referred to (e.g., "There are 3 minutes left in the Game.") at least one time for a 5-minute (or less) Game and at least two times for Games lasting longer than 5 minutes.	Timer is used to time the Game. **And neither of the following:** • Timer is placed in a visible/ auditory location and teacher acknowledges when Game time has ended (e.g., "The timer went off and that is the end of our Game."). • Time is referred to (e.g., "There are 3 minutes left in the Game.") at least one time for a 5-minute (or less) Game and at least two times for Games lasting longer than 5 minutes.	Teacher attempts to use the timer but does not follow through (e.g., sets the timer but never acknowledges when it goes off).	No timer is used or an unreliable timing device is used. or Teacher does not play the Game during the scheduled observation.

Program Component Being Rated	Rating				
	4	**3**	**2**	**1**	**0**
Teams Teams are rated for classroom observations only, *not when coding a videotape of the* classroom.	*All* of the following: • Students are all on a team (1–2 may be on own team temporarily) • Teams appear balanced, with an equal number of shy and aggressive children (similar number of Spleems observed on each team) • Appropriate number of teams for the class size (e.g., a class size of 25 should have 4–5 teams) • Teams are identified with team name and students know their team. *Teams of individual students should not be identified by the student's name.*	*Three* of the following: • Students are all on a team (1–2 may be on own team temporarily) • Teams appear balanced, with an equal number of shy and aggressive children (similar number of Spleems observed on each team) • Appropriate number of teams for the class size (e.g., a class size of 25 should have 4–5 teams) • Teams are identified with team name and students know their team. *Teams of individual students should not be identified by the student's name.*	*Two* of the following: • Students are all on a team (1–2 may be on own team temporarily) • Teams appear balanced, with an equal number of shy and aggressive children (similar number of Spleems observed on each team) • Appropriate number of teams for the class size (e.g., a class size of 25 should have 4–5 teams) • Teams are identified with team name and students know their team. *Teams of individual students should not be identified by the student's name.*	*Less than two* of the following: • Students are all on a team (1–2 may be on own team temporarily) • Teams appear balanced, with an equal number of shy and aggressive children (similar number of Spleems observed on each team) • Appropriate number of teams for the class size (e.g., a class size of 25 should have 4–5 teams) • Teams are identified with team name and students know their team. *Teams of individual students should not be identified by the student's name.*	No teams are evident. or Teacher does not play the Game during the scheduled observation.
Response to Spleems	*All* of the following: • Teacher observes and tracks accurately the majority of Spleems (e.g., Spleems are not missed) or praise is given for no Spleems (at least one praise statement for a 5-minute or less Game or at least two praise statements for Games lasting longer than 5 minutes). • Spleems are responded to with low negative emotion (e.g., nonpunitive). If a teacher yells one time, this would be a "splat" and no credit is given for this item.	*Three* of the following: • Teacher observes and tracks accurately the majority of Spleems (e.g., Spleems are not missed) or praise is given for no Spleems (at least one praise statement for a 5-minute or less Game or at least two praise statements for Games lasting longer than 5 minutes). • Spleems are responded to with low negative emotion (e.g., nonpunitive). If a teacher yells one time, this would be a "splat" and no credit is given for this item.	*Two* of the following: • Teacher observes and tracks accurately the majority of Spleems (e.g., Spleems are not missed) or praise is given for no Spleems (at least one praise statement for a 5-minute or less Game or at least two praise statements for Games lasting longer than 5 minutes). • Spleems are responded to with low negative emotion (e.g., nonpunitive). If a teacher yells one time, this would be a "splat" and no credit is given for this item.	*One* of the following: • Teacher observes and tracks accurately the majority of Spleems (e.g., Spleems are not missed) or praise is given for no Spleems (at least one praise statement for a 5-minute or less Game or at least two praise statements for Games lasting longer than 5 minutes). • Spleems are responded to with low negative emotion (e.g., nonpunitive). If a teacher yells one time, this would be a "splat" and no credit is given for this item.	Teacher does not attempt to observe or track Spleems. or Teacher reacts to most Spleems and/or a specific child harshly. or Teacher does not play the Game during the scheduled observation.

Program Component Being Rated	Rating				
	4	3	2	1	0
	• Teacher makes students' aware that student behavior is being monitored (e.g., announces a Spleem verbally or praises PAX behavior) • Spleems are addressed appropriately. Specific behavior is identified 75% to 80% of the time, without reference to individual students (e.g., "Blue team, Spleem for talking"). Give credit to teacher for this item if there are no Spleems observed.	• Teacher makes students' aware that student behavior is being monitored (e.g., announces a Spleem verbally or praises PAX behavior) • Spleems are addressed appropriately. Specific behavior is identified 75% to 80% of the time, without reference to individual students (e.g., "Blue team, Spleem for talking"). Give credit to teacher for this item if there are no Spleems observed.	• Teacher makes students' aware that student behavior is being monitored (e.g., announces a Spleem verbally or praises PAX behavior) • Spleems are addressed appropriately. Specific behavior is identified 75% to 80% of the time, without reference to individual students (e.g., "Blue team, Spleem for talking"). Give credit to teacher for this item if there are no Spleems observed.	• Teacher makes students' aware that student behavior is being monitored (e.g., announces a Spleem verbally or praises PAX behavior) • Spleems are addressed appropriately. Specific behavior is identified 75% to 80% of the time, without reference to individual students (e.g., "Blue team, Spleem for talking"). Give credit to teacher for this item if there are no Spleems observed.	
Prizes Prizes can be nonactive as long as they are true rewards (e.g., Positive Behavioral Interventions & Supports [PBIS] bucks).	_All_ of the following: • Prize is drawn randomly _from a group of prizes_ (can be voted on by the class) or teacher _makes it appear_ to students that prize is drawn randomly. • Prize is appropriate length of time (prizes for Games lasting 5 minutes or less are not longer than 1 minute; prizes for Games lasting more than 5 minutes are not longer than 2 minutes. Prizes that don't interfere with learning (such as backward chair sitting or prince/princess for the day) are appropriate for extended periods of time. • Prize is controlled, appropriate, and safe for the classroom (no running, screaming, pushing) and the majority of students stop the prize when time is up.	_Five to six_ of the following: • Prize is drawn randomly _from a group of prizes_ (can be voted on by the class) or teacher _makes it appear_ to students that prize is drawn randomly. • Prize is appropriate length of time (prizes for Games lasting 5 minutes or less are not longer than 1 minute; prizes for Games lasting more than 5 minutes are not longer than 2 minutes. Prizes that don't interfere with learning (such as backward chair sitting or prince/princess for the day) are appropriate for extended periods of time. • Prize is controlled, appropriate, and safe for the classroom (no running, screaming, pushing) and the majority of students stop the prize when time is up.	_Three to four_ of the following: • Prize is drawn randomly _from a group of prizes_ (can be voted on by the class) or teacher _makes it appear_ to students that prize is drawn randomly. • Prize is appropriate length of time (prizes for Games lasting 5 minutes or less are not longer than 1 minute; prizes for Games lasting more than 5 minutes are not longer than 2 minutes. Prizes that don't interfere with learning (such as backward chair sitting or prince/princess for the day) are appropriate for extended periods of time. • Prize is controlled, appropriate, and safe for the classroom (no running, screaming, pushing) and the majority of students stop the prize when time is up.	_Less than three_ of the following: • Prize is drawn randomly _from a group of prizes_ (can be voted on by the class) or teacher _makes it appear_ to students that prize is drawn randomly. • Prize is appropriate length of time (prizes for Games lasting 5 minutes or _less_ are not longer than 1 minute; prizes for Games lasting more than 5 minutes are not longer than 2 minutes. Prizes that don't interfere with learning (such as backward chair sitting or prince/princess for the day) are appropriate for extended periods of time. • Prize is controlled, appropriate, and safe for the classroom (no running, screaming, pushing) and the majority of students stop the prize when time is up.	No prize is used. or Prize is delayed beyond the observation. or Teacher takes the prize away from a winning team. or Teacher does not play the Game during the scheduled observation.

Program Component Being Rated	Rating				
	4	3	2	1	0
	• Prize is given to the students in an appropriate time frame immediately after the Game (within 5 minutes of timer going off). • Teacher is enthusiastic (smiles, laughs, or other overt behaviors indicating pleasure or positive response) about giving the prizes, builds suspense for the prize, and/or participates in the prize. • Students are familiar with GBG prizes and/or are excited about the prize. • Teacher provides "precorrects" to students about how to participate in the prize appropriately (e.g., "Remember no running"). • Teacher provides "precorrects" to students about how to participate in the prize appropriately (e.g., "Remember no running").	• Prize is given to the students in an appropriate time frame immediately after the Game (within 5 minutes of timer going off). • Teacher is enthusiastic (smiles, laughs, or other overt behaviors indicating pleasure or positive response) about giving the prizes, builds suspense for the prize, and/or participates in the prize. • Students are familiar with GBG prizes and/or are excited about the prize. • Teacher provides "precorrects" to students about how to participate in the prize appropriately (e.g., "Remember no running").	• Prize is given to the students in an appropriate time frame immediately after the Game (within 5 minutes of timer going off). • Teacher is enthusiastic (smiles, laughs, or other overt behaviors indicating pleasure or positive response) about giving the prizes, builds suspense for the prize, and/or participates in the prize. • Students are familiar with GBG prizes and/or are excited about the prize. • Teacher provides "precorrects" to students about how to participate in the prize appropriately (e.g., "Remember no running").	• Prize is given to the students in an appropriate time frame immediately after the Game (within 5 minutes of timer going off). • Teacher is enthusiastic (smiles, laughs, or other overt behaviors indicating pleasure or positive response) about giving the prizes, builds suspense for the prize, and/or participates in the prize. • Students are familiar with GBG prizes and/or are excited about the prize. • Teacher provides "precorrects" to students about how to participate in the prize appropriately (e.g., "Remember no running").	

Program Component Being Rated	Rating				
	4	3	2	1	0
After the Game: Reviewing Spleems	**_All_ of the following:** • *Number* of Spleems each team received are reviewed. • Teacher informs each team explicitly whether they won the Game based on having three or fewer Spleems (e.g., "Team 1, you won the Game" or "Blue team, you get to participate in the prize" or "Every team won the Game"). • *Types* of Spleems observed throughout the Game are summarized either by team or classwide, or, if no Spleems, then PAX behaviors are reviewed. • Teams are guided in determining on what they need to work for the next Game (e.g., "Remember, the next time we play the Game, raise a quiet hand when you have a question."). • If a team loses the Game, the teacher responds to the loss with low negative emotion (e.g., "Don't worry. You'll have another opportunity to play the Game later today").	**_Four_ of the following:** • *Number* of Spleems each team received are reviewed. • Teacher informs each team explicitly whether they won the Game based on having three or fewer Spleems (e.g., "Team 1, you won the Game" or "Blue team, you get to participate in the prize" or "Every team won the Game"). • *Types* of Spleems observed throughout the Game are summarized either by team or classwide, or, if no Spleems, then PAX behaviors are reviewed. • Teams are guided in determining on what they need to work for the next Game (e.g., "Remember, the next time we play the Game, raise a quiet hand when you have a question."). • If a team loses the Game, the teacher responds to the loss with low negative emotion (e.g., "Don't worry. You'll have another opportunity to play the Game later today").	**_Three_ of the following:** • *Number* of Spleems each team received are reviewed. • Teacher informs each team explicitly whether they won the Game based on having three or fewer Spleems (e.g., "Team 1, you won the Game" or "Blue team, you get to participate in the prize" or "Every team won the Game"). • *Types* of Spleems observed throughout the Game are summarized either by team or classwide, or, if no Spleems, then PAX behaviors are reviewed. • Teams are guided in determining on what they need to work for the next Game (e.g., "Remember, the next time we play the Game, raise a quiet hand when you have a question."). • If a team loses the Game, the teacher responds to the loss with low negative emotion (e.g., "Don't worry. You'll have another opportunity to play the Game later today").	**_Less than three_ of the following:** • *Number* of Spleems each team received are reviewed. • Teacher informs each team explicitly whether they won the Game based on having three or fewer Spleems (e.g., "Team 1, you won the Game" or "Blue team, you get to participate in the prize" or "Every team won the Game"). • *Types* of Spleems observed throughout the Game are summarized either by team or classwide, or, if no Spleems, then PAX behaviors are reviewed. • Teams are guided in determining on what they need to work for the next Game (e.g., "Remember, the next time we play the Game, raise a quiet hand when you have a question."). • If a team loses the Game, the teacher responds to the loss with low negative emotion (e.g., "Don't worry. You'll have another opportunity to play the Game later today").	Teacher does not review Spleems after the Game. or Teacher does not play the Game during the scheduled observation.

*A "splat" is a major Spleem or a severe negative behavior.

Good Behavior Game Rubric Rating Form

School: _____   Date: _____

Teacher: _____   Coach: _____

Grade Level: _____

Directions: Please see Form D Good Behavior Game Implementation Rubric for detailed definitions and specific examples to complete each of the seven ratings presented here.

Good Behavior Game Observation

☐ __PAX Quiet __clear/concise directions
__identifies Spleems
__sets timer in view and says how long
__announces start of game
Preparing the Students for the Game p. 1

☐ __T can observe
__approp. skill level __educational purpose
Appropriate Activity* p. 1

☐ __observes and tracks/praise no Spleems __low negative emotion/nonpunitive
__T makes S aware Spleems being counted __Spleem addressed approp.
Response to Spleems p.2

☐ __timer used __ timer visible
__referred to
Timer (minutes played __) p. 1

☐ __random ____ T provides precorrects __approp. length __controlled
__approp. time frame __T enthusiastic __S familiar with prizes
Prizes* (Length __) p. 3

☐ __all S on team __balanced
__approp. # of teams __teams identified
Teams p. 2

☐ __reviews # of Spleems __T makes S aware who won __reviews types
__guides teams what to work on next game __T responds to loss approp.
After the Game: Reviewing Spleems p. 3

Notes:

*Choice of Activity: _____   *Prize: _____

_____

_____

_____

_____

_____

APPENDIX O

Lesson Log

Lesson Log for __/__ (two-digit month/two-digit year)

Grade	Teacher	L1	L2	L3	L4	L5	L6	L7	L8	L9	L10	L11	L12	L13	L14	L15	L16	L17	L18	L19	L20
K																					
K																					
K																					
1																					
1																					
1																					
2																					

Lesson Log for _ _ / _ _ / _ _ (two-digit month/two-digit year)

Grade	Teacher	L1	L2	L3	L4	L5	L6	L7	L8	L9	L10	L11	L12	L13	L14	L15	L16	L17	L18	L19	L20
2																					
3																					
3																					
3																					
4																					
4																					
4																					
5																					
5																					

APPENDIX P

Game Scoreboard

Teacher: _____ Week of: _____ School: _____

Monday _____

Teams	Game 1	Game 2	Game 3	# of wins
Length of game: (minutes played)				

Tuesday _____

Teams	Game 1	Game 2	Game 3	# of wins
Length of game: (minutes played)				

Wednesday _____

Teams	Game 1	Game 2	Game 3	# of wins
Length of game: (minutes played)				

Thursday _____

Teams	Game 1	Game 2	Game 3	# of wins
Length of game: (minutes played)				

Friday _____

Teams	Game 1	Game 2	Game 3	# of wins
Length of game: (minutes played)				

Weekly Summary

Remember to save a copy of these data for your PAX coach.

Number of times played	
Total minutes played	

APPENDIX Q

Game Scoreboard Log

Instructions: In each table cell, insert Y (Log turned in by the teacher) or N (Log not turned in by the teacher).

Grade	Teacher	Game Scoreboards for Week of...																												
		11/15	11/22	11/29	12/06	12/13	12/20	1/03	1/10	1/17	1/24	1/31	2/07	2/14	2/21	2/28	3/07	3/14	3/21	3/28	4/04	4/11	4/18	4/26	5/02	5/09	5/16	5/23	5/30	6/06
K																														
K																														
K																														
1																														
1																														
1																														

Game Scoreboards for Week of ...

Grade	Teacher	11/15	11/22	11/29	12/06	12/13	12/20	1/03	1/10	1/17	1/24	1/31	2/07	2/14	2/21	2/28	3/07	3/14	3/21	3/28	4/04	4/11	4/18	4/26	5/02	5/09	5/16	5/23	5/30	6/06
2																														
2																														
3																														
3																														
3																														
4																														
4																														
4																														
5																														
5																														

APPENDIX R

Coaching Log

Coach Name: _____

Dates: From ___/___/___ to ___/___/___

Instructions: Submit the Coach Log to the Data Manager twice every month, on the 15th and the 30th.

Date (mo/day/year)	Teacher's Last Name	Contact Type* CT*	Contact Type* Inc	Duration (min)	1 Check in	2 PAX Element	3 Game	4 Lesson	5 PATHS Gen	6 Gen	7 PAX Element	8 Game	9 PATHS Element	10 Gen	11 Student	12 Class	13 Student	14 Needs Assessment	15 Track Implementation	16 Other	17 Relationship Building
							Modeling				Teacher Assessment/Feedback					Delivery					

Codes†

Date (mo/day/year)	Teacher's Last Name	Contact Type*		Duration (min)	Codes†																
		CT*	Inc		Modeling						Teacher Assessment/Feedback					Delivery						
					1	2	3	4	5	6	7	8	9	10	11	12	13	14	15	16	17
					Check in	PAX Element	Game	Lesson	PATHS Gen	Gen	PAX Element	Game	PATHS Element	Gen	Student	Class	Student	Needs Assessment	Track Implementation	Other	Relationship Building

CT = contact; Inc = incentive.

* 1 = face; 2 = phone; 3 = e-mail; 4 = teacher meeting; 5 = training; 6 = incentive.

When a 4 is included in the Inc column, include one or more of the following codes:

C1–C4 = competitions in December (C1), January (C2), March (C4) or May (C4): E = environment; G = generalization; K = Kid of the Day; P = PBIS; T = Tootle.

† A) provide rationale for element; B) discuss teacher observation of element; C) discuss student response to element; D) prompt in real time; E) set goal.

 PAX General Incentive Checklist

Tootles to You ...
You've Earned an Incentive!

Teacher: _____   School: _____

Grade: _____   Coach: _____   Date: _____

Thank you for doing the following:

☐ Using a PAX Cue authentically

    ☐ PAX Quiet   ☐ PAX Voices   ☐ PAX Hands   ☐ Thumbs Up/Down

_____

☐ Using PAX Stix authentically

_____

☐ Playing the Game (unprompted, playing at an alternative time)

_____

☐ Contributing to the schoolwide Tootle Board

_____

☐ Using the timer throughout the day

_____

☐ Implementing an additional PAX element

    ☐ PAX Tax   ☐ PAX Timer Surprise   ☐ Beat the Timer   ☐ PAX Roles

_____

☐ Making PATHS to PAX your own (e.g., creative addition/supplement to the program)

_____

☐ Other:

_____

 Guidelines for Creating a *PAX* Classroom Environment

Seven Questions to Ask Yourself

1. Is the "classroom vision" posted in a visible location?
   - Posted see/hear/feel/do chart(s)

2. Are the PAX Cues signs posted in a visible location and referred to frequently throughout the day?
   - PAX Quiet
   - Go PAX
   - PAX Voices
   - Stop Spleems
   - PAX Hands
   - PAX Promise

3. Are the PAX Stix used effectively?
   - Used throughout the day (e.g., random calling on students, in aid of transitions, for choosing "volunteers")

4. Is the PAX Quiet signal used effectively?
   - Used throughout the day (e.g., to get students attention, to aid transitions)
   - Harmonica used consistently; short, pleasant tone

5. Are the Thumbs Up/ Thumbs Down signs used effectively?
   - Placed on each student's desk/table
   - Referred to throughout the day

6. Is the timer used effectively?
   - Used throughout the day (e.g., Beat the Timer, for instruction)

7. Am I using PAX language and visual cues effectively?
   - "Thank you for being a PAX Leader."
   - "Nice PAX hands in the hallway."
   - "Was that a Spleem?"
   - Use of thumbs up or thumbs down.

A teacher who has created an effective *PAX* environment would answer YES to all of the above questions. Please contact your coach if you have any questions.

Coach Information (Name, email, phone)

 Classroom Environment Checklist

Teacher: _____ School: _____ Grade: _____

Coach: _____ Date: _____

During a brief classroom visit today, the following *PATHS to PAX* elements were observed in your classroom:

☐ PAX cues signs posted

    ☐ PAX Quiet   ☐ PAX Voices   ☐ PAX Hands   ☐ Go PAX
    ☐ Stop Spleems   ☐ PAX Promise

_____

☐ Posted "classroom vision" (see/hear/feel/do chart(s))

_____

☐ PAX Stix

_____

☐ Harmonica is used appropriately.

_____

☐ Thumbs-up/Thumbs-down signs are on each student's desk/table.

_____

☐ Timer is used throughout the day.

_____

☐ PAX language and/or visual cues are used.

_____

Program New Additions Flyer

PATHS to PAX

New Additions at (School Name)!

(Coach information: Name, e-mail, phone)

- **"Spotlight on . . .":** A teacher is chosen randomly biweekly for implementing key elements of the PATHS to PAX program successfully. This is their special time to shine! Their name and a certificate will be displayed in the lobby on the wall across from the staff bathroom. Please Tootle this teacher and hang it next to the "Spotlight on" certificate for all to see! When the next teacher is chosen, we will give the previous teacher his or her Tootles and start the process over again. The first teacher to receive this honor is (Teacher Name). Congratulations!

- **Grade-Level Good Behavior Game Competition:** As teachers submit their Game Scoreboards (weekly), they will be entered into a monthly count. The grade-level group with the highest percentage of Games played during that month will win a *prize*!

- Percent of Games played monthly = Actual Games played in month (calculated for all teachers in grade level group)/Possible Games played per month (three Games per day; days off taken into account).

- Make sure you turn in your Game Scoreboards at the end of *every* week!

- We calculated the totals for January and will be calculating February this week, so please turn in all Game Scoreboards as soon as possible!

- The grade-level groups are as follows: Pre-K, kindergarten, first grade, second grade, third grade, and fourth and fifth grades.

- **Individual Incentive for Playing the Game in Your Classroom!** Don't forget about the flyer distributed recently about a chance to earn your very own PATHS to PAX shoulder bag! You need to play the Game at least 30 times between now and Spring Break. (*Please turn in "honest" Scoreboards.*)

Program Update Flyer

PATHS to PAX at (School Name)   (Date)

The school year is almost finished and we are so impressed to continue to see many elements of the PATHS to PAX program throughout the entire school! We appreciate your dedication to the program and your commitment to seeing it through to the end of the school year! ☺

We have a new teacher who has been recognized in our PATHS to PAX spotlight. Congratulations (**Teacher Name**)! (Teacher Name) has completed the entire PATHS to PAX curriculum and has continued to play the PAX Good Behavior Game throughout the end of the school year. She also has continued with the Kid of the Day and Tootles. This is absolutely fantastic! She has wonderful relationships with her students and is very welcoming and friendly to all who enter her classroom. (Teacher Name) is truly a phenomenal teacher and it has been a pleasure working with her this year! Thank you, (Teacher Name), for all that you do!

We have a new grade-level winner in our PATHS to PAX Scoreboard competition. We actually had two grade levels (kindergarten and third grade) that played the Game more than 100% (more than three Games/day at times) for the month of May, so our overall grade-level winner was chosen randomly. Congratulations (**Teacher Names**) for turning in your Game Scoreboards and playing the Game more than 100% during the month of May! Thank you for continuing to play the Game throughout the end of the school year, and for turning in your Game Scoreboards! We will drop off your gift certificates this week!

Update: Ninety-two percent of teachers played the GBG at least 40 times from April 19 to May 14 and received a PATHS to PAX t-shirt. This is fantastic!!! Please continue to play the GBG at least three times per day and turn in your GBG Scoreboards through the end of the school year! Thanks! ☺

Tootles to those teachers who completed their PATHS to PAX lessons! Almost *all* teachers are finished teaching the lessons or finishing up with the lessons this week. Very impressive!!! ☺

Thank You!

Questions/concerns? Contact (coach name, e-mail, phone)

APPENDIX X

Teacher Spotlight

The PATHS to PAX New "Spotlight" Teacher Is . . .
(Teacher's Name)

Congratulations (Teacher's Name)!

(Teacher's Name) continues to impress with the quality of her PATHS to PAX Lessons and Good Behavior Games! She has implemented many aspects of the program successfully, including PAX cues and language, Kid of the Day, Tootles, and key Lesson topics (self-control, calming down, and so on).

(Teacher's Name) committed to teaching extra Lessons when testing was over to catch up to the pacing guide, and she has been keeping up the pace.

(Teacher's name) is genuine and friendly, and a phenomenal teacher. We would want to be in her class if we were in the third grade!

Thank you, (Teacher's Name)! Keep up the great work! ☺

Spring Fever Flyer

Do You Have SPRING FEVER?

PATHS to PAX is the solution! Now that April is almost over, many students (and teachers) may be feeling a bit of spring fever. Often, student off-task and problem behaviors begin to escalate at this point in the year, which leaves many of us feeling frustrated and irritated. Although it may not feel like it, this is the perfect time to increase playing the *Good Behavior Game*! It's a win–win situation; teachers get a chunk of time during which the majority of the students are focused on their work and showing PAX, and students get a quick (less than 1 minute) reward, which helps to increase PAX behavior in the future. The key to a successful GBG is your prize box! It is important to update the prize box periodically with *new* and *exciting prizes* that your students enjoy. Listed below are a few prizes observed recently in classrooms. Feel free to use these in your classroom

New Granny Wacky Prize Ideas

Flamingo Stand: Set the timer for 45 seconds; students balance on one leg with their foot resting on their opposite knee without holding on to anything. If they lose balance, they sit down. Anyone who is left standing when the timer goes off, wins!

Stuck in a Silent Box: Students pretend they are "stuck" in a silent box. They can pretend to bang, yell, knock, smoosh their face up to the side of the box to try and "get out." The key is that it's a silent box, so no matter how "loud" they scream, we should not be able to hear them!

Strike a Pose: The teacher calls out a pose and the students show off their best version for the camera while the teacher pretends to snap pictures. For example, "Show me happy," or "Give me your best goofy face!"

Coach Information (name, e-mail, phone number)

PAX GBG Prize List 1

Granny Wacky Prize Ideas...

Granny Wacky Prize Ideas from teachers:

1. Football fan (cheering fest)
2. Skip around the room
3. Small-ball toss (keep in air)
4. Make paper fortune tellers
5. Finger football
6. Snowman (freeze and then melt)
7. Silent ball
8. Crazy ball toss (throw ball through legs; catcher claps once before catching)
9. Tootle time (write Tootles to each other)
10. Read-aloud
11. High fives (everyone high fives)
12. Shake hands (everyone shakes each other's hand)
13. Swim around the classroom
14. Wonderball
15. Jack-in-the-Box (pretend you are a Jack-in-the-Box)
16. Squats
17. Pushups
18. Jumping jacks
19. Teach me how to Dougie
20. Stand-on-one-leg competition
21. Bunny hop
22. Tarzan (pretend to swing on ropes around the classroom)
23. Harmonica Jam (teacher has to play a tune on the harmonica for allotted time)
24. Snowball fight (paper balls or cotton balls)
25. Mime-in-a-box (act like a mime in a box)
26. Dance-a-thon
27. River/bank game
28. Knockout (catch ball; whoever drops ball is out)
29. Jumping and wiggling in air
30. Quiet drum major
31. Going on a bear hunt
32. Sit on your desk
32. Air drawing (draw pictures in the air)
34. Finger walk (walk your fingers around the desk/classroom)
35. Downhill skiing (in the classroom, pretend to downhill ski with poles)
36. Skateboarding (pretend to skateboard around the class)
37. Airplane (fly around the class)
38. Race car (drive around the classroom)

PAX GBG Prize List 2

Granny Wacky Prize Ideas...

1. Sound byte (kids listen to music for 30 seconds and guess the song)
2. Sit in someone else's seat and call each other the wrong name
3. "The wave"
4. Teacher dances
5. Tasteful "Your Mama" jokes (not directed at individual students)
6. Parade around the classroom while waving
7. 7-up
8. Foul-line shots with paper balls
9. Paper ball trash can shoot-off
10. Slow motion (move in slow motion)
11. Relay race
12. Zombie walk
13. Talk to your teammates
14. Imitate each other
15. Pick a friend and jump together
16. "Five Little Monkeys"
17. Switch seats
18. Statue
19. Learn and sing a wacky, goofy song
20. Rolling pencils on desk
21. Break dance
22. Sitting in lockers/cubbies
23. Dance like a robot
24. Put your feet on your desk
25. Trash can slam-dunk contest
26. Throw paper at the teacher
27. Hot potato
28. Kneel on the table
29. Name That Tune
30. Dance to your favorite tune
31. Dance contest and kids vote
32. Say the ABCs backward
33. Bubble fest with partners (blowing bubbles with bubble gum)
34. Statue while teacher tries to make students laugh
35. Cha-cha slide/Electric Slide
36. Sock hop
37. Soldier crawl
38. Listen to the radio
39. Write on the board
40. Scream and jump
41. Fastest blinker or blinking contest
42. Hop in place on one foot
43. Musical chairs
44. Walk around and touch every desk
45. Duck Duck Goose

46. Tight rope (walk a line on floor)
47. Limbo
48. Clean up with Clorox wipes
49. Walk backward
50. "Mr. Dog" (hide "bone" and student has to find object)
51. Human tic-tac-toe (tape on floor; girls vs. boys)
52. Stand on head
53. Crab walk
54. Michael Jackson dancing
55. Congo line
56. Huggy bear
57. The jerk
58. Group hug
59. Coke and Pepsi
60. Guess Who's Missing
61. Pencil sharpening
62. Karaoke
63. Twenty questions
64. Appropriate joke telling
65. Show and tell
66. Throw balls around
67. Balance book/folder on head
68. Waddle around the class
69. Swim on the floor like a fish
70. Mirror (mock your friend/partner)
71. Jump rope
72. Fifteen-second nap
73. Talk on fake cell phone
74. Top Chef (pretend to make food and eat it)
75. Scribble fest (scribble on paper)

Administrator Classroom
Environment Checklist

Teacher: _____   Grade: _____

Observer: _____   Date: _____

Tootle Board _____

- ☐ *Current* adult Tootles posted
- ☐ *Current* peer Tootles posted
- ☐ No *current* Tootles posted

Kid of the Day _____

- ☐ System in place for choosing students randomly
- ☐ Student wearing an identifier (e.g., crown, sash)
- ☐ Student identified in the room (e.g., poster, display)
- ☐ Written Tootles posted for the Kid of the Day

Good Behavior Game _____

- ☐ Scoreboards: Evidence the Game is being played frequently (3 times a day)
- ☐ Use of the timer to start and end the game
- ☐ Teacher is observing: Evidence of tracking Spleem
- ☐ Teacher shows enthusiasm (e.g., for the Game, prizes, winning teams
- ☐ Appropriate use of Granny's Wacky Prizes (e.g., random choosing, kept short)

PAX Cues (8½ × 11-inch Laminated Cards) Posted _____

☐ PAX   ☐ PAX   ☐ PAX   ☐ PAX   ☐ GO PAX/ STOP
Quiet   Voices   Hands   Promise   Spleems Cues

Additional Evidence of PATHS to PAX Implementation

☐ Posted classroom vision (see/hear/feel/do)

☐ Use of PAX language

☐ Use of PAX Stix

☐ Use of PAX roles (job cards)

☐ Use of harmonica for PAX Quiet

☐ Use of thumbs up/thumbs down

☐ Use of timer throughout the day (e.g., Beat the Timer, for instruction)

Coach Action Plan

Coach: _____ School: _____ Teacher: _____ Date: _____

Strengths:

Influential Factors:

Hypotheses	Goals	Action Steps	Short-Term Indicators of Progress toward Goals	Assessment

Notes:

Paths to PAX Lesson Modeling Checklist

Name: _____ **School:** _____

Please respond to each question as you observe a *PATHS to PAX* Lesson.

1. Was the Lesson objective clearly stated? _____

   Objective: _____

2. How was the Lesson related to other learning?

   _____

   _____

3. Did you feel the Lesson content was appropriate and related to the topic throughout the entire Lesson? Explain.

   _____

   _____

4. How were the students assessed throughout the Lesson?

   _____

   _____

5. Did you feel the pacing of the Lesson was good? Not too fast or too slow? _____

   Length of Lesson: _____

6. Did you feel that the affect and energy of the teacher seemed genuine and appropriate during the Lesson? Explain.

_____

_____

Additional Notes

Think about things you might like to try.

_____

_____

_____

Coach Observation Form

Coach: _____ **Teacher:** _____ **Observer:** _____

School: _____ **Date:** _____

Did the coach	Yes	No	Needs Improvement	Fair	Proficient	Advanced
1. Answer questions about the program		X	1	2	3	4
2. Model techniques		X	1	2	3	4
3. Involve the teacher in modeled Lesson		X	1	2	3	4
4. Coteach a lesson with the teacher		X	1	2	3	4
5. Role-play with the teacher		X	1	2	3	4
6. Show and discuss video examples		X	1	2	3	4
7. Prompt the teacher in real time		X	1	2	3	4
8. Provide feedback about teacher behavior using notes or data from observation	X		1	2	3	4
9. Solve problems, such as with an individual child, multiple students, classroom situation, and so on		X	1	2	3	4
10. Help the teacher generalize skills to new situations		X	1	2	3	4
11. Set or review goals with the teacher with regard to using program components		X	1	2	3	4
12. Set a date for the next observation or coaching session		X	1	2	3	4

How well did the coach			Needs Improvement	Fair	Proficient	Advanced
1. Provide a warm-up to the session			1	2	3	4
2. Maintain or make efforts toward creating a positive working relationship with the teacher			1	2	3	4
3. Attempt to motivate and generate excitement about the program			1	2	3	4
4. Demonstrate the ability to adjust material to the skill level or emotional state of the teacher			1	2	3	4
5. Empathize with teacher concerns (e.g., about program, students)			1	2	3	4
6. Use strategies to assess and ensure the teacher's comprehension during discussion			1	2	3	4
7. Demonstrate a collaborative/teamwork approach while minimizing the "expert" approach			1	2	3	4
8. Use an inductive approach to guide the teacher's skill development			1	2	3	4
9. Demonstrate knowledge of program content			1	2	3	4
10 Adhere to the specified Coach Action Plan developed for this teacher			1	2	3	4

Quality Coaching Code Descriptions

Instructions: **For each numbered item, indicate which of the following steps the coach demonstrated. Assign each bulleted step either 0 point (not done) to 1 point (done) to arrive at a 0- to 4-point rating for each numbered item.**

Did the Coach

1. **Model techniques**
    - Provided rationale and brief highlights of skill before modeling
    - Demonstrated skill
    - Discussed skill components after modeling
    - Discussed student response to modeled technique

2. **Engage the teacher in modeled element**
    - Asked the teacher to share an example
    - Requested the teacher practice the skill students are learning (e.g., Turtle Technique)
    - Encouraged teacher participation in prize
    - Praised the teacher

3. **Conduct an element with the teacher**
    - Reviewed Lesson/Game with the teacher ahead of time
    - Discussed roles
    - Incorporated modeling of at least one target skill for the teacher
    - Provided praise and feedback

4. **Role-play with the teacher**
    - Provided a clear setup for a role-play scenario
    - Had the teacher practice as the teacher, with the coach acting as a student
    - Had the teacher practice best-case and worst-case scenarios
    - Provided praise and feedback

5. **Prompt the teacher in real time**
   - Made suggestions about how the teacher could incorporate program skills while class is in session
   - Encouraged the teacher to try the skills right then
   - Discussed student response
   - Provided praise and feedback

6. **Show and discuss video examples**
   - Showed the teacher video examples
   - Had the teacher identify strengths and areas of improvement for teachers in the video examples
   - Discussed how the examples might apply to the teacher's current classroom situation
   - Praised the teacher for participating

7. **Answer questions or provide information about the program**
   - Reflected question to be sure he or she understood correctly (when necessary)
   - Used warm a tone, appropriate body language, and so on, to convey openness to questions
   - Provided clear, accurate information
   - Asked the teacher if the question was answered clearly and satisfactorily

8. **Provide feedback about teacher behavior using notes or data from observation**
   - Asked the teacher what went well and what didn't go so well during the observation
   - Provided positive feedback about specific things the teacher did well
   - Provided constructive feedback about specific areas in which the teacher could improve
   - Made an effort to point out student improvement/responses to the teacher's use of skills

9. **Solve problems, such as those dealing with an individual child, multiple students, a classroom situation, and so on**
   - Identified a problematic situation
   - Identified possible solutions
   - Discussed the potential outcomes of each solution
   - Identified a solution for the teacher to try

10. **Help the teacher generalize skills**
    - Identified a skill to generalize
    - Discussed the rationale for generalization of the particular skill
    - Identified modifications to skills or new setting applications
    - Elicited the teacher's feedback with regard to potential generalization

11. **Set or review goals with the teacher with regard to using program components**
    - Identified new or reviewed previously established goals
    - Provided positive reinforcement for progress toward goals
    - Helped identify and address barriers to goals
    - Established new benchmarks and a timeline

12. **Set a date for the next observation or coaching session (*Note*: For the following two steps, assign 0 point [not done] or 2 points [done]).**
    - Inquired about or confirmed the next Lesson/Game or asked about a convenient time for discussion
    - Stated briefly the purpose of the next coaching session

How well did the coach

1. **Provide a warm-up to the session**
   - Greeted the teacher
   - Asked how the teacher is doing
   - Probed the teacher's response
   - Chatted briefly to help the teacher become comfortable

2. **Maintain or make efforts toward creating a positive working relationship with the teacher**
   - Used a warm tone of voice
   - Demonstrated friendly body language (arms unfolded, smiled, nodded head)
   - Used words of encouragement and praise
   - Used words to emphasize the collaborative relationship between coach and teacher

3. **Attempt to motivate and generate excitement about program**
   - Pointed out the teacher's skill development
   - Pointed out behavioral improvements in students
   - Referred to data (e.g., research, other teachers' successes) to highlight program effectiveness
   - Referred to incentives

4. **Demonstrate the ability to adjust the materials to the skill level or emotional state of the teacher**
   - Paced the coaching session at a level appropriate for the teacher's skill
   - Matched rationales to the teacher's level
   - Provided examples of how to apply the techniques that were appropriate for the teacher's skill level
   - Conducted coaching activities (e.g., modeling vs. coteaching vs. observation) that were appropriate for the teacher's skill level

5. **Empathize with teacher concerns (e.g., about program, students)**
   - Used reflective listening to validate concerns
   - Normalized the situation based on experiences of other teachers
   - Disclosed his or her own experiences with similar situations
   - Provided hope

6. **Use strategies to assess and ensure the teacher's comprehension during the discussion**
   - Asked whether the teacher had any questions
   - Elicited examples from the teacher
   - Had the teacher summarize or explain concepts in his or her own words
   - Repeated the teacher's summary or explanation to demonstrate understanding

7. **Demonstrate a collaborative/teamwork approach while minimizing the "expert" approach**
   - Asked the teacher for his or her perspective on the particular problem or issue being discussed
   - Reflected and praised the teacher's suggestions, and gave appropriate feedback
   - Generated other suggestions, building off the teacher's suggestions
   - Asked the teacher for feedback about the coaching session

8. **Use an inductive approach to guide the teacher's skill development (*Note*: For the following two steps, assign 0 point [not done] or 2 points [done]).**
   - Posed open-ended questions
   - Provided structure for the teacher to reflect on a specific classroom situation during which the coach observed something critical happen

9. **Demonstrate knowledge of program content**
   - Used printed information only as a reference; did not read verbatim
   - Provided additional relevant information and examples
   - Demonstrated a clear understanding of behavioral principles
   - Had a varied and strong repertoire of approaches, and demonstrated flexibility when conveying information

10. **Adhere to the specified Coach Action Plan (CAP) developed for the teacher**
    - Focused on at least one strategy from the CAP
    - Used at least 50% of the strategies from the CAP
    - Collected data to inform progress toward CAP goals
    - Deviated from the CAP based on clear need or urgency

References

Aber, J. L., Brown, J. L., & Jones, S. M. (2003). Developmental trajectories toward violence in middle childhood: Course, demographic differences, and response to school-based intervention. *Developmental Psychology, 39*(2), 324–348.

Adelman, H. S., & Taylor, L. (2000). Shaping the future of mental health in schools. *Psychology in the Schools, 37*(1), 49–60.

Atkins, M. S., Frazier, S. L., Leathers, S. J., et al. (2008). Teacher key opinion leaders and mental health consultation in low-income urban schools. *Journal of Consulting and Clinical Psychology, 76*(5), 905–908.

Barrish, H. H., Saunders, M., & Wolf, M. M. (1969). Good Behavior Game: Effects of individual contingencies for group consequences on disruptive behavior in a classroom 1. *Journal of Applied Behavior Analysis, 2*(2), 119–124.

Blakely, C. H., Mayer, J. P., Gottschalk, R. G., Schmitt, N., Davidson, W. S., & Roitman, D. B., et al. (1987). The fidelity–adaptation debate: Implications for the implementation of public sector social programs. *American Journal of Community Psychology, 15*, 253–268.

Bradshaw, C. P., Zmuda, J. H., Kellam, S. G., & Ialongo, N. S. (2009). Longitudinal impact of two universal preventive interventions in first grade on educational outcomes in high school. *Journal of Educational Psychology, 101*(4), 926–937.

Breslau, J., Lane, M., Sampson, N., & Kessler, R. C. (2008). Mental disorders and subsequent educational attainment in a US national sample. *Journal of Psychiatric Research, 42*(9), 708–716.

Brown, S. A. (1993). Recovery patterns in adolescent substance abuse. In J. S. Baer, G. A. Marlatt, & R. J. McMahon (Eds.), Addictive behaviors across the life span: Prevention, treatment, and policy issues (pp. 161–183). Thousand Oaks, CA: Sage Publications.

Catalano, R. F., Berglund, M. L., Ryan, J. A., Lonczak, H. S., & Hawkins, J. D. (2002). Positive youth development in the United States: Research findings on evaluations of positive youth development programs. *Prevention & Treatment, 5*(1), 98–124.

Chorpita, B., Becker, K. D., Phillips, L., & Daleiden, E. (2011). *Practitioner guides.* Satellite Beach, FL: PracticeWise.

Christenson, S. L., & Thurlow, M. L. (2004). School dropouts prevention considerations, interventions, and challenges. *Current Directions in Psychological Science, 13*(1), 36–39.

Conduct Problems Prevention Research Group. (1999). Initial impact of the fast track prevention trial for conduct problems: II. Classroom effects. *Journal of Consulting and Clinical Psychology, 67*(5), 648–657.

Conduct Problems Prevention Research Group. (2010). The effects of a multiyear universal social–emotional learning program: The role of student and school characteristics. *Journal of Consulting and Clinical Psychology, 78*, 156–168.

de Haan, E. (2008). I doubt therefore I coach: Critical moments in coaching practice. *Consulting Psychology Journal: Practice and Research, 60*(1), 91–105.

Dolan, L. J., Kellam, S. G., Brown, C. H., Werthamer-Larsson, L., Rebok, G. W., Mayer, L. S., & Wheeler, L. (1993). The short-term impact of two classroom-based preventive interventions on aggressive and shy behaviors and poor achievement. *Journal of Applied Developmental Psychology, 14*(3), 317–345.

Domitrovich, C. E., Bradshaw, C. P., Poduska, J. M., Hoagwood, K., Buckley, J. A., Olin, S., & Ialongo, N. S. (2008). Maximizing the implementation quality of evidence-based preventive interventions in schools: A conceptual framework. *Advances in School Mental Health Promotion, 1*(3), 6–28.

Domitrovich, C. E., Gest, S. D., Gill, S., Jones, D. J., & DeRouise, R. S. (2009). Teacher factors related to the professional development process of the Head Start REDI intervention. *Early Education and Development, 20,* 402–430.

Durlak, J. A., Weissberg, R. P., Dymnicki, A. B., Taylor, R. D., & Schellinger, K. B. (2011). The impact of enhancing students' social and emotional learning: A meta-analysis of school-based universal interventions. *Child Development, 82*(1), 405–432.

Dusenbury, L., Branningan, R., Falco, M., & Hansen, W. B. (2003). A review of research on fidelity of implementation: Implications for drug abuse prevention in school settings. *Health Education Research, 18,* 237–256.

Elias, M. J., Zins, J. E., Graczyk, P. A., & Weissberg, R. P. (2003). Implementation, sustainability, and scaling up of social–emotional and academic innovations in public schools. *School Psychology Review, 32*(3), 303–319.

Embry, D. D., Staatemeier, G., Richardson, C., Lauger, K., & Mitich, J. (2003). *The PAX Good Behavior Game.* Center City: Hazelden.

Fixsen, D. L., Naoom, S. F., Blasé, K. A., Friedman, R. M., & Wallace, F. (2005). *Implementation research: A synthesis of the literature.* Tampa, FL: University of South Florida, Louis de la Parte Florida Mental Health Institute, National Implementation Research Network.

Furlong, M. J., Whipple, A. D., Jean, G. S., Simental, J., Soliz, A., & Punthuna, S. (2003). Multiple contexts of school engagement: Moving toward a unifying framework for educational research and practice. *The California School Psychologist, 8*(1), 99–113.

Furr-Holden, C. D. M., Ialongo, N. S., Anthony, J. C., Petras, H., & Kellam, S. G. (2004). Developmentally inspired drug prevention: Middle school outcomes in a school-based randomized prevention trial. *Drug and Alcohol Dependence, 73*(2), 149–158.

Gillham, J. E., Reivich, K. J., Freres, D. R., Chaplin, T. M., Shatté, A. J., Samuels, B., & Seligman, M. E. (2007). School-based prevention of depressive symptoms: A randomized controlled study of the effectiveness and specificity of the Penn Resiliency Program. *Journal of Consulting and Clinical Psychology, 75*(1), 9–19.

Gorman-Smith, D., Beidel, D., Brown, T. A., Lochman, J., & Haaga, A. F. (2003). Effects of teacher training and consultation on teacher behavior towards students at high risk for aggression. *Behavior Therapy, 34,* 437–452.

Gottfredson, D. C. (1997). School-based crime prevention. In L. W. Sherman et al. (Eds.), *Preventing crime: What works, what doesn't, what's promising: A report to the United States Congress,* (pp. J15–J19). Washington, DC: US Department of Justice, Office of Justice Programs.

Gottfredson, D. C., & Gottfredson, G. D. (2002). Quality of school-based prevention programs: Results from a national survey. *Journal of Research on Crime and Delinquency, 39,* 3–35.

Greenberg, M. T., Domitrovich, C., & Bumbarger, B. (2001). The prevention of mental disorders in school-aged children: Current state of the field. *Prevention & Treatment, 4*(1), 1a.

Greenberg, M. T., & Kusche, C. A. (1996). The PATHS Project: Preventive intervention for children. Final Report to the National Institute of Mental Health, grant R01MH42131.

Greenberg, M. T., & Kusche, C. A. (2006). Building social and emotional competence: The PATHS curriculum. In S. R. Jimerson & M. J. Furlong (Eds.), *Handbook of school violence and school safety: From research to practice* (pp. 395–412). Mahwah, NJ: Erlbaum.

Greenberg, M. T., Kusche, C. A., Cook, E. T., & Quamma, J. P. (1995). Promoting emotional competence in school-aged children: The effects of the PATHS curriculum. *Development and Psychopathology, 7*(01), 117–136.

Greenberg, M. T., Kusche, C., & Riggs, N. (2004). The PATHS curriculum: Theory and research on neuro-cognitive development and school success. In J. Zins, R. Weissberg, & H. Walber (Eds.), *Building school success on social and emotional learning* (pp. 170–188). New York: Teachers College Press.

Greenberg, M. T., Kusche, C. A., & Speltz, M. (1990). Emotional regulation, self-control and psychopathology: The role of relationships in early childhood. In D. Cicchetti & S. Toth (Eds.), *Rochester symposium on developmental psychopathology* (Vol. 2, pp. 21–56). New York: Cambridge University Press.

Greenberg, M. T., Weissberg, R. P., O'Brien, M. U., Zins, J. E., Fredericks, L., Resnik, H., & Elias, M. J. (2003). Enhancing school-based prevention and youth development through coordinated social, emotional, and academic learning. *American Psychologist*, 58(6–7), 466–474.

Grossman, D. C., Neckerman, H. J., Koepsell, T. D., Liu, P. Y., Asher, K. N., Beland, K., & Rivara, F. P. (1997). Effectiveness of a violence prevention curriculum among children in elementary school: A randomized controlled trial. *Journal of American Medical Association*, 277(20), 1605–1611.

Hahn, R., Fuqua-Whitley, D., Wethington, H., Lowy, J., Liberman, A., Crosby, A., & Dahlberg, L. (2007). The effectiveness of universal school-based programs for the prevention of violent and aggressive behavior. *Morbidity Mortality Weekly Report*, 56, 1–12.

Hamre, B. K., & Pianta, R. C. (2001). Early teacher–child relationships and the trajectory of children's outcomes through eighth grade. *Child Development*, 72(2), 625–638.

Han, S. S., & Weiss, B. (2005). Sustainability of teacher implementation of school-based mental health programs. *Journal of Abnormal Child Psychology*, 33(6), 665–679.

Hawkins, J. D., Von Cleve, E., & Catalano, R. F. (1991). Reducing early childhood aggression: Results of a primary prevention program. *Journal of the American Academy of Child & Adolescent Psychiatry*, 30(2), 208–217.

Herschell, A. D., Kolko, D. J., Baumann, B. L., & Davis, A. C. (2010). The role of therapist training in the implementation of psychosocial treatments: A review and critique with recommendations. *Clinical Psychology Review*, 30(4), 448–466.

Hoagwood, K. E., Olin, S. S., Kerker, B. D., Kratochwill, T. R., Crowe, M., & Saka, N. (2007). Empirically based school interventions targeted at academic and mental health functioning. *Journal of Emotional and Behavioral Disorders*, 15(2), 66–92.

Ialongo, N., Poduska, J., Werthamer, L., & Kellam, S. (2001). The distal impact of two first-grade prevention interventions on conduct problems and disorder in early adolescence. *Journal of Emotional and Behavioral Disorders*, 9(3), 146–160.

Ialongo, N. S., Werthamer, L., Kellam, S. G., Brown, C. H., Wang, S., & Lin, Y. (1999). Proximal impact of two first-grade preventive interventions on the early risk behaviors for later substance abuse, depression, and antisocial behavior. *American Journal of Community Psychology*, 27(5), 599–641.

Jennings, P. A., & Greenberg, M. T. (2009). The prosocial classroom: Teacher social and emotional competence in relation to student and classroom outcomes. *Review of Educational Research*, 79(1), 491–525.

Joyce, B., and Showers, B. (1995). *Student achievement through staff development: Fundamentals of school renewal.* 2nd ed. White Plains, NY: Longman.

Kam, C. M., Greenberg, M. T., & Kusche, C. A. (2004). Sustained effects of the PATHS curriculum on the social and psychological adjustment of children in special education. *Journal of Emotional and Behavioral Disorders*, 12(2), 66–78.

Kavanagh, D. J., & Bower, G. H. (1985). Mood and self-efficacy: Impact of joy and sadness on perceived capabilities. *Cognitive Therapy and Research*, 9(5), 507–525.

Kellam, S. G., Brown, C. H., Poduska, J. M., Ialongo, N. S., Wang, W., Toyinbo, P., Petras, H., Ford, C., Windham, A., & Wilcox, H. C. (2008). Effects of a universal classroom behavior management program in first and second grades on young adult behavioral, psychiatric, and social outcomes. *Drug and Alcohol Dependence*, 95(1), S5–S28.

Kellam, S. G., Rebok, G. W., Ialongo, N., & Mayer, L. S. (1994). The course and malleability of aggressive behavior from early first grade into middle school: Results of a developmental epidemiologically-based preventive trial. *Journal of Child Psychology and Psychiatry*, 35(2), 259–281.

Kelly, J. A., Heckman, T. G., Stevenson, L. Y., Williams, P. N., Ertl, T., Hays, R. B., & Neumann, M. S. (2000). Transfer of research-based HIV prevention interventions to community service providers: Fidelity and adaptation. *AIDS Education and Prevention: Official Publication of the International Society for AIDS Education*, 12(5 Suppl.), 87–98.

Kemp, T. J. (2009). Is coaching an evolved form of leadership? Building a transdisciplinary framework for exploring the coaching alliance. *International Coaching Psychology Review*, 4(1), 105–110.

Kusche, C. A., & Greenberg, M. T. (2012). The PATHS curriculum: Promoting emotional literacy, prosocial behavior, and caring classrooms. In S. R. Jimerson, A. B. Nickerson, M. J. Mayer, & M. J. Furlong (Eds.), *Handbook of school violence and school safety: International research and practice* (2nd ed., pp. 435–446). New York: Routledge.

Ladd, G. W., Kochenderfer, B. J., & Coleman, C. C. (1996, 1997). Classroom peer acceptance, friendship, and victimization: Distinct relation systems that contribute uniquely to children's school adjustment. *Child Development, 68*(6), 1181–1197.

Leach, D. J., & Conto, H. (1999). The additional effects of process and outcome feedback following brief in-service teacher training. *Educational Psychology, 19*, 441–462.

Lochman, J. E., Boxmeyer, C., Powell, N., Qu, L., Wells, K., & Windle, M. (2009). Dissemination of the coping power program: Importance of intensity of counselor training. *Journal of Consulting and Clinical Psychology, 77*(3), 397–409.

McKay, M. M., & Bannon, W. M., Jr. (2004). Engaging families in child mental health services. *Child and Adolescent Psychiatric Clinics of North America, 13*(4), 905–921.

Miller, W. R., Yahne, C. E., Moyers, T. B., Martinez, J., & Pirritano, M. (2004). A randomized trial of methods to help clinicians learn motivational interviewing. *Journal of Consulting and Clinical Psychology, 72*(6), 1050–1062.

Mortenson, B. P., & Witt, J. C. (1998). The use of weekly performance feedback to increase teacher implementation of a pre-referral academic intervention. *School Psychology Review, 27*(4), 613–627.

National Research Council & Institute of Medicine. (2009). *Preventing mental, emotional, and behavioral disorders in young people*. Washington, DC: National Academic Press.

Neal, A. M., & Brown, B. J. W. (1994). Fears and anxiety disorders in African American children. In S. Friedman (Ed.), *Anxiety disorders in African Americans* (pp. 65–75). New York: Springer.

Neil, A. L., & Christensen, H. (2009). Efficacy and effectiveness of school-based prevention and early intervention programs for anxiety. *Clinical Psychology Review, 29*(3), 208–215.

Neufeld, B., & Roper, D. (2003). *Coaching: A strategy for developing instructional capacity: Promises & practicalities*. Aspen, CO: Aspen Institute.

Noell, G. H., Duhon, G. J., Gatti, S. L., & Connell, J. E. (2002). Consultation, follow-up, and implementation of behavior management interventions in general education. *School Psychology Review, 31*(2), 217–234.

Noell, G. H., Witt, J. C., Gilbertson, D. N., Ranier, D. D., & Freeland, J. (1997). Increasing teacher intervention implementation in general education settings through consultation and performance feedback. *School Psychology Quarterly, 12*, 77–88.

O'Broin, A., & Palmer, S. (2009). Co-creating an optimal coaching alliance: A cognitive behavioural coaching perspective. *International Coaching Psychology Review, 4*(2), 184–194.

O'Neil, R., Welsh, M., Parke, R. D., Wang, S., & Strand, C. (1997). A longitudinal assessment of the academic correlates of early peer acceptance and rejection. *Journal of Clinical Child Psychology, 26*(3), 290–303.

Pankratz, M., Hallfors, D., & Cho, H. (2002). Measuring perceptions of innovation adoption: The diffusion of a federal drug prevention policy. *Health Education Research, 17*, 315–326.

Parcel, G. S., Ross, J. G., Lavin, A. T., Portnoy, B., Nelson, G. D., & Winters, F. (1991). Enhancing implementation of the Teenage Health Teaching Modules. *Journal of School Health, 61*(1): 35–38.

Park-Higgerson, H. K., Perumean-Chaney, S. E., Bartolucci, A. A., Grimley, D. M., & Singh, K. P. (2008). The evaluation of school-based violence prevention programs: A meta-analysis. *Journal of School Health, 78*(9), 465–479.

Peisner-Feinberg, E., Burchinal, M., Clifford, R., Culkin, M., Howes, C., Kagan, S., & Yazejian, N. (2001). The relation of preschool child-care quality to children's cognitive and social developmental trajectories through second grade. *Child Development, 72*, 1534–1553.

Petras, H., Kellam, S. G., Brown, C. H., Muthen, B., Ialongo, N. S., & Poduska, J. M. (2008). Developmental epidemiological courses leading to antisocial personality disorder and violence and criminal behavior: Effects by young adulthood of a universal preventive intervention in first- and second-grade classrooms. *Drug Alcohol Dependence, 95*, S45–S59.

Pianta, R. C., & Stuhlman, M. W. (2004). Teacher–child relationships and children's success in the first years of school. *School Psychology Review, 33*(3), 444–458.

Poglinco, S. M., Bach, A. J., Hovde, K., Rosenblum, S., Saunders, M., & Supovitz, J. A. (2003). *The heart of the matter: The coaching model in America's choice schools*. Consortium for Policy Research in Education (CPRE) Research Reports. http://repository.upenn.edu/cpre_researchreports/35.

Riggs, N. R., Greenberg, M. T., Kusche, C. A., & Pentz, M. A. (2006). The mediational role of neurocognition in the behavioral outcomes of a social–emotional prevention program in elementary school students: Effects of the PATHS curriculum. *Prevention Science, 7*, 91–102.

Ringwalt, C. L., Ennett, S., Johnson, R., Rohrbach, L. A., Simons-Rudolph, A., Vincus, A., & Thorne, J. (2003). Factors associated with fidelity to substance use prevention curriculum guides in the nation's middle schools. *Health Education & Behavior, 30*(3), 375–391.

Ringwalt, C. L., Pankratz, M. M., Hansen, W. B., Dusenbury, L., Jackson-Newsom, J., Giles, S. M., & Brodish, P. (2007). The potential of coaching as a strategy to improve the effectiveness of school-based substance use prevention curricula. *Health Education & Behavior, 36*(4), 696–710.

Rogers, E. M. (2003). *Diffusion of innovations* (5th ed.). New York: Free Press.

Rose, D. J., & Church, R. J. (1998). Learning to teach: The acquisition and maintenance of teaching skills. *Journal of Behavioral Education, 8*, 5–35.

Sankaran, S., Dick, B., Passfield, R., & Swepson, P. (2001). *Effective change management using action research and action learning: Concepts, frameworks, processes and applications.* Lismore, Australia: Southern Cross University Press.

Scott, T. M., & Martinek, G. (2006). Coaching positive behavior support in school settings. *Journal of Positive Behavior Interventions, 8*, 165–173.

Schaeffer, C. M., Petras, H., Ialongo, N., Masyn, K. E., Hubbard, S., Poduska, J. & Kellam, S. (2006). A comparison of girls' and boys' aggressive–disruptive behavior trajectories across elementary school: Prediction to young adult antisocial outcomes. *Journal of Consulting and Clinical Psychology, 74*(3), 500–510.

Schaeffer, C. M., Petras, H., Ialongo, N., Poduska, J., & Kellam, S. (2003). Modeling growth in boys' aggressive behavior across elementary school: Links to later criminal involvement, conduct disorder, and antisocial personality disorder. *Developmental Psychology, 39*(6), 1020–1035.

Sholomskas, D. E., Syracuse-Siewert, G., Rounsaville, B. J., Ball, S. A., Nuro, K. F., & Carroll, K. M. (2005). We don't train in vain: A dissemination trial of three strategies of training clinicians in cognitive–behavioral therapy. *Journal of Consulting and Clinical Psychology, 73*(1), 106–115.

Showers, B. (1985). Teachers coaching teachers. *Educational Leadership, 42* (7), 43–48.

Stirman, S. W., Crits-Christoph, P., & DeRubeis, R. J. (2004). Achieving successful dissemination of empirically supported psychotherapies: A synthesis of dissemination theory. *Clinical Psychology: Science and Practice, 11*(4), 343–359.

Storr, C. L., Ialongo, N. S., Kellam, S. G., & Anthony, J. C. (2002). A randomized controlled trial of two primary school intervention strategies to prevent early onset of tobacco smoking. *Drug and Alcohol Dependence, 66*, 51–60.

Substance Abuse and Mental Health Services Administration, Center for Mental Health Services. (2007). *Promotion and prevention in mental health: Strengthening parenting and enhancing child resilience.* DHHS publication no. CMHS-SVP-0175. Rockville, MD: Inter-university Consortium for Political and Social Research.

Sutherland, K. S., & Wehby, J. H. (2001). The effect of self-evaluation on teaching behavior in classrooms for students with emotional and behavioral disorders. *Journal of Special Education, 35*(3), 161–171.

Sutherland, K. S., Wehby, J. H., & Yoder, P. J. (2002). Examination of the relationship between teacher praise and opportunities for students with EBD to respond to academic requests. *Journal of Emotional and Behavioral Disorders, 10*(1), 5–13.

Swanson, C. B. (2004). Graduation rates: Real kids, real numbers. Washington, DC: Urban Institute.

Tobler, N. S., Roona, M. R., Ochshorn, P., Marshall, D. G., Streke, A. V., & Stackpole, K. M. (2000). School-based adolescent drug prevention programs: 1998 Meta-analysis. *Journal of Primary Prevention, 20*, 275–337.

Tobler, N. S., & Stratton, H. H. (1997). Effectiveness of a school-based drug prevention programs: A meta-analysis of the research. *Journal of Primary Prevention, 18*, 71–128.

Tschannen-Moran, M., Hoy, A. W., & Hoy, W. K. (1998). Teacher efficacy: Its meaning and measure. *Review of Educational Research, 68*(2), 202–248.

US Public Health Service. (2000). *Report of the Surgeon General's conference on children's mental health: A national action agenda.* Washington, DC: Department of Health and Human Services.

US Public Health Service. (2001). *Youth violence: A report of the Surgeon General.* Washington, DC: Department of Health and Human Services.

Webster-Wright, A. (2009). Reframing professional development through understanding authentic professional learning. *Review of Educational Research, 79*(2), 702–739.

Weissberg, R. P., Barton, H. A., & Shriver, T. P. (1997). *The social competence promotion program for young adolescents: Primary prevention works.* Thousand Oaks, CA: Sage Publications.

Weissberg, R. P., & Greenberg, M. T. (1998). School and community competence-enhancement and prevention programs. In R. P. Weissberg, M. T. Greenberg, W. Damon, I. E. Sigel, & K. A. Renninger (Eds.), *Handbook of child psychology: Child psychology in practice*, vol. 4, 5th ed. (pp. 887–954). Hoboken, NJ: Wiley.

Weisz, J. R., Jensen-Doss, A., & Hawley, K. M. (2006). Evidence-based youth psychotherapies versus usual clinical care. *American Psychologist, 61,* 671–689.

Wilcox, H. C., Kellam, S. G., Brown, H., Poduska, J. M., Ialongo, N. S., Wang, W., & Anthony, J. C. (2008). The impact of two universal randomized first and second-grade classroom interventions on young adult suicide ideation and attempts. *Drug and Alcohol Dependence, 95*(1), S60–S73.

Wilson, D. B., Gottfredson, D. C., & Najaka, S. S. (2001). School-based prevention of problem behaviors: A meta-analysis. *Journal of Quantitative Criminology, 17,* 247–272.

Wilson, S. J., & Lipsey, M. W. (2007). School-based interventions for aggressive and disruptive behavior: Update of a meta-analysis. *American Journal of Preventive Medicine, 33*(2), S130–S143.

Zins, J. E., Weissberg, R. P., Wang, M. C., & Walberg, H. J. (2004). *Building school success through social and emotional learning: What does the research say?* New York: Teachers College Press.

About the Authors

Kimberly D. Becker, PhD: Dr. Becker is a clinical psychologist and an assistant professor in the Division of Child & Adolescent Psychiatry at the University of Maryland School of Medicine. Since 2007, Dr. Becker has been involved in implementation science related to school-based interventions delivered by mental health providers, teachers, and other school staff. Dr. Becker's work related to the PAX Good Behavior Game (GBG) began in 2009 within the context of a large-scale implementation of the PAX GBG in Baltimore City public schools. During that time, Dr. Becker and her colleagues developed and refined the coaching model described in this manual. Dr. Becker has also led the development and testing of an online training for coaches to support teacher use of the PAX GBG.

Celene E. Domitrovich, PhD: Dr. Domitrovich is the Director of Research and Innovation for the Early Childhood Innovation Network (ECIN) and a member of the research faculty in the Department of Psychiatry at Georgetown University. She also holds a faculty appointment with the Prevention Research Center at Penn State University. Dr. Domitrovich is the developer of the preschool version of the Promoting Alternative Thinking Strategies (PATHS) Curriculum. She has conducted randomized trials of this and several other school-based preventive interventions. She is interested in the development of integrated intervention models and understanding the factors that promote high-quality implementation of evidence-based interventions in schools. Dr. Domitrovich has published numerous articles in peer-reviewed journals and has written several federal reports on evidence-based interventions and implementation. She served two terms on the board of the Society for Prevention Research and received the CASEL Joseph E. Zins award in 2011 for Action Research in Social Emotional Learning.

Dennis D. Embry, PhD: Dr. Embry is senior scientist at PAXIS Institute in Tucson and a co-investigator at Johns Hopkins Center for Prevention as well as co-investigator with the Promise Neighborhood Research Consortium, the University of Manitoba, University of South Carolina, overseeing 50 major prevention projects in the United States and Canada. He is a member of the Substance Abuse and Mental Health Services Administration/Center for Substance Abuse Prevention experts group, and a nominee for the President's Advisory Council on Prevention for Health Care Reform. Current publications emphasize achieving sustainable, cost-efficient, populationwide prevention effects across physical, mental, emotional, and behavioral disorders. He is an emeritus National Research Advisory Council Senior Fellow of New Zealand.

Nicholas S. Ialongo, PhD: Dr. Ialongo is currently a professor in the Department of Mental Health at the Johns Hopkins Bloomberg School of Public Health (JHBSPH). He trained as a child and family clinical psychologist at Michigan State University. In addition to his academic duties at the JHBSPH, Dr. Ialongo directs a National Institutes on Mental Health and Drug Abuse–funded Advanced Center for Intervention and Services Research, and is the principal investigator on the 20-year follow-up of the second-generation Johns Hopkins Preventive Intervention Research Center trial.

Jennifer P. Keperling, MA, LCPC: Mrs. Keperling earned her masters of arts degree in clinical psychology in May 2004 and became a Licensed Clinical Professional Counselor (LCPC) in January 2006. Since 2009, Mrs. Keperling has been a faculty member and research associate at the Johns Hopkins University Bloomberg School of Public Health, and has gained experience implementing both parent and child group evidence-based interventions (e.g., the Incredible Years) within the school setting, coaching classroom teachers in implementing evidence-based programs (e.g., the Good Behavior Game, PATHS), and leading other evidence-based groups and counseling interventions (e.g., Cognitive Behavioral Intervention for Trauma in Schools, Coping Power) with children, adolescents, families, and teachers in Maryland public schools. Before working at Johns Hopkins University, Mrs. Keperling was a school-based mental health counselor for 5 years at the University of Maryland School Mental Health Program. In this role she provided individual and group counseling to students in a Baltimore City elementary/middle school. Currently, Mrs. Keperling provides coaching and consultation services to classroom teachers for the Good Behavior Game + My Teaching Partner Project, a video-based coaching model that provides training and coaching to early career teachers to help address classroom management issues and to demonstrate the engagement of students with different learning styles.

Dana D. Marchese, PhD: Dr. Marchese earned her PhD in school psychology at the University of Missouri. She completed her predoctoral training at the University of Maryland, School of Medicine, in the Department of Psychiatry and with the University of Maryland Center for School Mental Health. Dr. Marchese earned her bachelor of science degree in psychology and criminal justice from Towson University and her master of science degree in clinical community counseling from Johns Hopkins University. Before obtaining her doctoral degree, Dr. Marchese worked for the Johns Hopkins University Center for Prevention and Early Intervention, coordinating and implementing evidence-based interventions with children and families in Baltimore City schools. She has experience coaching and consulting with teachers to increase implementation of evidence-based practices in the classroom. Her dissertation work was to develop a series of modules on best practices in classroom management with elementary school classroom teachers using the Classroom Check-up Consultation Model. Currently, Dr. Marchese is a faculty member and research associate at the Johns Hopkins University Bloomberg School of Public Health.

Wendy M. Reinke, PhD: Dr. Reinke is licensed psychologist and an associate professor at the University of Missouri. She earned her degree in school psychology from the University of Oregon. She completed postdoctoral training in prevention science at the Johns Hopkins Bloomberg School of Public Health. Dr. Reinke has experience consulting with teachers and implementing school-based, evidence-based interventions. She is the founder and co-director of the Missouri Prevention Center, and co-investigator of the Johns Hopkins Center for Prevention of Early Intervention. Her area of focus is in the prevention of disruptive behavior problems in children. Dr. Reinke has published more than 70 peer-reviewed articles and three books related to school-based interventions, teacher consultation, and prevention of disruptive behavior problems.

About the Coaches

Sandy Hardee, MS: Mrs. Hardee earned her master of science degree in curriculum and instruction from McDaniel College. She earned her bachelor of science degree in health science, with a dual concentration in secondary education and community health, from Towson University. On first leaving Towson University, Mrs. Hardee worked as a middle school program director for Students Sharing Coalition, Inc.—a Baltimore City nonprofit service-learning organization that focused on issues related to poverty and homelessness. She then taught middle school health in Howard County for 5 years. Shortly after leaving the public school system, Mrs. Hardee worked as a coach for a social–emotional and behavior management program with the Center of Prevention and Early Intervention at the Johns Hopkins Bloomberg School of Public Health called *PATHS to PAX*. Both programs used the positive behavioral interventions and supports (PBIS) framework and had more than 25 years of research to support the benefits of use in classrooms. Currently, Mrs. Hardee is working as a coach for teachers who teach grades kindergarten through eighth grade on a project called *Double Check*, an Institute of Education Sciences goal-2 funded grant that helps teachers apply PBIS and culturally proficient strategies to reduce disproportionality.

Brenda C. Kelly, PhD: Dr. Kelly earned her bachelor of science and doctoral degrees from the University of Maryland, College Park, and her master of education degree from Towson University. She is a new faculty member at Johns Hopkins Bloomberg School of Public Health . Most recently, Dr. Kelly served as the program director for Ready at Five, an affiliate of the Maryland Business Round Table of Education and the Maryland State Department of Education as a Race to the Top specialist for the Office of School Innovations. Before her retirement, she directed the Office of Early Learning for Baltimore City public schools (City Schools) from school year 2000–2001 to school year 2009–2010, where she was instrumental in building the early childhood programs in the district. Her passion for education and student wellness has returned her to the field to support research work on school-based preventive and early treatment interventions for children and adolescents, and to help disseminate the knowledge gained to improve prevention and treatment research, dissemination, and training practices.

Michael Muempfer, MA: Mr. Muempfer is currently the PBIS specialist for the Montgomery County public schools district in Maryland. He also continues to consult for the PAXIS Institute as a National PAX Good Behavior Game trainer. Before this, Mr. Muempfer was a school climate specialist for 3 years, specializing in PBIS, student/staff engagement, school safety, and school environment at the high school level. He has also worked as a PATHS to PAX coach for teachers in Baltimore while at Johns Hopkins Bloomberg School of Public Health for 3 years. Mr. Muempfer has worked and consulted with more than 50 elementary, middle, and high schools in Maryland specializing in PBIS, PAX Good Behavior Game, PATHS, Check-In/Check-Out, Check and Connect, Olweus Bully Prevention Program, Life Skills, Youth Mental Health First Aid, and classroom/behavior management. He has also consulted with schools in Washington, DC; Washington; New York; New Jersey; Texas; and Kansas. Mr. Muempfer began his career in education as a classroom teacher in the Baltimore City school district for 8 years, where he taught grades 3 through 5. He is a graduate of Penn State University and received his masters degree in educational leadership from Notre Dame of Maryland University.

Kelly Schaffer, MS: Mrs. Kelly Schaffer received her bachelor's degree in elementary education from Coastal Carolina University and a master of science degree in instructional technology from Towson University. She has a total of 18 years of experience working in Baltimore City public schools. Mrs. Schaffer began her career teaching second and third grade at George Washington Elementary School for 5 years. She then spent 2 years coaching teachers and working with students integrating technology in the classroom. Mrs. Schaffer taught second grade for 2 years at Bay Brook Elementary School. She was a coach for the PATHS to PAX Program 5 five years with the Center for Prevention and Early Intervention at Johns Hopkins University. Currently, she is a mentor teacher and has been teaching second grade for 4 years at Tunbridge Public Charter School.

Index